Buddhist Art in India and Sri Lanka

— A Critical Study —

Emerging Perceptions in Buddhist Studies
(ISSN 0971-9512)

1.2. An Encyclopaedia of Buddhist Deities, Demigods, Godlings, Saints & Demons — with Special Focus on Iconographic Attributes; by Fredrick W. Bunce 2 Vols. (ISBN 81-246-0020-1; set)

3. Buddhism in Karnataka; by R.C. Hiremath; With a Foreword by H. H. The Dalai Lama. (ISBN 81-246-0013-9)

4-5. Pāli Language and Literature: A Systematic Survey and Historical Study; by Kanai Lal Hazra. 2 Vols. (ISBN 81-246-0004-X; set)

6. Maṇḍala and Landscape; by A.W. Macdonald (ISBN 81-246-0060-0)

7. The Future Buddha Maitreya: An Iconological Study; by Inchang Kim (ISBN 81-246-0082-1)

8. Absence of the Buddha Image in Early Buddhist Art; by Kanoko Tanaka (ISBN 81-246-0090-2)

9. A Few Facts About Buddhism; by Gunnar Gällmo (ISBN 81-246-0099-6)

10. Buddhist Theory of Meaning and Literary Analysis; by Rajinish K. Mishra (ISBN 81-246-0118-6)

11. Buddhism as/in Performance: Analysis of Meditation and Theatrical Practice; by David E.R. George (ISBN 81-246-0123-2)

12. Buddhist Tantra and Buddhist Art; by T.N. Mishra. (ISBN 81-246-0141-0)

Emerging Perceptions in Buddhist Studies, no. 13

Buddhist Art in India and Sri Lanka

(3rd century BC to 6th century AD)

— A Critical Study —

by

Virender Kumar Dabral

with a Foreword by

R.C. Sharma

D.K. Printworld (P) Ltd.

New Delhi

Cataloging in Publication Data — DK

Dabral, Virender Kumar, 1951 –
Buddhist art in India and Sri Lanka.
(Emerging perceptions in Buddhist Studies, ISSN 0971-9512; no. 13)
Includes Bibliographical references (p.)
Includes Index.

1. Art, Buddhist — India — History. 2. Art, Buddhist — Sri Lanka — History I. Title. II. Series: Emerging perceptions in Buddhist Studies; no. 13.

ISBN 81-246-0162-3
First published in India in 2000

Published and printed by :
D.K. Printworld (P) Ltd.
Regd. office : '*Sri Kunj*', F-52, Bali Nagar
New Delhi - 110015
Phone: (011) 545-3975, 546-6019; *Fax*: (011) 546-5926
E-Mail: dkprint@4mis.com

Foreword

Dr. Virender Kumar Dabral's book on the *Buddhist Art in India and Sri Lanka* is a welcome addition in the field of bi-lateral artistic conventions. Soon after its inception Buddhism crossed the geographical barriers to become the world religion and Sri Lanka was the first neighbouring country to embrace from the time of Aśoka. The visit of Mahendra and Saṁghamitra to Sri Lanka, consecration of the Holy Relics and planting a sapling *Bodhi* tree at Anurādhapura were the epoch making events which continued to vibrate the annals of history of both the countries and will resound in future as well. A stone slab in the Mathura Museum belonging to the Kuṣāṇa period illustrates this episode.

The pleasing personality of Buddha, his austerity and penance, attainment of Supreme Knowledge, its further dissemination for all, firm assurance for removal of sufferings and delightful preaching of the Middle Path (*Madhyamapatipāda*) along with focus on non-violence, peace and compassion attracted millions of people in and overland. His message was communicated to masses through scriptures, narration of stories including the Jātaka tales, building of *stūpa*s, monasteries and temples, installation of images, creation of a pavilion (*maṇḍapa*) of murals, incision of inscriptions, writing of manuscripts — sometimes with illustrations, designing beautiful artefacts of decorative and ritualistic use, etc.

The spread of Buddhism germinated the seed of aesthetic sensibility and artistic activity beside propounding the religious and canonical teachings and ideals. This was common in both the countries although in most of the cases the initiative was from the main land but Sri Lanka not only gave a positive response but added further grace and grandeur in multiple ways.

The comparative study of the artistic conventions of the two neighbours remain a coveted goal for any art lover or art historian. Dr. Dabral has done a commendable job by producing a wonderful book on this important and interesting aspect. He has lucidly and comprehensively presented almost all spheres of visual arts like architecture, painting, sculpture, etc. At the same time he has interpreted a good number of symbols, motifs and decorative rendering with a deeper insight.

Such works are of vital significance for appreciation of cultural interaction between India and Sri Lanka for more than two milleniums and will further strengthen the cordial relations. Dr. Dabral deserves best compliments for highlighting this aspect with the stamp of his scholarship.

Rathayatra
July 3, 2000

Prof. R.C. Sharma
(Former Director General/VC
National Museum/Institute

Preface

HISTORY of Art is the study and creation of literature, designs, paintings, sculpture, music etc. It is a very vast field as it reflects various human emotions and sentiments translated into concrete forms that become part and parcel of the social culture of a society. History of Art beckons the creative urges.

Art removes the montony of cumbersome thoughts and develops different beautiful and striking concepts, feelings and emotions through the genre of creative skill. Art is a creative skill or activity where imagination plays a very significant role in promoting paintings, languages, literature and history quite distinct from various sciences.

Visual art has an important effect on others role and it helps us to understand, learn and visualize the events of the history with relevant parameters. Visual art in India and Sri Lanka has developed various attitudes and exhibits different regional trends.

Buddhist Art delineates all the important aspects of Buddhism. The Great Master is portrayed in various forms of art and literature, which has enriched the Buddhist Art. It also reflects faithfully *Jataka*s in various places. Buddhism has been the main link between India and Sri Lanka, hence Buddhist Art became an indelible mark in the Indian peninsula. It is believed that without Buddhism there would have been no such development of architecture, sculpture, language and literature as distinguished art forms in Sri Lanka.

Indian art is an expression of Indian life and socio-religious tradition. Mauryan art is represented by the animals of Aśokan pillars. Amarāvatī art is highly elegant and sensitive. Gandhāra art is a hybrid, heterogeneous. It is Graeco-Roman and its centres were Peshawar, Taxila and Afghanistan. Mathurā was a great centre of art and culture during Gupta period. The Kuṣāṇa art of Mathurā achieved perfection. Gupta art is of high aesthetic sense and chaste. Nālandā and Nagapattinam were also centres of Buddhism and Buddhist Art flourished and slowly it began to wipe out.

The sixth century BC was remarkable for the religious upheaveals, intellectual activities, uncertainties and excitement in many countries. It was an age of great thinkers and teachers, in China we had Lao Tzu and Confucius; in Greece Parmendies and; in India Mahāvīra and Buddha.

Buddhism's growth was slow in the beginning; but after Emperor Aśoka's war with Kaliṅga in 260 BC; its growth was rapid. Jainism's growth, though slow, has been steady. It flourishes still, while Buddhism has almost disappeared from India. Buddhism as a moralistic religion has great appeal. This aspect is the cause of its growth beyond the shores of India.

In the middle of the third century BC; history begins to emerge from tradition and there were no Brāhmaṇical temple or statues of Brāhmaṇical gods during pre-Buddhist period. It is believed that the advent of Buddhist must have led to the abandonment of the sacrificial forms of Hindu worship giving rise to veneration of Hindu deities and temples for their being sacrosanct. The first Hindu Temple was found in south India, i.e. fifth century AD.

There has been a 'cultural recrudescence' which caused a lot of trouble, degeneration, confusion, and worry in people's lives. Sinhalese culture is a replica of Indian culture. But in Buddhist art of Sri Lanka, many new developments of purely Sri Lankan origin, took place. Sri Lanka sculpture and painting owe their genesis to India. Borrowing was no doubt there but these were transformed by adopting their own method to suit local conditions. Thus, they became indigenous, or the creations of the people of Sri Lanka. But they have their limitations.

The Hīnayānist whether Śrāvaka or a Pratyekabuddha is determined, selfish and always strives towards his own *nirvāṇa* or emancipation, ignoring altogether all other beings of the world. The Mahāyānist makes compassion his motto and sets himself to work for the benefit of entire mankind. Both the Hīnayānists and the Mahāyānists believe that the Buddha as a *bodhisattava* remained in the Tuṣita heaven and obtained his enlightenment under the Bo-tree at Bodh Gayā and preached his First Sermon at Sārnāth. But they differ in their views regarding the divinity of Buddha. Though they are in agreement regarding the Buddhist triad of Buddha, Dharma and Saṁgha but they differ in the order in which these three are to be worshipped. The Hīnayānist worship in the order of Buddha, Dharma and Saṁgha, and the Mahāyānist in the order of Dharma, Buddha an Saṁgha.

Around the first century AD the Mahayana School of Buddhism was introduced in the island. During the period when the imperial Guptas held sway in India both Mahāyāna and Hīnayāna Schools prospered in Sri Lanka. During Fa-Hien's visit, there were many *dagaba*s and monasteries. The Sri Lankans started writing their own commentaries on Buddhist works in Pāli.

The sculptures of Sāñcī and Bhārhut represent Buddhist adaptation of Greek traditon but not Greek art. Real Buddhist sculpture took shape when Buddhist artists developed their own idiom and expression and were inspired by Buddhist monks. Buddha's figure is a naturalistic embodiment of many qualities, ideas and is able to express them with remarkable distinctions despite the vagueness of exaggeration or love of simplicity. Vahalkada was not in earlier *stūpa* but a later innovation of the Sinhalese artists.

Sri Lankans borrowed the form of Buddha images from Buddhist India and transformed the images to suit their traditions. The making of symbols to represent Buddha and the image of Buddha and its worship had begun by Buddhists in India and when it reached Sri Lanka in course of time it was perfected and embellished there. The Buddha is represented symbolically in Mathura, Amarāvatī and Sāñcī sculptures. The *dharma-cakra*, the Bodhi Tree and the Foot Print are among the symbols employed to convey the idea of the Lord's presence. These symbols are present in Sinhalese Buddhist art, but they are not intended for the purpose of symbolising the personality of the Buddha as in early Indian Buddhist art.

Buddha's life and his teachings formed the central theme of the Ajantā art of painting. The change of moods and style as a consequence of the development of religion are faithfully reflected in Ajantā paintings. The Sīgiriya paintings, on the other hand, seem to be older than the Ajantā. The composition of the Sīgiriya frescoes are narrative and decorative, based on verses and deciphered inscriptions. All artists and their works were considered an indulgence and luxury in mundane life. Luxury being foreign to Buddhism, monks and nuns were forbidden to see the so-called 'conversion pictures' or 'love scenes' which were at that time painted on walls and roofs. These principles slowly and gradually disappeared and today have become out dated. Sri Lankan and Indian artists were interested in beautiful forms and aesthetic ideals and were experts in dealing with flora-fauna, arboreal scenes and a battery of maiden damsels and goddesses to achieve the splendour of beauty and magnificence; they were in a way successful in delineating them.

Whatever ancient art and architecture is seen in Sri Lanka today, is borrowed from India. The earliest ones, if any, are nowhere to be seen in Sri Lanka. In architecture, sculpture and painting, we recognise Indian origin but do not find their development in the Buddhist Art of Sri Lanka. The initiation is only seen. A thorough probe has revealed that Sri Lanka has developed its own Buddhist Art forms which are totally original. It is also true that originality in art is nothing but a change, partial or complete, of borrowed elements in readaptation. Nevertheless, the Buddhist Art of Sri Lanka exhibits a partial borrowing, which has been modified, co-related, reinterpreted and readjusted to look as original and this has been done in a remarkable way.

A pilot survey of places was made where the Tathāgata once lived and toiled for humanity. The sites surveyed are Lumbini in Nepal where Buddha was born; Bodh Gayā where he attained enlightenment; Sārnāth where he attained "*Mahāparinirvāṇa*". These places together form a garland of holy gems that beckons pilgrims and research scholars from every nook and corner of the world.

I also had an opportunity to pursue higher studies in Sinhala Language and literature at the University of Paradeniya, Sri Lanka on a scholarship awarded by the Democratic Socialist Republic of Sri Lanka. Adequate material was also collected on the subject during my stay in Sri Lanka as I had an inclination to do a study on Sri Lanka which was almost untrodden. Hence, the book focuses mainly on Sri Lanka. Six years of study and seventeen years of teaching Sinhala language and literature has equipped me adequately to approach the subject of Buddhist Art and literature. My interest was also further developed and broadened while submitting a dissertation on "Buddhism — A Bond of Friendship Between India and Sri Lanka" to the National Museum Institute of History of Art, Consevation and Museology (Deemed to be a University), New Delhi as a requirement for M.A. (History of Art). A new horizon was opened while getting to know the thoughts of Sri Lanka's art historians and critics.

This further helped me a lot in pondering and making the study more subtle and compact.

Moreover, I must confess that this subject as a whole was unfamiliar for me; to explore it was an effort, but one well-work making.

While writing this book, I cannot forget Lt Gen R.K. Gaur, PVSM who has been very helpful in many ways. Words are inadequate to describe his unforgettable generosity and I salute him for his benign deeds.

Late Dr. G.N. Pant, Director, National Museum Institute of History of Art, Conservation and Museology (Deemed to be a University) had devoted a great deal of time and gave me valuable guidance and suggestions as and when I approached him.

I express my thanks to the staff of National Museum Institute of History of Art. Conservation and Museology, National Museum Library, Indian Council of Historical Research, American Institute of Indian Studies Ramnagar, Varanasi (now at Gurgaon), Museums at Mathura, Lucknow, Sarnath, Bharat Kala Bhavan, Varanasi, Banaras Hindu University, where I spent several years for collecting materials, photographs and other relevant evidence.

I sincerely thank my esteemed colleague and friend Firind Fariq for her help in giving valuable suggestions. I am profoundly thankful to her gesture.

Dr. Surendra Singh Yadav, Jagjit Singh, have been helping me in many ways. Their generosity is gratefully acknowledged.

My wife Vinita provided and collated the material from various sources which she had collected during her study at Allahabad University and National Museum Institute. My son Vineet and daughter Deepti helped me in preparing Index and reading the proofs at various stages. Their patience and love cannot be compensated. My mother's love and affection has been a source of inspiration to me.

I avail this opportunity to convey for sincere thanks to Shri Susheel K. Mittal of M/s D.K. Printworld (P) Ltd. for his painstaking efforts in bringing out this book in such an excellent form.

I am really moved with the efforts of Professor R.C. Sharma an eminent art historian, former Director General of National Museum and Director of Bharat Kala Bhawan, Banaras Hindu University, Varanasi who has been kind enough to write a foreword. I am sincerely grateful to him.

Virender Kumar Dabral

Contents

List of Plates

Pl. VIII : Bhārhut [Satnā-M.P.] *stūpa*. Great railing, crossbar, medallion, monkeys leading, captive element, second century BC. Sandstone, Calcutta, Indian Museum No. 164. AIIS-244.15

Pl. IX : Bhārhut [Satnā-M.P.] *stūpa*. Great railing, pillar medallion showing Alambusa Jātaka [No. 523], doe grazing *bodhisattva* had made water, becomes pregnant, gives birth of Isisinga, Insc. Risya-Sring Jātaka, second century BC. Sandstone, Calcutta, Indian Museum No. 225. AIIS-242.44

Pl. X : Bhārhut [Satnā-M.P.] *stūpa*. Great railing, south-west quadrant pillar, medallion at centre on Yavanajhakiya Jātaka, Virtuous wife of absent *bodhisattva* producing entrapped lovers before king. Insc. Name of Jātaka. Second century BC. Sandstone, Calcutta, Indian Museum No. 202. AIIS-243.49

Pl. XI : Bhārhut [Satnā-M.P.] *stūpa*. Great railing, south-west quadrant pillar, medallion at centre, expanded view Yavanajhakiya, Jātaka [or Maha-Umagga Jātaka]. Virtuous wife of absent *bodhisattva* producing entrapped lovers before the king. Insc.: Name of Jātaka, second century BC. Sandstone, Calcutta, Indian Museum 202. AIIS-483.89

Pl. XII : Bhārhut [Satnā-M.P.] *stūpa*. Great railing, pillars wife Yakṣī and Mahākapi Jātaka, second century BC. Sandstone, Calcutta, Indian Museum No. 3041. AIIS-242.24

Pl. XIII : Bodh Gayā [Gayā-Bihar], Mahābodhi tree coping stone with rosette, *c.* first century BC. Sandstone. 990 × .350m. Bodh Gaya Museum. AIIS-295.90

Pl. XIV : Bodhivr̥kṣa Temple at Anurādhapura, Sri Lanka. AIIS-338.18.

Pl. XXVII : Bodh Gayā [Gayā-Bihar], Railing pillar, *c.* first century BC Sandstone, 1.900 x .350 m. Bodh Gaya Museum No. 1365. AIIS-290.41

Pl. XXVIII : Bodh Gayā [Gayā-Bihar], Mahābodhi Temple, Vajrāsana, Under the modern Bodhi tree, *c.* third century BC. Sandstone 1.360 x .120m. AIIS-296.60

Pl. XXIX : Sīgiriya [Sri Lanka] Fresco on rock face, *c.* fifth century. AIIS-339.30

Pl. XXX : Sīgiriya [Sri Lanka] Fresco on rock face, *c.* fifth century. AIIS-339.12

Pl. XXXI : Sīgiriya [Sri Lanka] Fresco on rock face, *c.* fifth century. AIIS-339.17

Pl. XXXII : Sīgiriya [Sri Lanka] Fresco on rock face, *c.* fifth century. AIIS-339.11.

Pl. XXXIII : Sīgiriya [Sri Lanka] Fresco on rock face, *c.* fifth century. AIIS-339.27

Pl. XXXIV : Sīgiriya [Sri Lanka] Fresco on rock face, *c.* fifth century. AIIS-339.18

Pl. XXXV : Anurādhapura [Puversankulam] [Sri Lanka]. Buddha, seated *c.* fifth century, Stone, Ceylon, Anurādhapura Museum. AIIS-336.82

Pl. XXXVI : Anurādhapura [Sri Lanka], Samādhi Buddha on outer circular road, *c.* fourth century, Stone. AIIS-A40.89

Pl. XXXVII : Sāñcī, Eastern Gateway — Buddha walking on water, First century BC. AIIS-238.91

Pl. XXXVIII : Bhārhut [Satnā-M.P.] *stūpa*. Great railing, pillar, medallion at centre, Ruru or Miga Jātaka [No. 482], *bodhisattva* as standing rescues merchant, later preaches

Sri Lanka's Rulers

THE rulers listed below had effective role in the cultural activities of Sri Lanka. Hence only the relevant names pertaining to the study has been mentioned in order.

	BC
Vijaya	
Upatissa	
Abhaya	
Puṇḍakubhaya	
Mutasiva	
Devanāmpiya Tissa (Devanapa Tis)	250-210
Uttiya	
Mahāśiva	
Sena	
Guttika	
Elara	
Dutthagāmani (Duttagamunu)	161-137

Saddhatissa (Sadatis)	137-119
Lajja Tissa	119-109
Khallatanga	109-103
Vattagāmani Abhaya (Valagam Aba)	
Bahiya	103-89
Dathika	
Vattagāmini	89-77
	AD
Mahadathika Mahānāga	7-19
Kanittha Tissa	167-86
Mahāsena (Mahāsen)	274-301
Pāṇḍu	429-34
Parinda	
Dhātu Sena	455
Kassapa (Sigri Kasuba)	473-91
Moggallāna (Mugalan)	491-508
Kumāra Dhātu Sena	508-16
Aggabodhi-I	571-604
Aggabodhi-II	604-14
Aggabodhi-III	629-39
Aggabodhi-IV	667-83

List of Proper Nouns

THE proper nouns listed below are spelt in the form adopted by Sri Lankan scholars in order to maintain continuity and unformity.

Abhayagiri
Amarāvatī
Ambatthala
Anurādhapura
Arthaśāstra
Aśoka
Bhārhut
Bodh Gayā
Bodhisattva
Bodhi-tree
Brahmā
Ceylon
Culavaṁsa (*Chulavaṁsa*)
Dagaba
Dīpavaṁsa
Gāndhāra
Haṁsa (Hansa)
Hīnayāna
Jetawanarama (Jetavana)
Kaniṣka
Kuṣāṇa
Kuśinagara
Kuśinara (Kuśinagara)
Lumbinī
Magadh
Mahābhārata
Mahāvaṁsa
Mahāyāna

Mahinda
Maurya
Mihintale
Nāgārjuna
Parasamudra
Polonnaruwa
Pratyekabuddha
Rāmāyaṇa
Ruwanwaeli
Sāñcī
Saṁgamitta
Sārnāth
Śālabhañjikā
Śuṅga
Sīgiriya
Siṁha
Śrī Lakṣmī
Śrī Mahā Bodhī
Sri Lanka
Svarṇa
Svastika
Theravāda
Tuṣita
Vahalkade
Vaṅga
Vatadage

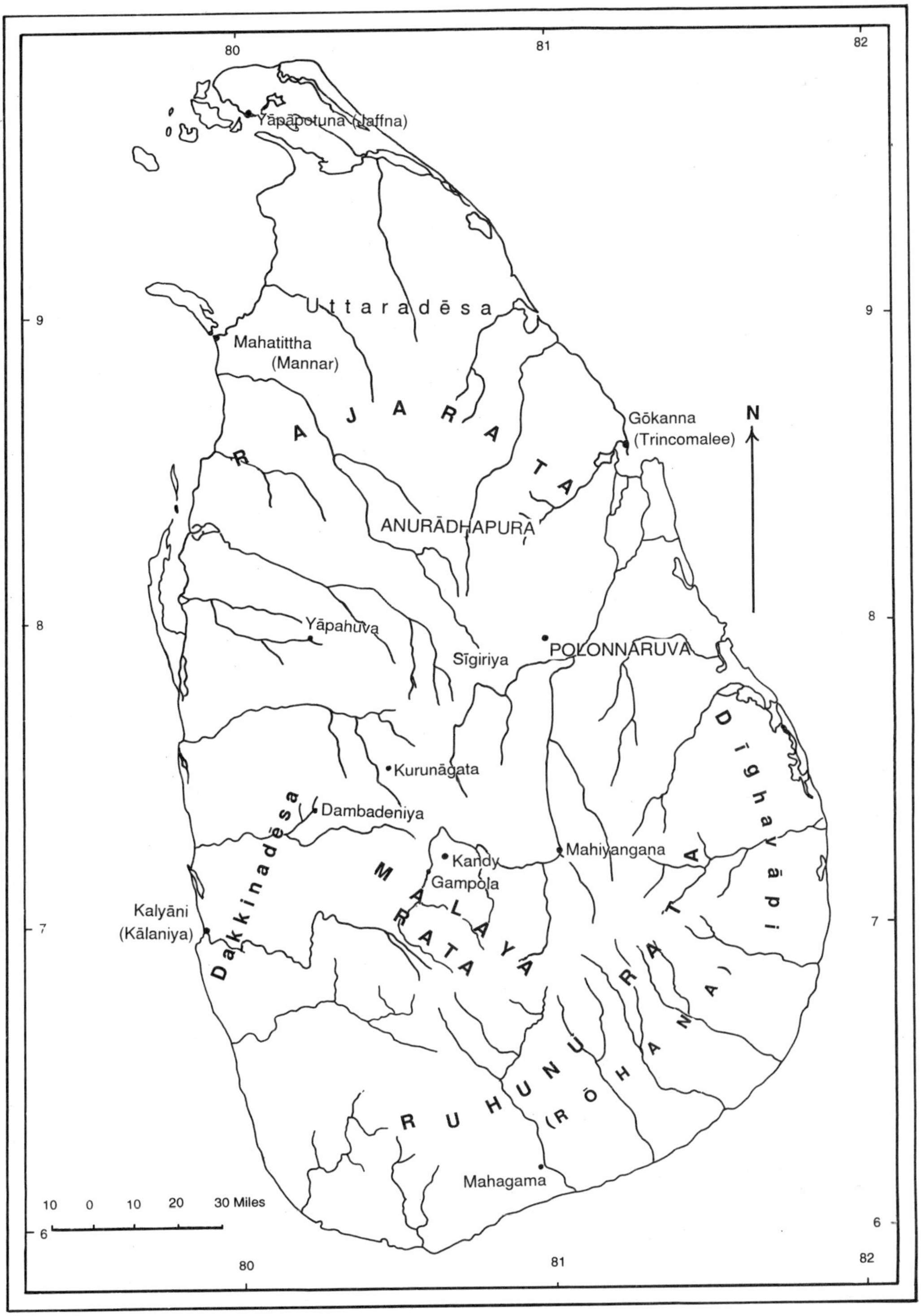

Ancient Sri Lanka

1
Introduction

INDIAN tradition has known modern Sri Lanka as Svarna Laṅkā, where everything man-made, streets, houses, palaces, fortifications were all made of gold, in short it is a golden land. But others called it by different names. To the Arabs it was 'Serendib'. Greeks name it 'Tapobane'. A few name it 'The Resplendent Isle', 'Pearl of Indian Ocean'. Chinese call it 'the island of *Jewel-ratnadīpa*'. Emperor Aśoka called it *Tambapanni*. Portuguese name it Ceilao, Seyallo. The Dutch completed the metamorphosis and called it 'Ceilon' and then it became 'Ceylon'. Now it is called the Democratic Socialist Republic of Sri Lanka.

India and Sri Lanka are two close neighbouring nations/countries which have influenced each other in a variety of ways. The most notable feature in their long relationship is the total absence of aggressive intentions towards each other. It is this factor which has acted as a cement in forging a strong bond in art and culture. Behind this factor lies Buddhism.

Sri Lanka is an island with an area of 25,332 square miles, 270 miles from north to south and 140 miles from east to west and is pearshaped. It is separated from the southern extremity of the Indian peninsula by the gulf of Mannar and the Palk Strait. The distance between the two countries is hardly 26 miles, so Sri Lanka becomes the closest neighbour of India.

Impact of India on Sri Lanka

In the Indian literature Sri Lanka occurs in Kauṭilya's *Arthaśāstra* where it was called *Pāra-samudra* (beyond the ocean). The history of Sri Lanka begins in the sixth century BC. The people living here were settlers who were closely connected with the Draviḍians of the mainland. They were to all intents and purposes of Indian origin. Hinduism and Buddhism were prevailing then in the Indian subcontinent and the social customs of India shaped those of the island according to her needs and deeds. The Sinhalese chronicles state that the ancestors of the Sinhalese migrated into this island from north India. The early mariners who arrived in Sri Lanka carried with them to their country not only Sri Lanka's pearls and precious stones but also wonderful tales.

Myths and legends

The mariners spread stories of a race of ogres and ogresses which were already dwelling in Sri Lanka and they had many irons in the fire. A story as narrated in the earlier period states that a merchant name Siṁhala came with a retinue of five hundred followers to the *Ratnadvīpa* island from the city of Siṁhakalpa. They were enticed by ogresses in the guise of alluring women who used to keep them as husbands. Siṁha, the father of Siṁhala, and his companions were warned of the probable danger but they paid no heed. But Siṁhala escaped by becoming the husband of one ogress. The ogresses devoured Siṁha. Siṁha's spouse went to Siṁhakalpa city assuming the form of a beautiful woman with an infant and made it known to the citizens that she had been deserted. She made an appeal to the king to take her back but the king remarked that all women were ogresses and yet he would be glad to keep her in the harem.

Fa Hien, a Chinese traveller gives the account that Sri Lanka had originally no inhabitants but only demons and dragons. Merchants of different countries came to Sri Lanka to trade. In days gone by, so the story runs, that there was a king who had a beautiful and charming daughter. This girl left the palace and travelled with a company of merchants, whilst they were travelling in the dense forest, the girl fells into the hands of a lion. The lion and the beautiful girl lived together and from their union had a son and a daughter. Siṁhabāhu was the son's name and he was bodily very heavy and had human characteristics but abhorred his father-lion. Siṁhabāhu made a plan to leave his father and escape with his mother and sister. The plan was successful and the three reached the Vaṅga country. The lion came to know that his son, wife and daughter had deserted him, became furious and began vexing the countryside. The king of Vaṅga was upset and offered a reward to anyone who would free his land from the terror of the lion. Siṁhabāhu, son of the lion, came forward and killed his own father and claimed the reward. He, thus, became a parricide and he had no love for the land where he committed this crime. Hence he left with his sister and mother and arrived in Lāṭadeśa (presently named as Gujarat). His sister Siṁhasivali had thirty two children of whom the eldest son was named Vijaya and next was Sumitta. Vijaya grewup and became a ruffian and leader of a company of vagabonds. With his band he started harassing the people. Siṁhabāhu warned him but Vijaya ignored this. The king of Lāṭadeśa arrested Vijaya and his retinue of about seven hundred followers and had their heads half shaved as a punishment and sent them away from his kingdom in a ship. Their wives and children were sent in another ship which drifted apart in the sea and the wives and children reached Nāgadīpa (Andaman and Nicobars) and Vijaya and his retinue touched north of Bombay and ultimately reached Sri Lanka. Vijaya is said to have landed at *Tambapanni* on the very day of the Buddha's *mahāparinirvāṇa*. It is very surprising to know that Vijaya reached on the very same day, i.e., the day of Buddha's passing away. It is recorded that Buddha knew about the arrival of Vijaya and he had made a prophecy that Vijaya would convert Sri Lanka into an abode of Buddhism and it would flourish under him in future. It is also believed that the Buddha had requested Indra, the king of Gods, to give protection to Vijaya and his retinue. Vijaya and his band of followers reached Sirisavatthu inhabited by demons. Some of his followers lost the way and Vijaya learnt that they were held captive by Kuveni, daughter of a Yakṣa king. They were released after heated exchange of words and this is known as the origin of the Sinhalese people. There are other stories also. One of the legends states that a princess had mated with a lion who gave birth to the eponymous hero and the race so produced came to be known as Sinhalese. Vijaya was also a king in South India who had landed in Sri Lanka.

Historians are also of the view that Vijaya, a powerful king of South India, arrived at Sri Lanka on the day of *mahāparinirvāṇa*. There is confusion whether Vijaya refers to the chief of the vagabonds or to the king from South India. But from all historical evidences and other relevant myths, Vijaya is the king from South India who had gone to Sri Lanka.

Rāmāyaṇa and Sri Lanka

> The legendary history of Ceylon begins with the *Ramayana*, the epic poem which recounts the ravishing of Sita by the demon King of Lanka, Ravana and her recovery by her husband Rama with the aid of the monkey chief Hanumanta.

But, though a few names in the island refer to the legend, such as Nuwara Eliya 'the glade of (Rāvaṇa's) city', Sītā Eliya, 'Sītā's glade' and Sītāwake, the epic itself seems to have had no[1] long standing impact, for it finds little mention in the folklore of the Sinhalese. Sri Lankans do not believe in the *Rāmāyaṇa*. There were kings, named, Rāvaṇa, Vibhīṣaṇa and there are places connected with the epic. Several folk tales rebuild the theory of making the existing Lanka, the Lanka of *Rāmāyaṇa*, nevertheless it is only mythology

1. Codrington, H.W., *A Short History of Ceylon*, p. 5.

and legend. However, it corroborates the fact that Lanka existed in earlier times.[2] It is a debatable issue and several interpretations give several concepts.

Arrival of Buddhism in Sri Lanka

Sri Lanka has borrowed[3] Indian culture, art and literature and changed them to suit the needs of her people. It is an adaptation.[4]

> Not without a reason Buddhism is recognised as one of the greatest gifts India bestowed on the world.

Sri Lanka was the first country to which the Mauryan emperor Aśoka[5] sent his son Mahinda[6] and daughter (or sister) Saṁghmitta to propagate Buddhism. Aśoka is described as *stūpair vicitraith giriśṛṅga-kalpaith in*

---

2. A.B. Surveer, *Anuradhapur Sanskriti* (*tr*), p. 3.
3. Wickramasinghe, Martin, *Aspects of Sinhalese Culture*, p. 10.
4. *Op. cit.*, p. 46.
5. Aśoka, the Great Mauryan Emperor and the illustrious king of India (273 BC-232 BC) was keen to spread the ideals of Buddhism throughout the world. The reign of the Great Emperor was an epoch in the history of Buddhism. Aśoka, a mighty builder, the builder of cities of innumerable *stūpas*, *vihāras* or monasteries, pillars was worshipper of Buddha. Devanāmpiyatissa, the second son of king Mutasiva was installed as Monarch of Sri Lanka in 309 BC.
6. Copleston Reginald Stephen, *Buddhism in Primitive and Present in Magadha and in Ceylon*, p. 156.

   Ceylon Chronicles maintain that Mahinda was the illegitimate son of Asoka. The Chinese pilgrim Hsuan Tsang states that he was Asoka's younger brother variously called Vigatasoka. (Thapar, Romila, *Asoka and the Decline of the Mauryas*, p. 24). Even in *The Discovery of India*, Pandit Nehru writes that Mahinda was Asoka's son. The Ceylon school thinks that the Third Council was held in the time of Asoka in about 247 BC "Ceylon tradition (as narrated in the Dipavamsa and the Mahavamsa) makes Bindusara, the husband of sixteen wives and father of 101 sons, of whom only three are named viz., Sumana (Susima according to the northern legends), the eldest, Asoka and Tisya (uterine brother of Asoka), the youngest son. The mother of Asoka in the northern tradition is Subhadrangi →

the Div. They carried a branch of the Bodhi tree and no arms. The king of Sri Lanka extended a royal welcome to these two. This is the only such incident known wherein a prince carried a branch of a tree and not a sword to an alien land, in the history of the world.

No doubt, the royal will to propagate the teachings of Buddha, was the cause of Mahinda's mission but at the same time this gesture amply mirrored the image of people's culture.[7] Today, Sri Lanka is the centre of Theravāda Buddhism which is also called Hīnayāna. Three quarters of the population of Sri Lanka are Sinhalese and nearly all of them are Buddhists. The Buddhist Art in India and Sri Lanka conveys an expression of the life and thought of the vast cultural background and socio-religious traditions.

SINHALESE CHRONICLES

The great Sinhalese Chronicles, the *Mahāvaṁsa*[8] and *Culavaṁsa*[9] provide full and accurate accounts of the chronology and details of the island's

---

→ the beautiful daughter of Brahmin of Champa, who bore Bindusara another son named Vigatasoka (Vitasoka), and not Tisya of Ceylon book" (Mookerji, R.K., *Asoka*, pp. 2-3). Romila Thapar writes: "The Mahavamsa states that although he put ninety-nine brothers to death, Asoka spared the life of the youngest of those Tissa. Tissa was later made vice-regent. In the Ceylonese sources, he is called Tissa but in other sources he is called by various names, Vitasoka, Vigatasoka, Sudatta and Sugatra." —*Asoka And the Decline of the Mauryas*, p. 27.

7. Gupta, S.P., *The Roots of Indian Art*, p. 12.
8. This chronicle has long been considered as work of the sixth century AD and the writer of the chronicle was Mahānāmā. The original is in Pāli and still preserved in Sri Lanka.
9. *Culavaṁsa* (*Chulavaṁsa*) is the continuation of the *Mahāvaṁsa*. The *Dīpavaṁsa* in Pāli is preserved in Burma. The chronicles books were handed down in Pāli and commentaries upon them in Sinhalese at two great monasteries at Anurādhapura, Great Monastery and North Monastery. The *Aśoka Avadāna* in Buddhist Sanskrit is preserved in Nepal. The author and date are unknown but presumed as early as the third century BC.

history.[10] These works are of great historical value[11] and are verse Chronicles of Ceylon history.[12]

The *Mahāvaṁsa* is primarily a religious history but it also describes the main political events such as invasions, action of intruders, conquests and civil wars. It is a poem written in Pāli and its four main themes are:

(i) Visits of Buddha to the Island

(ii) Indo-Āryan colonisation of the Island

(iii) Introducing Buddhism and its propagation

(iv) Epic of King Dutthagāmani

Fa Hien, the first Chinese pilgrim, wrote:

> The Ceylon Chronicles, the *Dipavamsa* and the *Mahavamsa* in particular may also be regarded as source material; since they describe at length the part played by Aśoka in spreading of Buddhism, more particularly in the coming of Buddhism to Ceylon.

Here again caution is necessary since these chronicles were written by the Ceylonese Buddhist monks who depicted Aśoka from the Orthodox Buddhist standpoint.[13] The principal Sinhalese works are *Nikāya, Saṁgraha, Pūjāvalī* and *Rājāvalī*. These are in the *Mahāvaṁsa* and *Culavaṁsa*. These chronicles are excellent guideposts to most of the major events in the country's early history. They also highlight the intimate relationship between the Sinhalese and Buddhism and the Buddhist Art which came to Sri Lanka in the third century BC.[14]

10. Coomaraswamy, A.K., *Buddha and the Gospel of Buddhism*, p. 300.

11. *Op. cit.*, p. 301

12. *Op. cit.*, p. 300.

13. Thapar, Romila, *Asoka and the Decline of the Mauryas*, p. 8.

14. Simon Richard, *Sri Lanka the Resplendent Isle*, p. 110.

Vijaya the first king known in the island's history hailed from India. The trade and culture that had then been going on and meticulously nurtured was also from India. Thus, the king while embracing Buddhism from Mahinda must have given a careful thought. And it is also true that before Mahinda no one from any other country or from any parts of the world had gone there with a religious mission. It is also important to know that the king Devanāmpiya Tissa had foreseen the importance of Buddhism and must have considered also that since emperor Aśoka made his son and daughter Buddhists; for the king of Sri Lanka thus, it was but natural to welcome Mahinda's mission.

RISE AND GROWTH OF BUDDHISM IN INDIA

At this point it is relevant to know about Buddhism and its growth to find out why it had such great appeal to the Sinhalese. Before the rise of Buddhism in the sixth century BC, India had gone through a long process of religious thought and philosophical speculations. The Vedic religion was one of various rites and rituals. Many people were dissatisfied with it and some of them became ascetics and wandered in search of enlightenment. A few of them returned from the woods and preached their ideas in the villages and towns. Among these two men became famous as teachers and founders of two great religions, i.e., Jainism and Buddhism. Mahāvīra became the founder of what came to be called Jainism and Gautama of Buddhism. Both were contemporaries. Mahāvīra and Buddha belonged to the republican tribes of the Licchavis and the Śākyas respectively. Both were brought up as sons of kings or chiefs and had recourse to all luxuries but gave up their princely life. They were keen to find the reasons why people suffer. Buddhism spread far and wide and wealthy merchants parted with their wealth for its rapid growth and contributed for the construction of monuments embellished with sculptures and masterly paintings. Under the patronage of emperor Aśoka, Buddhist monks later went on a mission to spread Buddha's teachings to other parts of Asia, China and Tibet. But Sri Lanka was the first country to have received Buddhism from the royal prince Mahinda. He was received with great honour because his father emperor Aśoka was the contemporary of Devanāmpiya Tissa. They were on friendly terms but never met each other.

CHRISTIANITY AND SRI LANKA

There is a legend that in the first century AD a new religion Christianity which spread in the West was brought to India. Jesus Christ preached Christianity which is based on worship of a single God. Christ emphasised love and Christianity spread in various forms all over Europe where it became the dominant religion. In India, Christianity first spread among the people of the Malabār coast, i.e., on Madras-Kerala coastal areas. It is very significant to note here that Christianity did not have any influence on Sri Lanka though it had the strongest influence on the coastal area of South India. The reason could be that Christianity was based on the earlier Jewish religion and there worship of God is paramount. The other valid reason apparently could be that Christ is believed to be not only the Messiah or Messenger of God, but in fact, the son of God. The Buddhists do not believe in God and in any dogmatic way of life. Christianity believes when people die their souls will go to heaven and be reunited with God. These beliefs and faiths look almost like Brāhmaṇism.

Christianity and Buddhism

Hence, Sri Lankan Buddhists or for that matter any Buddhists were not influenced by Christianity.

Here a comparison of the personality of Buddha and his movement Buddhism with Christ and Christianity is necessary. Both were venerated spiritual leaders and rose above forms and codes. Christ's inner life was undisturbed though he suffered much severe persecution later; but Buddha was disturbed at the sight of the suffering humanity. Christ's expression is emotional rather than intellectual. Christ teaches that the world is full of evil or spoiled and wished to remove the evil and establish the kingdom of heaven on earth. Buddha was never angry with the world. Buddha, on the other hand, teaches that birth, sickness and death are necessary for existence and can be overcome only when the cause or reason for these are found mastered. Buddha created a religious order and Christ did not and thus the whole of Asia from western India right across to Japan owes some of the best part of its civilisation and culture in the deepest moral sense to Buddha. Buddha's movement brought unity of Asian civilisations. Buddhism gave birth to a new variety of ideas and special order which advanced by leaps and bounds.

BUDDHIST ART

Buddhist Art reflects very faithfully the tenets of Buddhism. Ananda Coomaraswamy says:

> In the omission of the figure of Buddha, the early Buddhist art is truly Buddhist; for the rest, it is an art about Buddhism, rather than Buddhist art.
>
> Early Buddhist art says Ananda Coomaraswamy is popular, sensuous and animistic Indian art, adapted to the purpose of the illustration of Buddhist anecdotes and the decoration of Buddhist monuments.

Today Buddhist Art motivates the researchers and academics of India and Sri Lanka to exchange their views. It is the main nexus between the two countries. Various conflicting ideas have been ventilated but concrete analysis is yet to be achieved. Notwithstanding, it is also not to be forgotten that owing to changes in political scenario full justice is yet to be done to the study.

Since the advent of Buddhist Art in Sri Lanka, new horizons are being cultivated and nurtured, thus the study becomes more fascinating and interesting. Each art historian looks back at earlier ages and seeks to interpret them in the light of his own knowledge and experience. Art historians' perceptions of the past are therefore, often subjective.

The artists often tried to present the truths, convictions and beliefs that had taken their root in the minds of the people and were universally accepted as true. The religious fervour of Aśoka imparted much momentum to the spread of Buddhist lore. This instilled in the artists a desire to acquire knowledge of correct iconography and a knowledge of the *Jātaka*s for the major compositions which they were commissioned to paint or chisel. It is thus evident that in dealing with the Buddhist Art, a grasp of the ins and outs of the religious lore is a must.

The artist in all his creations had depicted inner pulsation of joy and it is beyond all question that the artists of that time in particular were to represent the most essential characteristics of the inner spiritual manifestation of the object they wished to represent in art. That is why it is said that the Buddhist Art as well as the Indian Art is a reflection of religious qualities. Both arts basically mirror their respective religions.

Aśokan monolithic columns

The Mauryan dynasty in the third century BC erected a series of monolithic columns which displayed sculpture. These columns show some unique characteristics and though carved from sand stone, were polished to a high degree of smoothness and veneer. The Mauryan sculpture mainly represents Buddha's life and previous life, i.e., depicting the *Jātaka*s.

The ealiest examples of Buddhist Art are the Aśokan monolithic pillars with capitals surmounted by animals, such as the bull, the lion or the elephant. The pillar erected by Aśoka at Lumbinī and his visit to Kuśinagara in 250 BC attests to his devotion to and patronage of Buddhism. He was on a *dharmayātrā* or a pilgrimage of piety.[15] The inscription on the pillars are in Brāhmī script and Prākṛt language.

15. Ahir, D.C., *Buddhist Shrines in India*, p. v.

> In spite of large literature, old and new in different languages, Pali, Sanskrit, English, French and German seeking from a variety of standpoints to interpret the unique personality and achievements of Aśoka, the interpretation is not yet adequate or final.[16]

Sir John Marshall says,

> the Sarnath Capital, on the other hand, by no means a masterpiece is the product of the more developed art of which the world was cognizant in the third century BC. [Plate I]

Without long practice in sculpture, it would not have been possible to reproduce such lions; the method of execution expresses marvellously the strength and liveliness of the lions through their expressive muscles and bones. The lions stand out as a natural development and are in complete harmony with the pillar as a whole.

BUDDHIST ART FOLLOWING COLLAPSE OF MAURYAN EMPIRE

The Mauryan empire lasted a little over a hundred years and after the death of Aśoka, began to break up in 185 BC, the last Mauryan king was killed by Puṣyamitra Śuṅgas, who started the Śuṅga dynasty in Magadh. The Śuṅga were of Brāhmaṇa descent and in turn were succeeded by the Kaṇvas in 28 BC. Bhārhut, Sāñcī, Sārnāth, Bodh Gayā represent the art of this period.

The early Buddhist Art of Bhārhut, Sāñcī, Gayā and Amarāvatī show no anthropomorphic representations of the Master. His presence is indicated by aniconic symbols such as the wheel, perfect enlightenment (*samādhi*), the *stūpa*, the *chatra* (parasol), the *triratna* (a tripod like symbol) symbolising one or the other event of his life. Buddha is shown with the fingers of his hand webbed.

16. Mookerji, R.K., *Aśoka*, p. vii.

The images of the Buddha were introduced in the south during first-second century AD in Amrāvatī School of art which is elegant and sensitive. The *mahā-caitya* (Amrāvatī *stūpa*) — second century BC to AD 250 shows affinity to Bhārhut. Buddhism had changed a great deal and it was no longer the simple religion which Buddha had taught. There were two sects, namely, Mahāyāna and Hīnayāna. Mahāyāna[17] was a sect with many ceremonies and included not only worship of Buddha but also of saints. Its monks were powerful.

> The earlier school of Buddhism was called Hīnayāna (Lesser vehicle) which stressed the Buddha's detachment from the world and his essential achievement of enlightenment. This state of non-existence and transcendence over the troubles of life could not be represented in an image, it must be known only through experience and so the depiction of the Buddha in his physical identity had no value or purpose. For this reason, we do not find references to the principal events in his life and previous incarnations. His presence was indicated symbolically by an empty throne, a pair of footprints, the wheel or the *pīpal* tree.[18]

But later Buddha's images, showing him as a monk of princely mien became the order of the day with stress on *ūrṇaroma*, a dot in between his eyebrows; coiffeur marked by a prominent protuberance; *uṣṇīṣa*, the top knot; *mudrās*[19] shown in various attitudes like preaching the doctrine (*dharmacakra*), *vitarka* (solving a riddle), *abhaya* (dispelling fear), *varada* (granting a boon), etc.

---

17. Mahāyāna (greater vehicle) stressed the role of *bodhisattvas* and one who delays entry to *nirvāṇa* and continues to take birth to assist other to gain salvation. This has parallel with the *guru* and disciple role of Hinduism.

18. *From Art in Diversity — Studies in the History of Art*, Longman, Cheshire, 1988, p. 8.

19. Perera, A.D.T.E., *Evolution of the Buddha Images*, p. 309.

Gāndhāra-Mathurā School of Art

The Kuṣāṇas, whose original home was in Chinese Turkistan, arrived in Afghanistan in the first century AD. The Kuṣāṇas arrived in the first century AD and established themselves at Taxila and Peśāvara and extended their reign up to Punjab, Kaniṣka. Their empire was vast extending up to Vārāṇasī in the East and Sāñcī in the South. It was the most powerful dynasty and Mathurā was an important centre of their kingdom. It was in this period that the Indo-Greek School of Buddhist Art achieved its greatest development.[20]

The Kuṣāṇa emperor was an ardent adherent and patron of Buddhism and it was during his time that the Fourth Buddhist Council was held.[21] Kaniṣka's statue at Mathurā shows him as a well built man. Kaniṣka's reign is also a landmark in the history of Buddhism. Tradition not only represents him as a great patron of religion but also associates him with the galaxy of Buddhist masters who shaped Buddhism and Buddhist Art.

Owing to new ideas and concepts, the arts, literature and other various social sciences entered into multifacet aspects of Indian life and far-reaching changes took place. As a result of conducive environment, a close contact was set-up with Iran and Western Asia. This affinity brought trade co-operation and new towns and villages began to crowd the map of Kuṣāṇa empire. Mathurā, Ujjayinī and many other towns became important centres for trade. Indian people were hand in glove with those of Western Asia and brought Greek sculpture to the cities of northern India and there were images of the Greek-Roman Gods. The Indian artists working in Gāndhāra were influenced by the images of these foreign deities. Their statues of Buddha and other scenes from Buddha's life reflect the Greek style. In other words,

20. Bagchi, P.C., *Aśoka and the Expansion of Buddhism*, p. 63.
21. First Council was held at Rājagṛha in 477 BC. Second Council was held at Vaiśālī in 372 BC. Third Council was held during Aśoka's reign at Pāṭaliputra in 247 BC.

the art of the sculptors who imitated Greek style came to be called Gāndhāra art. Afghanistan became the centre of Gāndhāra art.

Mathurā was already a centre of indigenous art and beautiful images of Buddha were made there. Thus, there were two Schools of art during the Kuṣāṇa period, the Mathurā School and the Gāndhāra School. These two Schools produced images not only of Buddha alone but of various other holy persons called the *bodhisattvas* whom the Buddhists respected [*Plate II* & *III*]. The *bodhisattvas* were holy persons who had lived on earth before Buddha. It is very surprising to know that Mathurā being the birthplace of Kṛṣṇa did not produce Kṛṣṇa images as it did of Buddha. Another point to note is that Mathurā School flourished in the early centuries of the Christian era. But hardly any special significance is seen. These two art schools lead us to believe that on account of the progress of the Mahāyāna Buddhism, Christianity and the Hinduism had no impact on Mathurā School. The literature produced by the Mahāyānist indicate that the movement led to the composition of numerous *avadānas* heralded the Buddhist faith.

BUDDHIST ARCHITECTURE

Since the time of Emperor Aśoka, religious architecture had come into vogue. Aśoka is said to have erected 84000 Buddhists structures of various kinds.[22] The *stūpa* enters into religious architecture and this is a respected symbol even today. This statement appears to be hyperbolical, nevertheless this was the starting point of Buddhist architecture. There were *stūpas* earlier even before Aśoka but he is credited to have constructed the original brick *stūpa* at Sāñcī and Dhamek *stūpa* at Sārnāth. The *stambha* or pillar carry symbols of faith.

Railings became the emblem of protection — meant to preserve anything special or of sacred nature. It was of significant value in Buddhist architecture as it encircled the *stūpa* and the sacred Bo-tree. Railing can be seen at

---

22. Mitra, R., *Buddha Gaya*, p. 233.

Sāñcī, Sārnāth, Gayā and Anurādhapura in Sri Lanka. This is a special characteristic of the Buddhist architecture.

SRI LANKA-ANURĀDHAPURA

Two great cities of Sri Lanka, Anurādhapura and Polonnaruwa, are testimony to the innumerable *stūpas*, monasteries and *vihāras*, *dagabas* representing different phases of time and social milieu. This has further whetted one's curiosity in visualising the trend of Buddhist Art in context with the Indian view. Anurādhapura, Polonnaruwa and Sīgiriya are known as 'ruined cities' of Sri Lanka. Polonnaruwa was the capital from eleventh century AD and here art flourished after seventh-eighth century AD. Anurādhapura is the most important and fascinating city to be studied and understood aptly. It is the city which has seen many ups and downs, natural calamities and it was attacked numerous times and restored. History tells us that the city of Anurādhapura represents the height of glory of Sri Lanka, in art and architecture.

Anurādhapura is the seat of Śrī Mahā Bodhi.[23] Devanāmpiya Tissa,[24] Dhātusena, Dutthagamani and host of many kings ruled Anurādhapura. It appears that the seat was reserved for the Monarch. The king was to be a superhuman who would have values, revered as a divine person and it was expected from the king that he should live according to the high standards of *bodhisattva* or a Buddha-to be. He had to make his mark. It is also a fact that great men have emerged from evil environment; perhaps their greatness was in some way an outcome of the struggle of their indomitable spirits with almost insurmountable obstacles. The last interlude of peace in the phase of the history of Anurādhapura period came in the reign of Aggabodhi-I (AD 571-604) and Aggabodhi-II (AD 604-14). Aggabodhi-I was a nephew of Mahānāga and his successor was his own nephew. They together built many

23. Bo-tree is known as Śrī Mahā Bodhi by the Sri Lankans.

24. In Sinhalese *devanāmpiya* means beloved of the Gods.

stūpas and monasteries. Aggabodhi-II is credited with the rebuilding of the Thuparama and the construction of six new *vihāras*. During AD 614 Aggabodhi died and Anurādhapura had to face turmoil. *Culavaṁsa* records that during Aggabodhi's rule 'when he was dead his subjects mourned, all in deep grief'. During this time the Tamil mercenary troops invaded the island.

NĀGA

The *nāgas*, prince and princess of Anurādhapura and Amarāvatī are only distinguishable from human beings by means of Cobra heads — *nāgapuṣpa*.[25] But it is true that the word *nāga* which was often found in Sri Lanka never appeared after the *Rāmāyaṇa*. The word *nāga* is a misnomer. This is applied to human beings and they are a tribe in the north-east of India. *Nāgas* are generally understood to be a form of non descript beings with the bodies of serpents attached to the upper parts of a human being but they are never represented in the Sinhalese carvings. Even at Bhārhut and Amāravatī these are missing. Cobras, elephants and supernatural beings in human form were also treated as *nāgas*.

The *Cambridge Encyclopaedia* states that

> The Buddha dies in Kushinagar in what is now Nepal at the age of eighty.[26]

Kuśinagara is in Uttar Pradesh, the most populated State of India and was never in Nepal. It also says that the name 'Ceylon' is still in use. It is also not correct; for Ceylon[27] has been renamed Sri Lanka.

---

25. *Nāgapuṣpa* is identical with *campaka* flower (A. Foucher). It is also called 'honeysuckle' or palmette motif on 'Aśokan pillar' (Gupta, S.P., *The Roots of Indian Art*, p. 14).

26. Robinson, F., (ed.), *The Cambridge Encyclopaedia of India, Pakistan, Bangladesh, Sri Lanka, Nepal, Bhutan and the Maldives*, published by Cambridge University Press, Cambridge, 1989, p. 327.

27. *Op.cit.*, p. 366.

Bodhisattvas

It is well-known that a group of Buddha flanked by two *bodhisattvas* are very frequent in Buddhist Art. In the numerous examples belonging to the medieval period of two satellites of Buddha, usually Avalokiteśvara and Maitreya, are clearly distinguished, the one by a lotus flower whence is epithet *padmapāṇi* and other by a *nāgapuṣpa* held in each case in the left hand. Moreover, Avalokiteśvara wears a figurine of Amitābha, Buddha of Boundless, Light, inserted in his diadem, whereas Maitreya has a *mukuṭa* with a decorative miniature *stūpa* in front.[28]

ART AS A REFLECTION OF CONTEMPORARY SOCIETY

The History of Art of a country is the story of its people; their culture, social panorama, environment, literature and their response both to internal and external influences. Sri Lanka and India are illustrating these through various forms. Today, Sri Lanka where Gokanna[29] one of the finest natural harbour is making an effort to adopt what it receives and was being received from the outside world to local needs. The artists in ancient India were masons, potters, blacksmiths and artisans and to them art was a part of social order. The Buddhist Art of India as well as Sri Lanka was matured and developed through public co-operation and donations. The Indian Art had attained a high degree of excellence from second century BC in plastic representation and pictorial sphere from second-fourth century AD, i.e., the beginning of Ajantā at its peak.

GUPTAS

In the fourth century AD, there was the Gupta Dynasty whose rule lasted for more than two hundred years. The period continued to see some of the great achievements of Indian culture which had begun in the earlier period.

---

28. Vogel, J.M., *The Sculpture and Paintings*, pp. 31-2..

29. Gokanna is Trincomalee.

Not only were the Guptas powerful monarchs, they were also patrons of learning and encouraged poets, writers, scientists and artists, all of whom contributed to Indian culture. This period is also called 'golden age' of India and marks the brightest period of art in India. This was also a period of Hindu renaissance. The Gupta kings were worshippers of Viṣṇu, though they allowed complete freedom of worship to Buddhists and Jains. They encouraged art and paintings. Sanskrit became the language of the learned. The Indian epics, the *Mahābhārata* and the *Rāmāyaṇa* and other Sanskrit works such as the Laws of Manu and Kauṭilya's *Arthaśāstra*, took their final form at this time. Kālidāsa wrote his dramas and poems[30] which later influenced Sinhalese literature. The Sīgiriya frescoes *gi* are the best examples.

During the Gupta period, there was a large Buddhist monastery at Sārnāth. Here some stone images of Buddha have been chiselled which are among the most beautiful pieces of stone sculpture that India has produced. The Buddhist monasteries at Ajantā and the walls of the caves were covered with paintings (known as *mural*s) depicting the life of Buddha. These have survived and their colours are almost as fresh as when they we painted. The Ajantā cave paintings depict the dignity of motherhood. Women are expressed in the fullness of their breasts and hips. This style of illustration is peculiar to the art of that period. In Sīgiriya frescoes, breasts as compared to those of Ajantā are a little heavy [*Plate IV*].

The artists of Sāñcī, Amarāvatī, Ajantā, Mathurā and their descendents utilised their capability and their artistic vision in the creation of the images or icons of Hindu gods and goddesses in order to promote socio-religious feelings among the people. The art of Ellorā and Mahābalipuram are excellent illustrations. The Amarāvatī art flourished during the Gupta Dynasty. The Sīgiriya frescoes of Sri Lanka have won laurels not only in the island but in

---

30. Kālidāsa was the sweetest Sanskrit poet and author of *Meghadūta*, *Raghuvaṁśa Kumārasaṁbhava* and *Ṛtusaṁhāra* were poems and drama *Abhijñāna-śākuntalam, Vikramorvaśīya*.

the entire world of arts. The paintings at Bāgh, Ajantā and Sīgiriya elevated the delicacy and depth of feelings. The great Buddhist Art reached its high watermark under

> Candra Gupta in AD 320 and an empire was established that controlled most of India until its decline in the sixth century.

This had influenced monasteries and caves.

It is also believed that the artists from India travelled to Sri Lanka. The flight of steps, columns, monolithic characters, etc., attest to this fact. The Mathurā School was concentrated in a small region. The workshops of Mathurā produced several images and had link with the past. The Mathurā School has produced beautiful *bodhisattvas* during the Gupta's rule and these were sent outside India also. Isurumuniya lovers of Sri Lanka reflect the characteristics of the Gupta School in India of the fourth and fifth century.

The interchange of art forms between India and her neighbour have always been active. This has led to the rise and development of new idioms. That the Gupta period has been the hallmark in illustrating this hypothesis is borne out by the paintings of Ajantā from second century BC to sixth century AD. Narrative compositions of *Jātakas* in the walls, ceilings, halls and columns are the glories of the world art.

Motifs of rosette are noticed at Mihintale in Sri Lanka. Steles are found in Bhārhut, Sāñcī, Bodh Gayā, Amarāvatī and Anurādhapura. These are vines, floral, animals and human beings. Gupta patronage of art and literature encouraged the evolution of the classical idiom which became the standard form for subsequent creative efforts.

Sanskrit being the language of the ruling class and sculpture marked the culmination of quest for spiritualism and perfection. "Pāli became the literary languge of Ceylon and still holds that position." Ceylonese literature was an off-shoot of Indian literature, the art of Ceylon — architecture, sculpture and paintings was derived from India. The Ceylonese alphabet also came from India. On the other hand, the Buddhist world owes a great debt to Ceylon.[31] Very few are interested in Pāli now.

Ajantā and Bāgh provided inscription for understanding Buddhist Art. It is not fair to turn a Nelson's eye to historical facts but to discern and bring a balanced and comprehensive understanding of the present and the past. A comparative study calls for a critical and analytical approach which may lead to up to date views. It is in this spirit that this study has been undertaken.

Each nation has a particular genius of its own and therefore, a particular way of self-expression. Hence, the analytical approach of Buddhist Art is broadly based on tradition, literature as well as arts of space, i.e., architecture, sculpture and painting. The main focus is on Sri Lanka Buddhist Art, which has not been thoroughly studied and understood. For making an accurate critical study, we have placed our reliance on a combined study of these.

31. Bagchi, P.C., *Aśoka and the Expansion of Buddhism*, p. 86.

2

Architecture

ARCHITECTURE is the art of designing and constructing an extremely attractive, fully useful and least costly building for a specific purpose at a particular place to suit and satisfy not only its builders but their descendants too. It is also called the art and science of planning, designing and constructing. "Architecture is the matrix of civilisation", says Percy Brown. Each great culture movement has made intellectual evolution and contribution to the art of building. Architecture is 'the science of construction'. It is a systematised body of knowledge related with the assessment, evalution and execution of the ways of building the construction.[1] Architectural study is of three dimensions, the study of the frameworks, the study of sculpture decoratives and the study of iconographic decorative. Architecture, more than any other subject, truly reflects the aspirations, the level of knowledge, degree of prosperity, the nature of the age and its beliefs. For example, take the *stūpa*. It reveals that people were religious and pious, enjoyed economic prosperity and well versed in matters ethical, moral and spiritual without forsaking their earthly traditional values.

---

1. Murty, K. Satya, *Handbook of Indian Architecture*, p.1.

Stūpa

Stūpa is the most distinguished feature of early Buddhist architecture.

The terms *stūpa*, *caitya* and *dagaba* are generally used by people as synonyms for *stūpa*. These are important terms in Buddhist architecture. There is difference in their meaning and the purpose for which they are used. *Caitya* is a shrine, an altar or a temple, a mound containing a relic, e.g., ashes, bones, hair and tooth. *Stūpa* is an architectural terms for a relic mound. *Stūpa*s in Sri Lanka are called *dagaba*s. *Dagaba* is a part of the *stūpa*. The *stūpa* is a whole monument, while the *dagaba* is the only area where the relic is deposited. The Buddhist burial mound is not an isolated but is the central part in Sri Lanka. *Dagaba* is derived from the primitive tumuli, or *stūpa*s for the burial of the dead which existed in Sri Lanka long before the advent of Buddhism. King Devanāmpiya Tissa, the contemporary of emperor Aśoka received from the emperor the alms bowl and collar bone of Buddha amongst other sacred relics; it was necessary to enshrine these. Thus, the tumulis developed into a large hemispherical brick dome. This was crowned by a square block of brick work called the '*tee*', containing offerings. It is also true that all *dagaba*s do not contain relic. Both the *dagaba* and the Bo-tree are honoured by the people of Sri Lanka and both command respect especially from the Buddhists; hence, their practice of constructing a *stūpa* near the Bo-tree and *vice versa*. It is also a practice in Sri Lanka to construct a *vihāra* (a monastery or a hall) for the devotees. But from the architecture point of view, it was an essential part as heretofore. *Stūpa*s and *vihāra*s were constructed because of royal patronage. This, of course, was not always so. History proves that everywhere in the world the merchants and others did contribute liberally in order to elevate their religious longings. This was earlier also and holds good today. And they have become part and parcel of Buddhist Art. *Stūpa* is *dhātugṛha*, which in Sanskrit means a funeral mound. "The most impressive of the religious monuments, of course, are the *stūpa*s or *caitya*s."

"The concept of *stūpa* was clearly borrowed from India. Indeed, the *stūpa* in India was a pre-Buddhist type of building, but it had swiftly been adopted by Buddhists who built them to enshrine the relics of the Buddha and of other learned and saintly Buddhist monks".[2] Probably *stūpa*s were also built in fifth century BC with mud.[3] The *stūpa* is the most remarkable monuments of Buddhism. It is also found in *Ṛgveda*[4] and reached its maturity and perfection in Buddhist art.[5] The fact that the hemispherical portion is called *aṇḍa* (egg) recalls to mind the Hindu *hiraṇya-garbha*, (the golden egg) from which creation came into being. Robert Knox says,

> Stupas are the most characteristic monuments of ancient Indian Buddhism. They are solid mounds of varying sizes constructed of brick or stone masonry and often with sculpted stone panels attached to them. A tiny chamber, usually contained a casket, most often of stone but sometimes of pottery or metal, having the ashes of the Buddha, or a Buddhist dignitary. Stupas originate from the idea of the simple burial mound developing over many centuries, in both shape and embellishment into the enormous, elaborate structures found in the Andhradesa. Stupas are found all over Buddhist India, the Himalayan world, Sri Lanka and South East Asia.

The Amarāvatī *stūpa* is one of the largest in Andhra Pradesh, it was first built in the third century BC[6] by a missionary monk sent by Aśoka and after Aśoka came the Sātavāhanas who were sympathetic to Buddhism but were not Buddhists. At Sanghol too a Buddhist *stūpa* has been found and is

---

2. Silva, C.R.D., *Sri Lanka A History*, p. 60.
3. Gupta, S.P., *The Roots of Indian Art*, p. 11.
4. Barua, B.M., *Bharhut Book*, p. 8.
5. Agrawala, V.S., *The Heritage of Indian Art*, p. 14.
6. Ahir, D.C., *Buddhist Shrines in India*, p. 86.

believed to be of third century BC and is probably the work of Aśoka. Thus, there was no degeneration of Buddhist Art. Aśoka also built the original temple[7] at Bodh Gayā and added fragments of railings [*Plate V*].

The *stūpa* architecture bears a deep imprint of the different but important schools of Buddhism. The Hīnayāna phase of Buddhism influenced the early Buddhist *stūpa* architecture of *c*. 300 BC to *c*. AD 100.

The Sri Lanka's early *stūpa*s were domes made in the shape of bubble.[8] The top of the dome was surmounted by a railing[9] and finally the *stūpa* itself was crowned by an umbrella (*chatra*).[10]

*Stūpa*s models were found at Anurādhapura (Sri Lanka), Bhārhut [*Plate VI*], Sāñcī, Mathurā, Bodh Gayā, Amarāvatī and Nāgārjunikoṇḍa. The three chief components of the *stūpa* were circular or square base, the hemispherical dome and the *hārmika*. Because of the Mahāyāna influence *stūpa*s were decorated with human and animal figures. The images of [*Plate VII*] Buddhas and *bodhisattva*s and chief events of the master's life were carved on *stūpa*s and on the *toraṇa*s, observes, K.D. Bajpai. Generally, animals which had some link with the Buddha's life or which are mentioned in *Jātaka*s are mostly seen [Plate *VIII*]. In this way four types of *stūpa*s were created. *Śārīrika stūpa* enshrined the corporeal remains of Buddha or his close disciples. *Pāribhogika stūpa* enshrined the items used by Buddha namely, bowls, plates, etc. Commemorative *stūpa*s were made at sacred spots where some religious or historical events had occurred. Votive *stūpa*s were erected as a mark of respect to Buddha at places where he had visited.

Bhārhut is one of India's earliest and most significant monuments [*Plate*

---

7. Rhys Davids, T.W., *Buddhist India*, p. 131.
8. Silva, C.R.D., *Sri Lanka A History*, p. 61.
9. *Ibid.*
10. *Ibid.*

X]. It is important as a 'library' of Buddhist mythology.[11] Bhārhut is also important as we find inconographic motifs including Brāhmaṇical ones.[12] [*Plate IX*] There are various types of the *śālabhañjikā* and *nāga* (an anthropomorphic serpent figure) images on the railing posts and are supported by symbolic animals. The Hindu gods and goddesses with their *vāhanas*[13] are also associated. The bas-reliefs at Sāñcī and railings are also quite similar. "The Mahastupa at Bharhut was discovered by Cunninghan in 1873 and fully exposed in 1874."[14] It has now been connected with the Buddhism, but it is believed that the *stūpa* originated in *Ṛgveda* times.

*Yakṣa*s or *yakṣī*s have become models of beauty in art and literature. The *yakṣa*s and *yakṣī* images are seen not only in Bhārhut but also in Sāñcī, Mathurā, and Amarāvatī and it is felt that these are essential features of Buddhist Art. They were meant to invoke wealth, prosperity and beauty.

At the eastern gateway of Bhārhut one of the *lokapāla*s or Guardians of the Four Gateways of the Sky, is shown carrying the 'bell-shaped' standard, surmounted not by lions, but by Garuḍa, the eagle of Viṣṇu, the Sun-God, who has for his emblem the blue lotus. The lotus throne of the Buddha is nearly always represented in Indian Art with the outer fringe of petals turned downwards, and the whole flower is frequently shown naturalistically with petals turned down upon the stalk in a form closely resembling the so-called bell of the Aśokan Capitals. At Bhārhut and at Sāñcī the petals and stamens of the flower are often carefully carved upon the so-called 'bell-capital'.[15] Sāñcī and Bhārhut hold extremely exalted place not only in the

---

11. Craven, R.C., *A Concise History of Indian Art*, p. 65.
12. *Ibid.*
13. *Ibid.*
14. Agrawala, V.S., *Studies in Indian Art*, p. 77.
15. Havell, E.B., *A Handbook of Indian Art*, p. 41.

Buddhist world but in the history of Indian art.[16] Bas-reliefs are carved with *Jātaka* stories [*Plate XI*], for example, *Sasa Jātaka*, *Mahā Kapi Jātaka* [*Plate XII*], *Vessanatara Jātaka*, etc. Sāñcī followed Bhārhut tradition. The Bhārhut carvings are shallow and two-dimensional.

> The reliefs of Bharhut portray many such popular demonstrations of religion in which chariots, elephants, horses, luminous celestial sights, etc., find their proper place.[17]

> One of the medallion — carvings of Bhārhut depicts the Bodhi tree of Bhagavato-vipasino according to Buddhaghosha's description, one reads in the story of luminous celestial graves like citraleta, Nalanda, etc., which were sighted by the people.

Vaiśālī was one of the largest cities of Buddha's time. Reliefs are there showing the incident of his last journey from Vaiśālī to Kuśinagara.

> The monks of the Mahavana monastery attended the consecration of the Mahastupa built by Dutthagamani in Ceylon.[18]

The second century BC was an epoch in the Indian and the Sri Lankan history which witnessed many incidents that changed its course.

One of the greatest landmarks in the History of Buddhist Art is Bodh Gayā; the most sacred of all places where Prince Siddhārtha of the Śākya clan attained Supreme Wisdom (*sambodhi*) under a *pīpal* tree [*Plate XIII*]. This place is so sacred that nothing in the world is equal to it and in the words of Buddha before his *parinirvāṇa*; he spoke of four places which the pious believe that they should visit namely, Lumbinī, Bodh Gayā, the Deer Park at Sārnāth and Kuśinagara. Bodh Gayā is a serene and beautiful

---

16. Mitra, D., *Buddhist Monuments*, p. 92.
17. Ray, Niharranjan, *Maurya and Posts Maurya Art*, p. 59.
18. Mitra, D., *Buddhist Monuments*, p. 74.

place humming with life as the cradle of the Buddhist world. This is the place from where Saṁghmitta took a sapling of the Bo-tree, which she planted later at Anurādhapura in Sri Lanka [*Plate XIV*]. The sacred tree as it is called and the *vajrāsana*, the diamond seat on which Prince Gautama reached his final victory over worldly desire and realised the Bliss of Supreme Knowledge. Holy shrines and monuments show a glimpse of its past splendour. It is believed that

> Asoka built the original temple; it has been so often changed and added to, that only fragments of railing and probably the very remarkable sinhasana, or throne remain of the work done in his time.[19]

Buddhapad's only one stone was *in situ* and it is between the Pañca Pāṇḍu Temple and the grave of the second *mahant* right opposite the Great Temple.[20] Open pavilion, four monolithic pillars and some fragments of rear postures were of Aśokan period.[21]

Sārnāth is also an attraction for historians. The Dhammekh *stūpa*, Dharmarājika *stūpa*, the Main shrine, Aśoka's pillar with the Lion Capital are located there. The Dhammekh *stūpa* is most elegant, impressive and fascinating. Its exteriors are decorated with a variety of motifs, fine scrolls with well polished human and animal figures. The Dharmarājika *stūpa*, built by emperor Aśoka contains the relic of Buddha.

The *stūpa*s at Sāñcī and Amarāvatī besides those of Bhārhut and Nāgārjunikoṇḍa include narrative themes of Hīnayāna period. Sāñcī and Bhārhut do not give a single icon in human form. R.C. Sharma remarked,

> Both are belonging to second-first century BC. All we see him through

19. Davids Rhys, T.W., *Buddhist India*, p. 131.
20. Mitra, R., *Buddha Gayā*, p. 100.
21. *Ibid.*

various symbols of well-known events of his life.

Emperor Aśoka's selection of Sāñcī was perhaps influenced by his queen Vidiśā. The queen was a devotee of Buddha and it is stated in the Sri Lankan Chronicles that a monastery Vediśāgiri was constructed and is identified with the hill of Sāñcī. Sāñcī is

> having specimens of almost all kinds of Buddhist architectural forms. With its nucleus dating from third century BC and establishment continued to flourish till the twelfth century AD, despite all political changes due to the rise and fall of many dynasties.[22] [*Plate XV*]

There is no special mention of Buddha having a link with Sāñcī; still it is the most important site. Sārnāth *stūpa* and Sāñcī *stūpa* and Capital of Aśokan pillar [*Plate XVI*] were built with chunar sandstone.

> The torana or the arched gateway is one of the most lovely creations of Indian architect and its best surviving representations are at Sāñcī.[23] [*Plate XVII*]

The goddess Lakṣmī is seen on the *toraṇa* gateway in a seated as well as standing posture. The *Jātaka* tales and the connected stories intermingle on the frames. Kālidāsa, the celebrated dramatist and poet has compared the '*toraṇa*s to the rainbow *surapatidhanuṣcharuṇa*'.[24]

> Whether it is the eastern or the northern gateway, the salabhanjika or the motif of the damsel gathering flowers under the sala tree is very prominent. In fact, the charm of this torana lies in this motif that is represented frequently not only here but in Mathura also, in some of the Kushana toranas which though now lost, have survived

22. Mitra, D., *Buddhist Monuments*, p. 96.
23. Sivaramamurti, C., *Sources of History Illumined by Literature*, p. 117.
24. *Op. cit.*, p. 118.

> partially in the torana salabhanjika brackets that originally adorned them.[25]

Actually *toraṇa*s are also found in Amarāvatī and are decorated with

> turbans, necklaces, earrings, facial features and the position of hands joined in adoration will be noted, the fan-shaped headgear of the toranasalabhanjika at Sanchi has its counterpart in Mathura and Amaravati.[26]

> Ceylonese architecture in general is of a mixed timber and masonry tradition leaving behind only the barest vestiges of its original ornamentation. Thus, the richest aspects of the tradition that are left to us in the archaeological record of ancient Sri Lanka consist to a large extent, of which we might call architectural and planning concepts. This includes not only the elaborately planned monastic complexes, the royal citadels and pleasure gardens and the extensive network of irrigation works, but also a number of building types which reflect the high level of development of formal architecture achieved by the ancient builders, architects and engineers. The most familiar examples of these are colossal dagabas or stupas and the Vatadages or circular stupa temples.[27]

Earlier there were no architects, engineers or surveyors hence, the rural village folk as well as urban people had to depend upon their memories[28] and used to construct the chapel, house or any building that was required.

---

25. *Op. cit.*
26. *Op. cit.*, p. 140.
27. Bandaranayake, S., *Buddhist Tree Temples in Sri Lanka*, p. 136.
28. Sirisena, W.M., *Sri Lanka and South East Asia*, p. 144.

The distinctive architecture type of Sri Lanka is the brick-built shrine with vaulted roof and massive walls rising from a heavily moulded plinth.

It has no parallel in India or in any other Asian region. Paranavitana surmises that it was evolved in Sri Lanka from prototypes of which no traces are found in Indias. The Thuparama[29] *dagaba* at Polonnaruwa though it is of twelfth century is the finest example of this type of *stūpa* construction. This is a special feature of Sinhalese *stūpa*s from second century BC to fourth century AD.

Sri Lankan Architecture can be categorised in two parts, secular architecture and religious architecture. Secular architecture paid attention to the design of houses, palaces, forts, porches, etc., i.e., utilitarin buildings necessary for a comfortable way of life. Religious architecture deals with *stūpa*s, temples, mosques, chapels, etc. Religious architecture mainly depends upon the design of shrines, memorials, etc., required for the moral upliftment of people. A.D.T.E. Perera says,

> The colossal Buddha shrine was one of the common types of the classical period of Sinhala religious architecture.

ANURĀDHAPURA

Anurādhapura in Sri Lanka is known as the city of *stūpa*s. Anurādhapura was attacked several times and was restored after every attack. The original features of this city, though missing, can be visualised; nevertheless three main historical cities[30] of the island were circumscribed with broad moats, earthen ramparts and stone walls of which Anurādhapura is one. It is a city of *dagabas*. *Dagaba* is a popular term used instead of *stūpa*. Railings, pillars, cross bars, drum, drum slabs, the dome, guardian lions, etc., make the

29. This *dagaba* is different from the Thuparama of Anurādhapura.

30. Anurādhapura, Polonnaruwa and Sīgiriya.

elements of *dagabas*. In Sri Lanka, a *dagaba* is a bell-shaped[31] as eastern gateway of Bhārhut with a terminal sphere in a solid mound [*Plate XVIII*].

The word *anu* in Sinhalese means ninety, but the word 'Anurādhapura' does not mean 'the city of ninety kings'. It is true also that no less than ninety kings followed each other in the royal sacred city. The name is probably derived from Anurādha a constellation[32] of stars under which the city was founded. This is the most important of the 'Lost Cities' and is the first in the great trinity of beauty in the island followed by Polonnaruwa and Sīgiriya. Among the 'Eight Sacred Places' in this city of ruins, the first in significance is the Sri Maha Bodinwahanse [Bo-tree] in the *mahāvihāra* or Great Temple which is situated very near to the modern city of Anurādhapura. *Mahāvaṁsa* says,

> Endowed with many miraculous powers, it has stood for ages in the delightful Mahamegha garden in Lanka, promoting the spiritual welfare of the inhabitants and the propagation of the true religion.[33]

To the left of the Bo-tree lie the ruins of the maligawa — Lohapasada or Brazen Palace [*Plate XIX*] another sacred place. This monastery was built by King Dutthagāmanī in 100 BC. According to the *Mahāvaṁsa*, this is the most remarkable building in the world. The *Mahāvaṁsa* concludes, "Palace, parasol, throne and pavilion were beyond price". There are today monolithic stones damaged, columns.

There are *pokunas* (ponds, tanks or wells), image houses, *vihāras* and monasteries, but no shops and markets nearby. *Pokunas* also have a significant role in the history of Anurādhapura. Anurādhapura is also called 'dry zone' and for irrigation purposes *pokunas* were essential. *Pokunas* were also meant to deceive the enemies at night. Some of these are huge and are

---

31. Khosla, Sarla, *Gupta Civilisation*, p. 248.
32. Surveer, A.D., *Anurādhapur Sanskriti* (tr.), pp. 1-3.
33. Williams, Harry, *Ceylon Pearl of the East*, p. 127.

known as *sāgars*. Till date, it has not been possible to trace the original boundaries of these *sāgars*. These are also for religious ablutions. At Mihintale, there is 'snake *pokuna*' and on a bas-relief is a huge five-headed cobra. The Maha Saeya [*Plate XX*] at Minintale near Anurādhapura, the Thuparama *dagaba*, the Ruwanwaeli *dagba*, the Mahā Nāga *dagaba*, Yatthala *dagaba*, the Sanda Giri *dagaba*, the Miriswaeti *dagaba*, the Laṅkārāma *dagaba* are some important *dagaba*s in Anurādhpura.

Ruwanwaeli dagaba: [*Plate XXI*]

It is also called 'Gold Dust', 'Gem Sand'. King Dutthagāmanī (161-137 BC) erected this *dagaba* in order to enshrine the sacred footprint and to house precious relics of Buddha. It is mentioned in the *Mahāvaṁsa* that the king ordered,

> round stones to be brought by means of his soldiers, had them well beaten down with pounders, and to ensure greater durability he caused that layer of stones to be trampled by enoromous elephants whose feet were protected by leather shoes. He had clay spread upon the layer of stones; over them a network of iron.

It is also called by several names in Sinhalese like *hemamali*, *sonnamali*, *ratnawali*, *mahāstūpa*, or great *stūpa*.[34] Its height is 275 feet and it is 254 feet in diameter. It is densely covered with trees which had taken root in the clefts of the masonry and huge heaps of displaced bricks lie in decay around its base. It is entirely built of bricks. King Dutthagāmanī died in 137 BC and the work of this *dagaba* was finished by his brother and successor Saddha Tissa (137-110 BC). The Dome was constructed by the king and his brother Saddha Tissa constructed the spire.[35] King Lajji Tissa (119-109 BC) son of Siddha Tissa, erected three altars and frontispieces or Vahalkadas. Several

34. Surveer, A.B., *Anurādhapura Sanskriti* (tr.), p. 117.
35. *Ibid.*, p. 118ff.

kings have been adding and restoring and renovating the *dagabas*. King Moggallāna (AD 608-14) presented a new cloth to the *dagaba* and Kassapa-II (AD 652-61) fixed a jewelled pinnacle on the spire. There are different sizes of bricks, heads of elephants, but no sign of plasters, A.D.T.E. Perera maintains that there are remains of the original elephant wall surrounding the *dagaba*. But it is not seen now. There are evidences, however, there are statues of kings carved, the figures of protecting deities on relief on which lotus flowers, birds and leaves are visible. The salient feature of stelae at Anurādhapura is its crowning animal motif, i.e., lion or a humped bull or an elephant or a horse. There is a bird *haṁsa* standing on a pillar.

Moonstone

The functions of the animals and birds are not depicted but at times these are carved on the semicircular slabs termed as 'moon stones' (in Sinhalese it is *sandakadapahana*). Sun-and-moon stone and in Pāli — *patika*. The moonstone [*Plate XXII*] has the shape of the half moon. These are placed at the entrances of religious edifices. It is also found at Polonnaruwa Vatadage and Hatadage. In India, we do have this at the University site at Nāgārjunikoṇḍa at the entrance as it has traditional value.

Moonstones are semicircular slabs of stones richly decorated in low relief and placed at the foot of a stairway leading to a major shrine, with a standard pattern consisting of several concentric bands of ornament beginning with an outer zone of luxuriant foliage followed by a spirited procession of animals — the horse, elephant, ox and lion remarkably for their poise and probably symbolising the four quarters of the world. This band of animals is followed by a belt of stylised vegetation and then a row of *haṁsa* (sacred geese) with flowers dangling from their beaks. The innermost bands are all inspired by the lotus plant and culminating in stylised lotus petals of great delicacy. The vitality of the carvings is matched by an extraordinary restraint.

The moonstones were flanked by guardstones, which are stones with rounded tops and carvings of vases of flowers or large dwarfs or

> Naga kings holding vases of flowers. The staircase itself was decorated with carvings and flanked on either side by balustrades leading down to the guardstones. The entire set of decorative carvings and architectural format of the entrance was clearly design to impress the pilgrim entering the shrine.[36]

In shape the slabs are the major segment of a circle. Elephants are lively and geese are calm in poses. The sun-and-moon stone at Anurādhapura is half sun curved and the central part is having lotus decoration. Procession of geese-*haṁsa* are also curved on the moonstone. There are similar designs in Sāñcī and Bhārhut.[37] But the moonstone is a creation of Sri Lankan artists.[38] S. Paranavitana speaks out that the moonstone will be inside the building in front of the entrance where the image of the Buddha's statue is kept.[39] The animal symbolism could be as that of the Aśokan pillars.

The Miriswaeti *dagaba* is the fourth in size of the great *stūpas* at Anurādhapura. This was also erected by king Dutthagāmanī. 'The elephants stable' monoliths are here. The word *miri* in Sinhalese means chillis.

The *Sela caitya* is in front of the Thuparama *dagaba* and was constructed by Lajji Tissa (199-109 BC) second son of Saddha Tissa. The Abhayagiri *dagaba* is the mightiest of all. It is 450 feet in height and 360 feet in diameter. This is the original measurement. The Jetavana and the Abhayagiri *dagabas* at Anurādhapura are the largest *stūpas* in Asia.[40] Its name northern *stūpa* is also confusing for, geographically it is the eastern *stūpa*. The Jetawanarama *dagaba* for a long time was called the northern *stūpa* under the impression that it was the Abhayagiri. Now the position is clear and

---

36. Silva, C.R.D., *Sri Lanka A History*, p. 62.
37. Surveer, A.B., *Anurādhapura Sanskriti*, p. 117.
38. *Op. cit.*, p. 85.
39. *Ibid.*
40. Bandarnayake, S., *Buddhist Tree Temples in Sri Lanka*, p. 136.

they retain the first names of eastern and northern *stūpas*.[41] There are four huge altars larger and finer than those of the Ruwanwaeli. A few carvings are of high standard of workmanship, i.e., cobras, elephants, horse, geese and bulls and the human figures on the altars of Nāgas [*Plate XXIII*] and Nāginīs show devil-human war. It is a beautiful *dagaba* and architecturally well-shaped, symmetrical and simple. King Kanittha Tissa built Vahalkades and King Voharaka Tissa (AD 215-37) repaired *chatta* and Dhātu Sena (AD 463-79) again repaired *chatta*. Prakrama Bāhu also restored this *dagaba*.

The Jetawanarama dagaba

This *dagaba* is remarkable only for its gigantic size; it is the third of the trinity of vast *dagabas* of which the Abhayagiri and Ruwanwaeli are the other two. It is 250 feet in height and 600 feet in diameter. It was erected by King Mahā Sena (AD 277-304) and plaster work was done by King Mahā Nāga (AD 561-64). At the cardinal points there are four Vahalkades and two rectangular pillars [*Plate XXIV*]. There is seven-headed cobras and *nāgas* and cobras are protecting the relics.

Ambatthala dagaba

It is created on the Mihintale Hill by King Mahā Dathika Mahā Nāga (AD 9-21) and this is the spot where *arhat* Mahinda stood and was received by King Devanāmpiya Tissa. No ornamentation is there. King Kanittha Tissa constructed an edifice on this *dagaba*.

King Devanāmpiya Tissa had constructed two *dagabas* the Thuparama *dagaba* in 245 BC and the Pathama *cetiya* in Anurādhapura and one at Mihintale (*Plate XXV*). The Pathama *cetiya* is not traceable.

The Thuparama dagaba

This *dagaba* was constructed in order to enshrine two relics of Buddha, his

41. Williams, Harry, *Ceylon Pearl of the East*, p. 136.

right collar bone and the eating plate. 'Tee' bricks have been used and probably it came from Burma. King Lajji Tissa (119-109 BC) Aggabodhi-II (AD 598-608) and Aggabodhi-III (AD 624-40) took keen interest in preserving invaluable relics and gems. It is a beautiful 'bell-shaped' structure in a graceful proportion with pillars, circles, topes, octagonal pillars and monolithic shafts. The dates of these artfacts have not been indicated, however, these must have been kept after completion of the *dagaba*. The carvings are magnificent. It has been constructed of bricks and earth-mud. Railings, pillars and the Indian topes especially railings are magical protection against evil spirits.[42] Three refuges are Buddha, the Law and the Community of monks which are generally exhibited and are protected.

Maha Saeya

King Devanāmpiya Tissa built this *dagaba* at Mihintale in 243 BC. Its shape is a hemisphere on three low circular platforms. Reliefs are surmounted by an umbrella or a *chatta*, like all other *dagaba*s. There are no 'Vahalkades' and no stone pillars but wooden pillars are visible. It is recorded in the *Mahāvaṁsa* that King Lajji Tissa 'encased with stone' and disappeared. It is also believed that Mahinda's ashes were laid down and a *dagaba* was also erected but this *dagba* appears to have been lost. Similarly, Saṁghmittha Thupa said to have been built near Thuparama *dagaba* is also not found.

> The stupas which feature prominently in the Buddhist architecture of the Anuradhapura period, some of which survive almost in their entirety had been subjected to periodical repairs which have obliterated their original features. Hence, they do not present us with an opportunity to study the original designs of that period.[43]

It is true that after Indianisation, a distinctive Sri Lankan style was

42. Fergusson, *History of Indian and Eastern Architecture*, p. 194.

43. Basnayake, H.T., *Sri Lanka Monastic Architecture*, p. 175.

developed in constructing *dagabas* or *stūpas* and though it has Indian originality still we cannot say that these are identical.

BODHI TREE

Saṁghamitta Theri, daughter of Emperor Aśoka came with a branch of Bodhi-tree from Bodh Gayā to Anurādhapura. The emperor had keen interest in propagating the Buddhism far and wide, hence he encouraged his daughter to embrace Buddhism. This was a starting point for women to become *theris* or nuns. But it was wide off the mark. It is also said that a particular sect of women in Sri Lanka wanted to become *theris* surreptitiously but it was discouraged. This is called Bodhinwahanse in Sinhalese. The sacred tree is about 30 feet in height and the length and breadth of the mound are 71 feet and 57 feet respectively.[44] It is considered as the oldest tree in the world.[45] Sir J. Tennet writes in his *Ceylon*, but that which renders the fallen city illustrious even in ruins, is the possession of the Jaya Sri Maha Bodin — Wahanse, 'the victorious, illustrious, Supreme Lord, the sacred Bo-Tree', the planting of which forms the grandest episode in the sacred annals of Ceylon.[46] The *dagabas* or *stūpas*, Bo-tree are an indispensble part of every Buddhist monastery in Sri Lanka and occupy sites of considerable beauty. "With their domes of dazzling white their tapering and graceful spires and their gilded pinnacles", says Dr. Paranavitana, "they form a picturesque though familiar feature of the landscape" [*Plates XXVI to XXVIII*].

Anurādhapura has three large *pokunas*.[47] These are also called lakes. Nuwarawewa, Tissawewa are famous. Near to Tissawewa, which

44. Harishchandra, W. Brahmachari, *The Sacred City of Anurādhapura*, p. 31.

45. *Ibid.*

46. *Op. cit.*, p. 32.

47. *Pokunas* means tanks, these are also called *weva* in Sri Lanka.

commemorates the name of King Devanāmpiya Tissa is Isurumuniya rock temple. This temple was also built by King Devanāmpiya Tissa; and is the most interesting temple in this 'ruined city'. "Of all the pretty corners of Anurādhapura", writes John Still, "this little group of black rocks is the most picturesque." A first-century AD rock inscription refers to it as 'Isiramanne'. This means 'Hermit's Delight' according to Paranavitana. These are three statues of Buddha. One statue is hewn out of the rock and also its seat. The two standing statues are made of wood. Thick rock was excavated and like Kalu-gal Vihāra at Polonnaruwa and Dambulla. Water tanks except for observing religious purification ceremonies or rites serve no other useful purpose. These are frescoes and some sculpted images.

VIHĀRAS

Buddha too did not favour the Vedic sacrifices and the many rituals which people had to perform. He objected to the importance given to the *varṇa*s because those who belonged to the lower *varṇa*s, the śūdras and others were ill treated by the upper *varṇa*s. Buddha thus started monasteries which were places where monks lived and spent their lives praying and preaching Buddhism. The monasteries (*vihāras*) were also used as schools. The Buddhist monasteries became important centres of education for the monk and wealthy merchants donated money to the Buddhist and beautiful monuments.

The rock-cut caves or *vihāra*s are also preserved in rock-cut halls at Ajantā, Lomas Ṛṣi Cave, Bhaja, Bedsa. The Lomas Ṛṣi Cave in the Barabar Hills belongs to a group of small rock-cut cells which were dedicated during the reign of Aśoka. The interior walls of these caves have fine polish of the Mauryan style. The Ajantā cave Nos. IX, X, XIX and XXVI are churches (*caitya*s as they are called) and the remaining are the *vihāras.* Vincent A. Smith does not favour the term *vihāra*s to the caves of Ajantā because they do not fulfil the architectural composition. Actually Ajantā's caves are famous for paintings. But earlier these were cave dwellings for the monks. Of course, not all the caves conform to the plan of *vihāra*s but basically the caves are *vihāra*s as the monks reside there; there is no doubt about this. *Vihāra*s commenced from the sixth century BC and relate a connected tale of their gradual evolution and ornamentation.

> Viharas have always been a symbol of strength and spread of Buddhism, reflecting the thought, culture, aspiration and intellectual development of a people.[48]

Pāli literature tells about the architectural details regarding the monastic establishment. There were doors, door posts, and lintels, with arrangement for bolts, lock and key with windows made by railings, network or slips of wood,[49] and window blinds and shutters,[50] solid benches against the walls of a room or under the verandah against the outside wall of the house. The basic requirement was a cell containing a bed and a pillow that too rock-cut pillow.[51] Early the monks used to sleep on rock bed and rock caves usually were their shelters. "After the first century AD, the use of caves for residential purposes went out of fashion, as from the first century BC, both in the north and the south-east, *vihāra*s began to built."

The most ancient *vihāra*s of Sri Lanka were the Mahāvihāra and the Abhayagiri *vihāra* in Anurādhapura. The Mahāvihāra was famous for its literary activity and was also a great centre of orthodoxy; while the Abhayagiri *vihāra* was generally associated with heretical beliefs. These and other *vihāra*s built in the early centuries of the Christian era, had foundation of stones as many of the remains at Anurādhapura show while the upper parts were made of brick, wood or clay.[52] The *vihāra*s of Polonnaruwa period were also the largest built in Sri Lanka and are made

---

48. Barua, D.K., The Dalai Lama's Foreword in *Vihāras in Ancient India*.
49. *Op. cit.*, ff.
50. *Op. cit.*
51. Dehejia, Vidya, *Early Buddhist Rock Temple*, p. 74.
52. Mendis, G.C., *The Early History of Ceylon*, p. 28.

of brick and lime mortar. The *vihāra* originally is the private apartment of a single *bhikkhu.*[53] The Tautirimale *vihāra* built during (247-207 BC) was the abode of hermits and king Devanāmpiya Tissa had lots of influence on this *vihāra* in maintaining it. Even today, people are a mixture of Sinhala and Tamil. The monks sent by Emperor Aśoka had planted eight Bo-trees here according to the legends but no historical evidences exist. Nevertheless, this is based on the story of aborigines.

There are several Buddhas and *bodhisattva* images on rock boulder but are not complete. The images are mutilated and in a dilapidated situation hence no compact study could be carried out. The *Mahāvaṁsa* refer the Tautirimale *vihāra* and is also called Tivanka Bamunugame.

Loha Maha Prasadaya means the Great Brazen Palace built by Dutthagamani was an excellent monastery.[54] It had nine stories and in each of them were one hundred apartments. The apartments were furnished with silver.[55] There was a beautiful ivory throne, emblem of the sun in gold, moon in silver, the stars in pearls, and roof was covered with brazen tiles.[56] Thus, it was called Loha Maha Prasadaya. All the stories were furnished with couches, chairs and other necessaries of great value.

> Even the laver and its ladle kept at the entrance, for washing the hands and feet of monks were made of gold.[57]

The art historians and scholars feel that the origins of the *vihāra* dates back to second century BC. A.M. Hocart, C.P. Bell and John Still agree with this and did comprehensive study. It is true that the archaeological finds of India

---

53. Mookerji, R.K., *Ancient Indian Education*, p. 438.
54. Harishchandra, W. Brahmachari, *Sacred City of Anurādhapura*, p. 40ff.
55. *Ibid.*
56. *Ibid.*
57. *Ibid.*

and Sri Lanka have not attracted art historians' attention as much as those of Egypt. There is a lot of difference in the Buddhist architectural remains of Sri Lanka and India.

The history of these two countries have been reconstructed and re-written several times leaving loopholes behind and thus inevitable imbalance is always seen. Bell, Hocart and Paranavitana have done marvellous work and their greatest contribution to ancient culture of Sri Lanka is a valuable work. Generally, we leave the question unanswered when we are told that the India's art, architecture and culture have been borrowed by Sri Lanka. There is some limit to the borrowing and some limit to accepting of such action as reactions vary. Still it can be certainly said that the idea of building shrines over the relics of Buddha and his disciples, worship of Bo-tree, residential units for monks and such like were taken from India, assimilated and given a different form and shape. Also in many cases, a different name. Though the concept was from India, the execution and final shape given to it, is definitely Sri Lankan.

Thus, the Sri Lankan Buddhist architecture can be called purely local or indigenous.

List of the Dagabas in Sri Lanka [from third century BC to sixth century AD]

S.No.	*Name of the Dagaba*	*King who initiated*	*Place*	*Date (approx)*
A	B	C	D	E
1.	The Aabastala *dagaba*	King Uttiya	Mihintale	275 BC
2.	The Thuparama *dagaba*	Devanāmpiya Tissa	Anurādhapura	244 BC
3.	The Maha Saeya	-do-	Mihintale	243 BC
4.	The Patharama *cetiya*	-do-	Anurādhapura	256 BC
5.	The Mahiyangame *dagaba*	King Uddachulabhya	Anurādhapura	—
6.	The Saṁghamitta *stupa*	King Uttiya	Anurādhapura	—
7.	The Jetavana *dagaba*	—	Anurādhapura	3rd *c.* BC
8.	The Mahānaga *dagaba*	King Mahā-Nāga	Anurādhapura	- do -
9.	The Kaelaniya *dagaba*	King Yattnale Tissa	- do -	- do -
10.	The Ruwanwaeli *dagaba*	King Duttha Gāmanī	- do -	2nd *c.* BC
11.	The Miriswaeti *dagaba*	-do-	- do -	158 BC
12.	The Sela *caitya*	Lajji Tissa	- do -	—
13.	The Digha Vapi *dagaba*	Saddha Tissa	—	—

14.	The Idikatu *dagaba*	King Kalakanni (48-28 BC)	Mihintale	—
15.	The Aet *dagaba*	—	- do -	—
16.	The Lankārāma *dagaba*	—	Anurādhapura	1st c. AD
17.	The Abhayagiri *dagaba*	King Mahā Sena (AD 277-300)	- do -	3rd c. AD
18.	The Ambatthala *dagaba*	King Maha-Dathika Mahā Nāga (AD 9-12)	Mihintale	—

The Sinhalese names of various parts of dagaba

Tun mal pesawa — The three storey ornaments, ornamental bangles

gaeba— the dome

hataraes kotuwa — The square or tee

devata kotuwa — base of the spire

kota — The spire

sat — The spire umbrella

kota kaeraella — The pinnacle or the end of spire

Important Vihāras of Sri Lanka

Awukane Vihāra

IN ANURĀDHAPURA

Abhayagiri

Jetawane Vihāra

Thuparāma Vihāra

Ruwanwaeli Vihāra

Isurumuni Vihāra

Loha Mahā Prasadaya

Sīgiriya Gallery at Sīgiriya

Table on Stūpa — India

Location	*Name of Stūpa*	*Date (approx)*
Sāñcī	Great *stūpa* No. 1	*c.* 250 BC
- do -	Great *stūpa* 1	*c.* 150 BC
- do -	*Stūpa* 2	*c.* 150 BC
- do -	*Stūpa* 3	*c.* 50 BC
Bhārhut	Original *stūpa*	*c.* 250 BC
Bodh Gayā		*c.* 75 BC
Amarāvatī	*Stūpa*	*c.* 3rd c. AD
Sārnāth	*Stūpa*	*c.* 6th c. AD

3

Painting

> There is no art in the world more variegated than the art of painting. In painting, the painters masterpieces (carana) is more artistic than the rest of his pictures. An artistic design occurs to the painters of masterpieces that such and such pictures should be drawn in such and such way. Through this artistic design, there arise operations of the mind (or artistic operations) accomplishing such things as sketching the outline, putting on the paint, touching up and embellishing. Then in the picture known as the masterpiece is effected a certain (central) artistic figure.[1]

ART reveals its inner emotion through creation which becomes reality; this reality is the figure and soul of the figure is line; hence line is the essence of painting. Line, colour, ornamentation, modelling make a painting. It never misses that quality of abstraction which is indispensable to mural decoration as it is indeed to all truly great paintings. Painting is a picture which someone has produced using paints.

Painting is the picture painted by a particular artist or a group of

---

1. Buddhaghosal, in *New Light on Early Buddhism* by B.G. Gokhale, p. 85.

artists and the style in which they are painted. Painting among all arts is the highest and it is through profound devotion to painting that one can achieve, i.e., merit, wealth, pleasure and eternal bliss. It is a mirror of the artist's personality and exhibits his temperament towards society and society's culture is also reflected there. It requires high level of skill which is generally inborn qualities or acquired through experience. It helps in creation and production of literature, music, sculpture, etc. which are considered beautiful for the promotion of cultural avenues. The basic principles of paintings are:

Saḍaṅga	Line and colour
Rūpabhedha	Distinction of forms
Pramāṇam	Proportion of line, mass and design
Bhāve	Emotion and aesthetic feelings, sentiments and expression
Lāvaṇya	Realisation of beauty or grace
Sadṛśya	Resemblance
Varṇikabhaṅga	Combination and harmony of colours

The paintings generally are not understood by the people and this is so with all works of art. Therefore, it is an arduous task to understand the indefinable ideal of beauty which the painting propagates. A painting is an emotional urge to give form to the feelings felt or perceived, imagined and thus create the piece of art.

Ajantā and Bāgh in India and Sīgiriya in Sri Lanka are mute witnesses to the flowering of painting in Buddhist Art. The painters of Ajantā, Bāgh and Sīgiriya (Sri Lanka) were the reflection of this process. Madanjeet Singh says that

> the Ajantā paintings have been linked with those of Bagh. These three sites actually have some resemblance. Many art critics and

> historians feel that the art of Ajanta or Sigiriya, have some ideas and themes[2]

and do not care to know

> the present state of the development of literature and art in Ceylon.[3]

> The interest of most of them in the Sigiriya frescoes is not purely aesthetic but springs from the appeals of sex, patriotism and sentiment.[4]

Sīgiriya frescoes depict divine maidens. 'Taint of personality' is visible in these paintings. The paintings of Sīgiriya, Ajantā and Bāgh produced 'didactic' images of thinking, feeling, sensitiveness, sensation, sensuousness and intuition. These paintings had a mission and a purpose and thus their appeal was irresistible and unmistakable. Indian paintings are naturalistic. Poets like Kālidāsa perceived life and emotions in mountains and clouds, trees and wind, nature and beauty.

Sīgiriya: A picture gallery

The oldest and best preserved medieval Sinhalese paintings belonging to the fifth century AD are the Sīgiriya frescoes. Sīgiriya frescoes on the rocks are most beautifully conserved of all ancient paintings of Sri Lanka. This was the capital city of Sri Lanka for eighteen years in the fifth century AD under the tutelage of Kāśyapa monarch. The ruins here reveal the old kingdom and heritage of religious and secular tradition. Appreciation of the culture and art of Sri Lanka would be limited without Sīgiriya. Sīgiriya is situated between the Sinhalese capitals of Anurādhapura, Polonnaruwa and Kandy. Dr Paranavitana says,

---

2. Wickramasinghe, Martin, *Aspects of Sinhalese Culture*, p. 1.
3. *Ibid.*
4. *Op. cit.*, p. 58.

> there are 21 figures in all some of them of a fragmentary character. The figures are of profusely jewelled females depicted as rising from clouds; they are cut off at the waist. This circumstance indicates that the figures represent a class of celestial beings.

Dr. Paranavitana is the only and the first archaeologist who could decipher the verses (*graffiti*) here and his works till date are the authority and well authenticated.

Dhātusena was a nobleman of the Moriya clan in Sri Lanka. Pāṇḍu, a Tamil king ruled from Anurādhapura, and Dhātusena was a novice in robes at the great *mahāvihāra* monastery as disciple of his uncle, who was a monk. It is recorded in the chronicles that the uncle foresaw that his young nephew would ascend the throne in future. A war ensued between Dhātusena and the Tamil king who was overthrown. Dhātusena came to the throne and ruled for eighteen years (AD 455-73). The *Culavaṁsa* records that King Dhātusena built *vihāra*s and his greatest achievement was the construction of Kalawewa, a reservoir. He had two sons, Moggallāna and Kāśyapa. Moggallāna was his illegitimate son and the king favoured him as his successor. But Kāśyapa, the second son, rebelled and with the help of his associates was able to put his father to death. Kāśyapa too ruled for eighteen years and became a powerful monarch and built a magnificent palace at Sīgiriya. It is an engineering feat. It is believed that Kāśyapa fortified Sīgiriya and shut himself through fear of his brother Mogallāna who arrived from India with his supporters and fought with Kāśyapa resulting in the defeat and suicide of the parricide and usurper. Mogallāna ruled for eighteen years and was succeeded by his son. It is also said that Kālidāsa was his contemporary and was his son's friend.

Sīgiriya frescoes depict some themes like Ajantā and Bāgh. Blue colour which is prominent at Ajantā and Bāgh are missing in Sīgiriya. The three colours dominant at Sīgiriya are red, yellow and green. The comparison of Ajantā paintings with those of Sīgiriya are natural because both frescoes are dated to the fifth century AD. Hence all critics recognise the fact that the art of Sīgiriya is closely related to that of Ajantā.[5] The noble ladies painted in pale yellow or orange carrying flowers and their attendants are also women [*Plate XXIX*]. A painting of a lady carrying a lotus at Sīgiriya may be compared to the painting of the lady in Cave II at Ajantā. There the main difference is of colours. By observing colours it may be said that the paintings are not identical. Apparently, these look identical. Havell said of Sīgiriya ladies that they are of 'Botticellian grace' and

> there can be no doubt that they are extremely remarkable productions of their age and well deserving of careful study and serious criticism. There is nothing to indicate who the Ceylonese artists were, when they came, or how they learned their skill.[6]

Apart from Sīgiriya frescoes wall paintings have been noticed (in second century BC) at Anurādhapura in the eastern side of the Ruwanwaeli *dagaba*. Three colours yellow, red and blue and white are also used. H.C.P. Bell, the first art historian of Sri Lanka, says that the females depicted at Sīgiriya were the wives of king Kāśyapa.

Coomaraswamy maintains that there are two schools of art 'the Bhārhut or idealistic' and 'the Ajantā or impressionist'. Sīgiriya is an ancient rock, of about 200 meters high and one has to walk through a series of staircases. Many Buddhist scholars including Coomaraswamy believed that Buddha ignored art. Buddha did not ignore art but it has been misinterpreted also. It is very much evident from the novice who have to attain monkhood that they have to study Sanskrit. Study of Sanskrit is important for them before ordination and thus poetry is also to be studied besides other relevant subjects. Poetry is the combination of

---

5. Smith, V.A., *A History of Fine Art in India and Ceylon*, p. 111, (Pref.).
6. *Ibid.*

emotions and feelings and in many places it depicts the life of women, drinking scenes, harem scenes, etc. Thus, it is not palatable to accept the argument that Buddha ignored art altogether.

S. Paranavitana says that the females are 'Lightning Princess' attend by 'Cloud Damsels'.[7] [*Plate XXX*] We believe with Bell that it was

> beyond question that artists trained in the same school — possibly the very same hands — executed both the Indian and Ceylon frescoes.[8]

If this is taken as correct then there should not have been much differences in colours. Because colours signify the period and the role of the artists, their interest and emotions and feelings. The possibility could be that some of the artists must have been shifted or might have gone to travel here and there and during the course of journey or even in Sri Lanka might have come across local people interested in painting. They might have been told how to decorate the palaces with paintings or their dwellings and thus the painting style was borrowed and adopted according to their needs. It is acceptable, as 'great art is contagious. Civilisation confirms its cycle'. According to E.F.C. Ludowyk,

> the frescoes in Sigiriya have been linked with the murals at Ajanta. The painter in Ceylon does not repeat Indian painter in form, composition or colour; he uses the same mode but with a difference. This is to be felt in the contrast between the distance placed between the painter and picture in Sigiriya and the involvement of the Ajanta artist in his own luxuriance. The stylised women in Sigiriya seem restrained and hieratic. The very sensuousness of their figure appears to be held in check by the touch of hardness in the definition of the curve, and given a dimension different from

7. Silva, K.M.D., *A History of Sri Lanka*, p. 56.
8. Gunasinghe, Siri, *Ajantā Shadows on Sīgiriya*, pp. 494-509.

> that of physical representation.[9]

It is generally felt that the Buddhist paintings of the second century BC are in Ajantā and the finest specimen of Gupta period (fifth-sixth century AD) are at Bāgh, Ajantā and Sīgiriya. During this period, some murals were also seen at Mihintale near Anurādhapura but were in a dilapidated condition. H.C.P. Bell also maintains that in Ajantā and Sīgiriya paintings

> Dress and ornaments pose and colouring are common to both alike.

But it is not so. Benjamin Rowland feels that the Bāgh, Ajantā and Sīgiriya also show the influence of Amarāvatī style. The influence is there but we cannot be sure that it is because of Amarāvatī style. The female beauty generally excels everywhere. No art can be original. It is difficult today and earlier too, it was not an easy task to make an original piece. However, attempts were made in different postures, in different ages, in different ways and means. By making combinations and permutations, we may achieve a thing which may be called an original. But while examining and analysing, it may invoke various interpretations and as a result of this the originality is lost and new horizons are in the offing. Then we may learn the influences which were responsible in making or writing like this. Thus, it is beyond all questions to accept that

> all great artists have been influenced by others. And even borrowing is not copying because the borrowed elements are changed and reintegrated by the artist according to his personality and imagination even if his art is religious and communal. The best work of an independent artist, even though he may have been influenced by a school or tradition, has an original flavour which is a blend of his imagination and personality.[10]

---

9. Ludowyk, E.F.C., *The Story of Ceylon*, p. 88.

10. Wickramasinghe, Martin, *Aspects of Sinhalese Culture*, p. 59.

Maintaining that the beauty of the female figures at Sīgiriya is at par with that Amarāvatī figures will not be appropriate because Amarāvatī females have round faces, fleshy cheeks, wide open eyes and heavy lips as against the oval faces with less heavily delineated features of the Sigiriya women. Overall Amarāvatī female form is more robust and of ampler proportions compared to the Sigiriya ones.

Breasts of Sīgiriya *apsaras* are tight whereas those of Ajantā are loose. The artists of Sīgiriya [*Plate XXXII*] had a natural flair for understanding female beauty and possessed ability to interpret it in their own ways. They had no 'academic training' whereas Ajantā's artists had a fair knowledge of *śilpa*.

Gunasinghe writing on 'Ajanta's shadows on Sigiriya' is not acceptable. Shadow is a word which does not describe the ins and outs of the painting or situation. These are not clear-cut ideas. We describe people and their activities or for that matter a piece of art as shadowy when very little is known about them. The Ajantā painters were experienced and worked for more than five hundred years from the beginning of the first century BC and they have left their mark in the variety of their styles. Sīgiriya paintings were completed in a short span of time. Gunasinghe writes,

> the Sigiriya murals were completed within a few short years, possibly by one company of artists, investing them with an unmistakable homogeneity, permitting us to speak of a style. The most distinctive characteristics of this style concern the fundamental of drawing and the application of colour and deserve more attention then has been accorded hitherto.

We can see only line works and brush and 'brush strokes are rapid bold and lively'. Hence, the paintings are simpler but expose secularism and delight. But these paintings never remain religious. The eyes of Sīgiriya damsels are natural, of almond shape and eyebrows are indicated by a thin line in a single curve [*Plate XXXI*]. Coiffure is not depicted at Sīgiriya and Ajantā. Still they exhibit genius; for, an illusion of utterance is created. They look as they want to utter something. There is some unnatural tendency, mystic and reminding of the inevitability of mortality that can be seen in the paintings of Sīgiriya damsels. Hair (coiffures) adds beauty to women and hairs of a lady always remained a popular subject with a poet, and artist. But here in Sīgiriya the absence of coiffures has not diminished the charm of the ladies. They, on the contrary, look superb. This further expands the peculiarity of Sīgiriya damsels. We see elements of nature transforming but never dying; never finishing.

A. Foucher says,

> I think you are also of the opinion that in order to better appreciate works of art, it is not unnecessary to understand them; and that the first thing one has got to do after having duly admired their beauty is to identify the subjects they represent.[11]

No hair style was adopted in Sīgiriya, it may be because paintings were made by the monks and they are clean shaven and this could have been one reason, which appears to be logically correct. Monks are not allowed to grow hair on their heads and to evince a natural tendency to abhor to coiffures in their paintings. This tradition of making paintings by monks also find mention in the *Dīpavaṁsa* and the *Mahāvaṁsa*. Whatever be the reason for not exhibiting paintings in the rooms of the monks, but they were permitted to paint and allowed full freedom in the field of painting, and so they

> painted with great skill, and the hands holding flowers, fruit, or musical instruments, are most gracefully rendered.

11. From a preface of a book *Studies in the Ajantā Paintings* by S. Dieter.

> They bear a strong resemblance to the paintings of Ajanta and Bagh.[12]

Ajay Mitra Shastri studied them and came to a conclusion that the paintings of Ajantā and Bāgh are almost identical. If we accept this opinion then we can also assume that the paintings at Ajantā, Bāgh and Sīgiriya almost resemble each other. But unfortunately it is not so. There are some features which are alike and many which are not. The Sīgiriya forescoes have a poetic dynamism and actually the purpose of these frescoes have not been studied and commented upon appropriately. But the beauty has been described as *par excellence* [*Plate XXXIII*].

> Thousands of eye witnesses who visited the art gallery at Sigiriya have gone into the ecstasy at the sight of the female figures. They have described these damsels as 'golden coloured or blue-lilly coloured ones resembling celestial maidens.' That is sufficient praise for the excellence for this art.[13] [*Plate XXXIV*]

The poetic dynamism is there because these paintings have a long history like sculpture and architecture and this provided literature to Sri Lankans especially poetry which was significantly religious and secular. This is evident in the *Sandeśya* poems. Most of the verses scribbled on the wall are by kings, nobles and learned clerics. The form and metre used in these verses evince the literary tradition and in most of the verses, like in paintings, women are identified as cloud in maidens. Archer has reset an anonymous writer:

> Your beauty charmed the heart.
> My eyes lingered and were lost.
> You took them to yourself.

---

12. Wijesekera, Nandadeva, "*Buddhist Art Painting and Sculpture*", pp. 14-17 in All Ceylon Buddhist Congress Diamond Jubilee (2462-2522).

13. Wijesekera, Nandadeva, *op. cit.*

If you had not accepted me as your lover,
I would have known you had never been in love.[14]

Dr. Godakumbure feels that by temperament, the Sinhalese is a poet. He speaks in poetry. The Sinhalese language lends itself easily to verification or composition in metre, and very often prose itself, turns into a sort of metrical language. It is flexible, it is varied and it has a nice vocabulary, able to convey every subtle and diverse shade of meaning, to make vivid to the imagination any picture the poet wishes to conjure up.

It is true that the female figures of Sīgiriya are endowed with great beauty, charm and are attractive. The female figures of Bhārhut, Sāñcī display a simple and innocent charm. The women of that age probably were not acquainted with the art of exposing their beauty. The figures of female attendants were true to their companions but were shown innocent. Same is the case with the bathing women represented in the Kuṣāṇa art of Mathurā and in Ajantā of the Gupta period and post-Gupta period. The artists were eager to depict women in the nude and enhanced the figure's sensual effect by adding ornaments, necklaces, wraps, partially concealing veils and by showing the anxious endeavours of the women to cover their hands whatever nudity was still apparent. The artists tried to reveal the secrets of female beauty through various forms and shapes. This is a blended form of sensuous motion with religion and spiritual flavour. The Sīgiriya and Ajantā female figures have an attractive look suggesting movements and inviting gestures. These features are sufficient to agree with the view of Sri Lankan writer Martin Wickramasinghe who writes about appeals of sex. It suggests an inclination for pleasures that are experienced through physical senses, especially sexual pleasure. These, of course, become sensuous because it gives pleasure to the mind or body. Sensuality glows everywhere not only in the stances, postures and glances of the women figures, but also in the luxuriance of pastoral landscape and

14. Ludowyk, E.F.C., *The Story of Ceylon*, p. 87.

in the luminous work of art where the lines and colours are pure and joyous.

> Painting is a branch of sensuality. Nobody can paint a nude who hasn't learnt the women body by heart with his hands and his lips and his own body. I take my art seriously. I'm unremitting in my preliminary studies.

Kālidāsa always has advocated beauty and we feel he is the only one to date who could understand the conception of beauty or *rūpam*, i.e., the characteristics of the best art. Kālidāsa too influenced Sinhalese literature and we can find *sandeśa kavi* in Sīgiriya frescoes. All frescoes paintings at Sīgiriya are 'Gupta'.

There is a school of thought which feels that Sīgiriya's real function was mystical or mystico-politico since no utility was seen or the intention of these frescoes have not been suitably dealt with. This school of thought also feels that it represents Mount Meru, the cosmic mountain at the pivot of the entire universe where according to Hindu (and may be Buddhists) cosmology, the planes of existence intersect. Sīgiriya has a transcendental meaning and is at the geometric centre of the island.

The most celebrated frescoes are on the Western Wall

> the procession of lovely, bare breasted women covered the entire-face of the rock; today, only a score or so remain. Some were defaced by vandals in 1967, but these have been carefully restored and the cloud maidens are now as beautiful as ever. It is said of these beautiful women that they inspire poetry. This is certainly true of the frescoes. The remains of the Mirror Wall are covered in graffiti, scratched upon it by visitors to the fortress over the centuries following Kasyapa's death. They are a far cry from the scrawls of contemporary vandals:

Dry as a flower/That fallen on a rock
Are the hearts of those beauties
Whose golden skin
Has caught my mind

Of the thousands of clouds maidens that covered the face of Sigiriya, only a few remain.[15]

The ladies are mum unable to speak or have no inclination. Sīgiriya ladies upper part is shown and lower part of their bodies are invisible. We can see flowers in the hands of golden hued women.

The emphasis of the paintings is on rotundity. Their breasts are in rounded form, moderately fat and bulbous. The figures are not numb. The nipples are broad but sharp pointed and the ladies look as they are of nubile age. It is true that the ladies do not belong to a lower strata but are of putative class which enraptures kings, nobles, avant garde and connoisseurs. The common class or the persons who do not have an aesthetic sense may consider these as nonsense. Some critics have been biased and even went on the records to say that the paintings are cheap. It is purely inimical. The paintings do not affect the Buddhist way of life. In *Dasadhamma Sutta*, Buddha speaks, "Beauty is nothing to me; neither the beauty of body nor that comes of dress." Paranavitana deciphered about 700' gi (verses). His *Sigri graffiti* is a monumental work in Sri Lanka and a reference for the art historians and litterateurs of the world.

We spoke/but they did not answer,
Those ladies of the mountain;
They did not give us
The twitch of an eyelid
Another answers consolingly
She answers no-one

15. Richard, Simon, *Sri Lanka The Resplendent Isle*, p. 33.

For her King has died.[16]

A 'Classical Style' developed in Sri Lanka with the culmination of Colas temple at Polonnaruwa and stone relief sculpture from stelae of second and third centuries AD and slowly it came in the Sīgiriya. There is a human figure and especially

> the female torso — they show a clear line of development from stylisation to classic realism, and in their finally evolved form they closely approximate to the classic style of the Sīgiriya paintings.[17]

In the Archaeological Museum at Anurādhapura we find fifth-sixth-century lime stone torsos of full breasted female figures which resemble the figures of female deities of Gongagotta and Vessagisiya.[18] Critics have assigned various names to the female figures of Sīgiriya. To some they are *apsaras*, to some they are damsels, queen or celestial or heavenly ones. We may call them by any name but they are beautiful. Their heads are decorated with coronets, a small crown, tiaras, tuft of feathers and may be jewellery, i.e., aigrettes crown the head, flowers and ribbons on the hair, ears, necklace, arms and wrists are loaded with ornament, jewellery stones and precious metals. Beneath their heavy breasts, their stomachs show creases and this is peculiar to beauty. The topknot of hair is rendered in a charming manner adorned with pearls and diamonds set in gold. All these enhance the sensuous of the female figure. The way they are decorated and depicted in high stylistic fashion indicates that the ladies belonged to high strata of society. They are not from an ordinary or low category. Bell feels that these ladies reflect the life and the atmosphere and ideals of high society. They may be wives of kings or be from palaces. Coomaraswamy calls them *apsaras*. He also agrees that Sīgiriya is the

---

16. Richard, Simon, *Op. cit.*, p. 35.
17. Bandaranayake, S., *The Rock and Wall Paintings of Sri Lanka*, p. 25.
18. *Op. cit.*, p. 26.

extension of Ajantā and Bāgh or Sittanasvasal in South India. Philip Rawson has a different opinion and according to him flowers are worn in their hair by the ladies in Ajantā paintings where the women are heavily jewelled and decorated. Contours are emphasised with black and the expression of eyes, lips and hands are given clarity. John Still writes that the Sīgiriya is a gigantic picture gallery and the 'largest picture in the world perhaps'.

Ajantā paintings

> There are excellent illustration in these paintings at Ajanta of the six limbs of painting *shadanga*: composed of, *rupabheda*: variety of form, *pramanam* proper proportion, *bhave*: depiction of emotion, *lavanya yojana*: infusion grace, *sadrisya*: likeness, and *varnikabhanja*; mixing of colours to produce an effect of modelling. The diversity of form at Ajanta is indeed credible. The painters here mastered the vast complex of human, animal and plant forms in addition to giving free scope of their imagination and were creating designs galore. The artist at Ajanta has control over not only the proportions of individual figures but also has the ability to group them and he has designed excellent compositions. Emotion is at its best in the narration of scenes from the legends; the grace of some of the figures bespeaks *lavanya yojana*. While figures are repeated as in the *Vessantara Jataka*, the element of portraiture is clearly made manifest and *sadrisya* in obvious.[19]

Ajantā paintings have three kinds: decorations, portraiture and narration. The decorative designs include fabulous creatures of mythological beings, *garuḍa*s, *yakṣa*s, *gandharva*s, *apsaras*. Portraits of *bodhisattva*s — Padmapāṇi Avalokiteśvara in Cave I shows the highest attainment in painting portraiture. The *Jātaka*s depicted in the Ajantā paintings belong

19. Sivaramamurti, C., *Indian Painting*, p. 37.

to the narrative class.

Technically the Ajantā paintings are tempera as Sīgiriya are frescoes. But in all these works, a rough mud plastic with cowdung and animal is first pressed and then a coat of fine plaster is laid and is allowed to dry. The painting is done by drawing outlines in red ochre, brown, red or black. The principal colours in vogue were red, yellow, black, blue, white and green. The scenes represented are the *Jātaka*s and life stories of Buddha. The subjects dealt here are of religious interest but other things of the world such as representation of ordinary and court life, mingled with mythological figures, animals and plants are also shown. The *Jātaka* stories gave opportunities to the artists to depict the world in all its varied aspects. Buddha, before he attained Buddhahood had passed through many births, i.e., a self-sacrificing monkey being Mahākapi to Shaddante the magnanimous six-tusked white elephant.

> The paintings at Ajanta have become world famous. Both from the point of technique and subject-matter, they are superb and speak eloquently of Indian aesthetic advancement during a period of over 800 years. The act of painting developed at Ajanta from the second century BC to seventh century AD. The paintings preserved here in several rock-caves not only portray Buddhist scenes but also throw welcome light on various secular aspects of life. The artists of Ajanta wanted to bring the fact home to the people that religion was concerned not only with the other world, it was also meant to make this life happy and peaceful.[20]

The wall paintings of Ajantā in some caves are inscribed with verses from Āryasura's work, the painting and the literary work are in close harmony of sentiment.[21] The Ajantā caves are the product of both the Theravāda

---

20. Bajpai, K.D., *Five Phases of Indian Art*, p. 116.

21. Coomaraswamy, A.K., *Buddha and the Gospel of Buddhism*, p. 313.

(Hīnayāna) and Mahāyāna Buddhism. The oldest *vihāras* at Ajantā caves are 30, 8 and 12. Hīnayāna caves 8 and 9. Mahāyāna (AD 450-550) caves are 6, 7, 11, 16, 17, 19, 26.

Cave 1 is a splendid example of Mahāyāna. Paintings depict the attacks made on Buddha before enlightenment.

Cave 2 representations from Bhārhut, Sāñcī, Amarāvatī, Mathurā, Sārnāth.

Cave 4 Padmapāṇi-*bodhisattvas*, men and women flying.

Cave 6 Two-storyed *vihāras*.

Caves 8, 9, 12 & 13 are Hīnayāna; were excavated in second century BC. Cave 9 has a fine facade, apse and aisles of second century BC.

Cave 10 Similar to Sāñcī. Elephants are under a banyan tree; of second century BC. The paintings show worship of the *bodhi* tree and illustrates *Chaddanta Jātaka*.

Cave 16 Gupta art is prominent.

Cave 17 It depicts Sinhala legend. It has three ships carrying King Sinhala army of elephant troops and cavalry to Sri Lanka.

Cave 27 Prince Vessantara with his consort geese in *Haṁsa Jātaka*

Caves 3, 4, 14, 28, 29 were never completed.

We do not see any dance form in Sīgiriya and Ajantā. Generally dance gives life to the painting, but in these two places, it is missing. Whereas at Bāgh, dance a (Hallisaka form) is depicted. Probably many of us believe that Amarāvatī and Bāgh styles are seen at Ajantā. The Hallisaka form of dance portrays mode of valour and zeal. The painting depicting *Mahājanaka Jātaka* at Ajantā has a group of dancers and *citras* in walls and *tribhaṅga* pose.

Śibi Jātaka — The Princes and his consort, *Nigrodhamiga Jātakas*, *Chaddanta Jātaka*, *Maccha Jātaka*, the *Sarabhaniga Jātaka*, the *Vessantara Jātaka*, and many other *Jātakas*, have been portrayed like in Nāgārjunikoṇḍa, Sāñcī, Bhārhut. Marshall says that,

> At Bagh as at Ajanta the paintings are done in tempera. Colours are same.[22]

> The colour composition, the anatomy of figures and their postures are simply remarkable in the paintings of Ajanta.[23]

Marshall opines that the Bāgh paintings and Ajantā paintings relate and deal with identical subjects,

> the same poetry of emotion and the same wonderful diversity in the poses of their figures, the same feeling for colour.

The Ajantā tradition was followed in Sri Lanka till nineteenth century regarding the subjects, i.e., *Jātaka* and the *Buddha-carita*. The Sātavāhana period comes (second century BC-second century AD) and changes are noticed in Ajantā and Sāñcī.

> The paintings cover the walls, pillars and ceilings and illustrate scenes from the life of master and his previous lives, comprising the Jātakas and *avadanas*. There are also floral and animal motifs dexterously created.[24]

> The Jataka cave temples are actually magnificent art galleries and the murals found there constitute an illustrative commentary on Jatakas and *avadanas* of Buddhist literature.[25]

---

22. Marshall, Sir John, *The Bagh Caves*, p. 16.
23. Bajpai, K.D., *Five Phases of Indian art*, p. 116.
24. Sivaramamurti, C., *Indian Painting*, p. 24.
25. Sivaramamurti, C., *The Art of India*, p. 176.

Sarla Khosla in her book *Gupta Civilisation* and Madanjeet Singh in *The Cave Painting of Ajanta* refers to the visit of Kālidāsa to Ajantā while he was associated with the court of Candragupta II.

> Kalidasa's lyrical compliment to a young women in his *Kumarasambhava*, "like a painting on which the final outline had been carefully drawn to mask the modelling of the limbs by the master painter Kamadena."[26] Kalidasa himself describes "Her lip is ruddy as an opening bud. . . . The glow of youth is spread on all her limbs."

> *lokasmin hi cittakamma to uttarim annam cittam nāma natthi*

> there is nothing finer in the world than the art of painting

The two great Indian epics the *Rāmāyaṇa* and the *Mahābhārata* have references to paintings, royal palaces and artistic antiques and architectural forms.[27] Aśoka sent out his missionaries to propagate Buddhism and simultaneously he took the initiative in displaying art

> and is credited to have sent eighteen guilds of artists, craftsmen and painters with his son, Mahinda to Ceylon so as to turn Anuradhapura, the ancient capital of that country into an art gallery [Chittasala].[28]

Ajantā paintings, to be precise, the Indian paintings, were all derived from religious inspirations. The Sīgriya monasteries were serving as schools to teach Buddhism, philosophy and art and culture. The three places where we can find purely Buddhist characteristics are Ajantā,

---

26. Singh, Madanjeet, *The Cave Paintings of Ajantā*, p. 107.
27. Deshpande, M.N., "Ajantā the Kaleidoscopic Enigma of Art Historians", p. 17. (pp. 1-27) in *The Art of Ajantā New Perspectives*, Vol. I.
28. *Ibid.*, p. 18.

> the caves of Sigiriya and at a place called Tamankaduwa in the Island of Ceylon.[29]
>
> The world of the Ajanta princess in their palaces, royal processions with decorated elephant and horses, hunting scenes, loving couples, shopkeepers, porters with loads slung over their shoulders, ascetics in monasteries, peasants, beggars and hots of other people, surrounded by a fantastic variety of beasts and birds and flowers, were perpetuated by the trained hands of many craftsmen. The creation and interpretation of all this is masterfully drawn pictures on delicately painted walls is undoubtedly an indigenous contribution to Ajanta.[30]

There is a repetition of scenes but in different manifestations. It is 'the mirage of kindly light'.[31] There is a lyrical world of men, women, luminating *bodhisattva*'s, animals, creepers, flying celestial and human joys and sorrows take us 'to the homeland of our dreams':[32] Laurence Binyon, a learned connoisseur writes: 'the scale of the frescoes make a forcible and imposing impression'. We can see 'there is a grace, dignity and character'.

The foregoing descriptions and illustrations will enable us to form a judgement concerning the aesthetic value of the Ajantā painting. Ajantā paintings identify multiple stylish figures and varying compositional principles. Paintings in Cave 10 of Ajantā have resemblance to Bhārhut, Amarāvatī. The turbans, earrings and their facial expression and the headgear of *toraṇa śālabhañjikā* at Sāñcī too resemble those of Mathurā and Amarāvatī. Cave 17 and 18 will prove this statement. Ajantā belongs

---

29. Chandra Dey, Sri Mukul, *My Pilgrimages to Ajantā and Bāgh*, p. 199.
30. Singh, Madanjeet, *The Cave Paintings of Ajantā*, p. 103.
31. Ghosh A. (ed.), *Ajantā Mural*, p. 9.
32. *Ibid.*

to the 'arts of space' and this explains that there will be painting, sculpture and architecture. Sīgiriya and Bāgh, of course, do not fall in 'arts of space'. Hence, this is the main cause of variations in these paintings. It may also be conducive to us to know that Ajantā classicism is not derived from Gupta or Vākāṭaka art but from Āndhradeśa, i.e., from Kṛṣṇā valley artists.[33] Since all *Jātaka* tales are allegories and thus Ajantā art became narrative. It is not at all relevant to say that Gupta art is not responsible for classicism. As a matter of fact, the Gupta dynasty was solely responsible for maintenance of the art and literature. They did the maximum and this Gupta age is called 'golden age'.

Sir John Marshall has aptly summarised the qualities of the Ajantā school of painting and its contribution to the art of Asia.

> The school which these paintings represent was the source and fountainhead from which half the art of Asia drew its inspiration and no one can study their rhythmic composition, their instinctive beauty of line, the majestic grace of their figures and the boundless wealth of their decorative imagery without realising what a far-reaching influence they exerted on the art not of India alone and her colonies, but of every other country in which the religion of the Buddha penetrated. Nor are these paintings to be appraised only in relation to the art of Asia. They will bear comparison with the best that Europe could produce down to the time of Michael Angelo. . . .

The *Jātaka*s exhibited here concern the world of *deva*s, animals, vegetables, birds, landscapes and many other things. The figures are drawn with admirable skill and painted with a deep understanding of colour values. But essentially it is an art of line, as Percy Brown so well

33. Parimoo, Ratan, *Vidhurupandita-Jātaka from Bhārhut to Ajantā: A Study of Narrative, Semidogical and Stylistic Aspects*, p. 337 (pp. 315-41).

summarises its qualities, as all Indians and Eastern art is. The artists of Ajantā were so much the masters of line that to their subtle and fine touch the line yielded all pictorial secrets. Every degree of expression is rendered with a subtle handling of the line. Hence line is the important feature in Ajantā. On Ajantā Ajit Mookerjee writes:

> The graceful and festive damsels, the lovely *apsaras* with fully blossomed life 'brusting through the moon — breasts and wine — jar — heaps' — are yet another scene that attracts one's wistful attention. Human from first to last — they fly, they dance, they court, they 'make love unabashed'. Life in all its aspects was manifest to a high degree in these paintings and sculptures as well as in music, dance and drama.

Bāgh

The Gupta emperors, the patrons of art and literature, were responsible for creating a milieu of art in India and this great art of their flourished in Bāgh too. It is unfortunate that the most of the paintings in the Bāgh are not in existence now.

The Ajantā School was not only confined to their own place but went here and there. Bāgh and Ajantā as claimed are similar. We do not find inscription of any kind. Their hair style of male is that of the Gupta period. From the style and depiction of paintings at the caves, they can be dated to the sixth century. Paintings are in black and white. There is variety of designs in paintings with gaiety. There is 'hardly any trace of asceticism'.[34] The artists portrayed their subjects from life and tradition. Women in Bāgh paintings are sympathetic and are seen sharing their ideas with others. The Bāgh paintings reached excellence in fourth century AD. There

34. Smith, V.A., *A History of Fine Art in India and Ceylon*, p. 109.

is an expression of personality in the Bāgh paintings. Cave No.3 was for the Head monk, and this was used for sermons and gatherings whereas Cave No. 5 was for teaching.

J. Perera writes that religion has a great impact on painting and this has resulted in elevating the consciousness. This consciousness has further developed and created sub-consciousness which has link with *īśvar* or God. God is ultimately the guiding factor. In the field of art, it is a boon. Everybody cannot be artist or painter. Thus, he further elaborates and thinks a force is there which is contributing in this field.[35]

Maheshwari Dayal Khare has travelled extensively in the surroundings of the Bāgh and had done a marvellous study in conducting survey of Bāgh paintings. Mr. Khare agrees that a tangible study has not been conducted for Bāgh paintings and Sīgiriya paintings. However, he also agrees that Sīgiriya, Ajantā and Bāgh are identical but keeps the Bāgh paintings higher[36] than others. Bāgh paintings are morally sound and are natural. The *bodhisattvas* in *tribhaṅga*[37] pose have a special place in Bāgh. Spiritual feelings are awakened. The artists have not mentioned their names in these paintings. Many times it is also difficult to place their historical dates. In Cave No. 7 Pillars (*stambha*) are in ruined shape. The original paintings are not available but their remains convey the independence of the painters. The painters at Bāgh were not dependent and rather they were free to draw whatever they wanted. The Ajantā artists were not free. They had a particular aim and mission. Here in Bāgh no nakedness is seen but a wave of innocence is there. We will see that females are wearing blouse up to their neck. Necklace, armlets, bangles are heavily hanging. Bāgh caves have no *caityagṛha*. There are

35. Perera, J., *India's Contribution to World of Thought and Culture*, p. 623.

36. Khare, M.D., *Bāgh Kī Guphāyen*, p. 74.

37. *Op. cit.*, p. 75.

seven caves and the paintings in these caves were murals like those of Ajantā.[38] Conclusively,

> The caves at Bāgh were hewn out of sandstone rocks which happened to be topped by a deep bond of clay stone. Perhpas the heavy weight of the top-layer and seepage of water through it must have ruined most of the caves with their porticos and sculptured facades. But the remains still offer the wonderful specimens of mural painting. The Bāgh frescoes are taken by competent authorities to be contemporaneous with the late Ajanta frescoes. In craftsmanship they are similar. Their mastery over spontaneous technique of mural painting is no less. They have the same mood of reserve in the midst of joy. But while, the Ajanta frescoes are more religious in theme, depicting incidents from the previous lives of the Buddha, with their human association, the Bagh frescoes are more human, depicting the life of the time with its religious associations.[39]

We may conclude by saying that Sīgiriya frescoes were not religious. Ajantā and Bāgh frescoes had religious obligations. The Sīgiriya frescoes certainly have some similarities with Bāgh. This is purely based on the historical events, since Sīgiriya and Ajantā almost belong to the same period and Bāgh also came in offing. The other reason for similarities could be that with the artists or the paraphernalia gone with Mahinda, a retinue of artisans along with the others might have exchanged their ideas and thus paintings were done. The most dominant figures are the ladies. Ajantā and Sīgiriya ladies differ from those of Bāgh. Bāgh paintings depict purely Hindustānī charm and value. We call it Hindustānī because no sensuousness or any kind of emotion, feelings are not notices. Much work

38. Mitra, Debala, *Buddhist Monuments*, p. 99.

39. Barua, D.K., *Vihāras in Ancient India*, p. 98.

has not been carried out on Bāgh paintings and same is the case with Sīgiriya paintings. The Ajantā have been studied, thorough deep critical study has been conducted and compared with the world arts. It has thus become more significant than the two. It is believed owing to rains and rivers the paintings at Bāgh have been erased, thus the original features are missing and today the position is most discouraging. Therefore, Bāgh paintings were not studied properly; were ignored and no attention was paid by the scholars. Nevertheless, the three galleries, i.e. Ajantā, Bāgh and Sīgiriya make a triangle in understanding Buddhist paintings which have long and rich heritage. It is therefore very essential to keep these galleries alive by carrying out earnest comparative research.

4
Sculpture

Some men see things as they are and say why,
I see things that never were and say why not

— Somerset Maugham

SCULPTURE in general defines each attitude, each expression and each gesture. Sculpture is a form of freedom of expression and is not necessary that these should be at religious places. It is the art of making objects or figures using solid material like stone or shaping clay. Sculpture in general is a concrete shape given to iconographic descriptions. It interprets various iconographic forms and *rasa*s. Sculpture inspired much activity in painting and architecture.

The art of sculpture can only arrest a particular movement of the creative flow for its representation. It is perhaps for supplementing this abstraction that the Indian artist always associated his human creation or the deities with plant life or animal life, to indicate the uniformity and life that flows through nature and that throb through spiritual perception. History of culture has sculpture as its source material.

Urbanisation, occurred in the sixth century BC. Great social and cultural upheaval occurred during the lifetime of Buddha in the fifth century BC and Buddhism can be called a protestant movement of that period. Emperor Aśoka gave this religious movement his imperial patronage and set it up on its course to become a world religion.

It is not possible, with our present state of knowledge, to date the beginning of the art of sculpture in India. It was there during Harappan period, dated to third and second millennium BC in a most developed form. We have a continuous history of culture from the Mauryan period. It is a belief that sculpture brings hallucinatory vision; an experience of seeing something that really is not there. The sculpture became a powerful idiom to express and illustrate stories, *gāthās* and poems. The artists used this medium to bring home the message of religious literature to the common folk; they made the picture speak animals and birds in India are made to speak and think like a man.[1]

The *Jātakas*, the epic and the fables spoke through sculpture.

> Excellent stone sculpture comes into full being all at once, Minerva-like in the beginning of the third-century BC Maurya sculpture occupies a special place in the history of Indian art.[2]

Buddhists and Hindus have treated sculpture as religious art.[3] Stella Kramrisch says,

> The art of India is neither religious nor secular, for, the consistent fabric of Indian life was never rent by the Western dichotomy of religious beliefs and worldly practice.

There ought to have been sculptures before Buddha images or symbols

---

1. Sivaramamurti, C., *Birds and Animals in Indian Sculpture*, p. 8.
2. Agrawala, V.S., *The Heritage of Indian Art*, p. 12.
3. Wickramasinghe, Martin, *Buddhism and Art*, p. 107.

denoting Buddha originated. Perhaps the *yakṣa* or *yakṣī* images were there. There was always terracotta art. The earliest stone and bronze sculpture were from proto-historic period, e.g., priest and dancing girl of Mohenjo-Dāro seals and small objects made at Mohenjo-Dāro were found at sites in Iraq. The making of beads and amulets were also popular. Beads were made of clay, stone, paste, shell and ivory. The metal workers produced tools and implements in copper and bronze, such as spears, knives, arrow-heads, razors, vessels made of metal sheet were used, but these items were for upper strata society as these were expensive. Flat, rectangular seals made of clay or stone have been unearthed during archaeological excavations; usually the picture of a bull, tree or same scenes are seen on the seals which were used by merchants to sell their goods.

The Western Art historians and critics or the writers having Western interest have not been in a position to interpret Buddha sculpture or for that matter any piece of Indian sculpture aptly. The sculpture of Buddha in India and Sri Lanka differ. But it does not tantamount that the sculptures are passive. A School of thought emerged and gave their opinion that Buddha sculpture represents self-mortifications and betrays pessimism and sadness. The sculptors who made Buddha images at that time were well acquainted with the ideas about Buddha prevailing at that time. Notwithstanding, our modern views about Buddha sculptures and their setbacks, they still look subtle, calm and we can say that they portray gravity mixed with compassion. Buddha image has always been elegant and perfect. It is but natural that the gravity indicates passiveness, seriousness but great men have always been shown immersed in deep thoughts. Sculptures depicting serious expression always commands awe and reverence from the devotee; a cobra symbolises anger, enmity but when it merges with Buddha, it stresses Buddha's kindness, infinitive love, compassion, spiritual calm and quiet. A serpent in the sculpture stands for the infinite which may break up in thousands of parts. Most of the sculptures we see in museums were discovered at different places at different times in piecemeal[4] and it "is a story of considerable physical daring and adventure in"[5] reading and dating them and write their history.

> There is hardly anybody excepting the archaeologists who is interested in exploring the field of our ancient sculpture from an artistic point of view, though there are many artists, poets, journalists and even art historians who write and talk incessantly.[6]

Images of Buddha

Buddha images of ancient Sri Lanka differ from Indian images of the same posture. The sitting Buddha images of India are in the 'cross-legged' posture called *padmāsana.* In this posture the right foot is placed on the left thigh and the left foot on the right thigh. The Indian posture is proper and needs no elaboration, but the images of Sri Lanka particularly at Anurādhapura and Polonnaruwa vary and lead to confusion. Many believe that they are all 'cross-legged'. The Sri Lankan images of Buddha are not in *padmāsana* and are totally dissimilar to Indian ones. Havell says about Anurādhapura Buddha images,

> It represents the Buddha first emerging from the *yoga* trance, the left leg being released from the 'adamantine' pose of profound meditation, when both legs are firmly locked together.

The Anurādhpura image has been dated to fourth century and this is somewhat similar to the bas-reliefs of Amarāvatī and Nāgārjunikoṇḍa. It could be that the image of Buddha was carved in South India and was perfected in Sri Lanka. In many cases, it is seen that the things started in

---

4. Mookerjee, R.K., *Aśoka*, p. vii (Pref.).
5. *Ibid.*
6. Wickramasinghe, Martin, *Aspects of Sinhalese Culture*, p. 58.

India went to Sri Lanka where they reached perfection. Undoubtedly, it is true also. Anurādhapura image [*Plate XXXV*] is an independent development and has no parallel. It is *chef-d'oeuvre*.

Buddha statue teaches us in detail the features and peculiarities of the different schools. Some of us think that Sri Lankan sculptures are only copies of Indian sculptures. There is a tradition in every country, in every city and in every village. A family has also a tradition. Thus, tradition is a pre-requisite to understand sculpture; for, sculpture is a blend of imagination and personality.[7] S. Radhakrishnan writes,

> In the life of the Buddha, there are two sides, individual and social. The familiar Buddha image is of a meditating sage, *yogin* absorbed and withdrawn lost in the joy of his inner meditation. This is the tradition, associated with the Theravada Buddhism and Ashoka missions.[8]

Buddha images give us *śānta rasa,* peace and solemnity [*Plate XXXVI*].

Mathurā and Gāndhāra were the first places where Buddha images came in vogue and this travelled to far off places. Mathurā is a place of Kuṣāṇa sculpture and is directly linked with Bhārhut and Sāñcī. In Mathurā we have red sandstone. During first-third century AD, Mathurā and Gāndhāra were great centres of sculptures. Mathurā sculptures seek to communicate spiritual ecstasy. These images are combinations and compositions of sensuous and spiritual.

Mathurā became popular because Buddha visited it, but this place was not liked by Budha as the *yakṣa* cult was dominating there[9] and dogs were wild. Mathurā sculpture does not exhibit the Buddha in human form

---

7. *Op. cit.*, p. 59.
8. Bapat, P.V. (ed.), *2500 Years of Buddhism*, p. viii (Foreword).
9. Sharma, R.C., *Buddhist Art of Mathura*, p. 39.

and it can be urged upon that the sculptors were not able or not so keen in portraying human form. The chief characteristics of Mathurā art is that it took initiative to transform symbols in human form. Here was the process of evolution. Mathurā School also exhibits the different stages in the evolution of Buddha image. Although it is accepted that the Mathurā is the place from where Buddha image was initiated but there is also a belief that Buddha image came in vogue even during the lifetime of Buddha. *Divyāvadāna* states that at the request of King Bimbisāra, Buddha let his shadow fall upon a cloth and agreed to its outline being marked in order to facilitate the painting of his figure on it.[10] The *Mahāvaṁsa,* the Sri Lankan chronicle states that a golden statue of Buddha in the attitude of Enlightenment was kept in the relic chamber of Ruvanwaeli *dagaba*. It means that the origin of Buddha image can be traced to the time when he was alive. But Bhārhut and Sāñcī belonging to second-first century BC do not display a single Buddhist icon in human form. There were no Buddha images at Amarāvatī and at Nāgārjunikoṇḍa even during third century BC

> One of the greatest achievement of the Mathura School was the introduction in art the representation of the Master in human form.[11]

Mathurā sculptor gave the proper form and shape to Buddha image. Buddha was born as a king and led a monk's life. Cakravarti and *yogī* signs are seen in Buddha's images. Therefore, *mahāpuruṣa lakṣaṇa*s have been delineated. These are exhibited in all the images of Buddha. Aśvaghoṣa describes:

---

10. Anand, Mulk Raj, "Origin of the Buddha Image", *Marg*, Vol. XV, No. 2.
11. Sharma, R.C., *Buddhist Art of Mathura*, p. 168.

Long arms hanging up to knee	*ajānubāhu*
The elongated earlobes	*pralambakarṇapāśa*
Broad chest	*visalavasa*
Webbed fingers	*jalaṅgulikāra*

Soles, palm, finger tips decorated with wheel, etc. *cakrankahesta-pada*, knotted hair above the head [*usnisa*], spiral hair mark between eyebrows [*urna*].

The Mathurā artists have conceived Buddha as a superhuman being. Mathurā and Gāndhāra had close political and cultural links during the Kuṣāṇa period. We find Gāndhāra features in Mathurā sculptures like drapery covering both shoulders, moustaches, conical cap, events of the life of Buddha, curly and spiral lock of hair, variety of postures. Mathurā sculptures have incorporated curly hair, drapery covering one shoulder, the *abhaya* pose and monk's *saṁghātī*. Buddha images of the Kaniṣka period show the body straight and stiff, shaven head, the left hand held akimbo resting on the waist, right hand held in protection *mudrā* (*abhaya*), lower garment reaching below the knee. The *bodhisattva* image of Mathurā of second century AD looks majestic. The bare

> torso with the belly portruding slightly over the belt, has a sensitive roundness and softness and conveys the impression of living flesh.[12]

SĀRNĀTH

The Sārnāth School followed the Mathurā. During the Gupta period Sārnāth emerged as a blooming school and produced many magnificent and graceful Buddhist images. The most remarkable and distinguishing feature of the Sārnāth style is the foldless wet drapery.[13] The principal

12. Morley, Grace, *Indian Sculpture*, p. 50.
13. Sharma, R.C., *Buddhist Art of Mathura*, p. 241.

episodes of Buddha's life have been sculpted into three on a single stone in three registers at Sārnāth. On the lower register we can see Queen Māyā Devī is having a dream and Prince Siddhārtha is born. In the middle register Prince Siddhārtha on his horse in leaving the palace and in the third or upper register Buddha is seated and delivers the First Sermon at Deer Park. This sculpture of fifth century AD is in Sārnāth tradition. Seated Buddha is shown in three forms. *Samādhi* is the highest form of ecstasy. Always in the meditation and totally absorbed in it. In *dhyāna-mudrā* the hands are crossed and placed on the lap. In *bhūmisparśa-mudrā* the right hand is moved forward across the right knee to touch the earth. The posture in which hands are raised and placed in front of the chest is *dharmacakra-mudrā*. In *abhaya-mudrā* the right hand is raised and palm is turned outward. In *varada-mudrā* the right hand is extended. In *vitarka-mudrā* the *bodhisattva* is great. *Uṣṇīṣa* is protuberance on the top of the head.

Dhyāna-mudrā means meditation, *bhūmisparśa-mudrā* signifies calling the earth to witness, *dharmacakra-mudrā* points to the setting the wheel of the law in motion, *abhaya-mudrā* indicates dispelling fear, *varada-mudrā* denotes charity while *vitarka-mudrā* conveys argument.

The Lion capital (third century BC) adopted by the Government of India as State Emblem is the most magnificent sculpture of Mauryan art. On the abacus four animals — an elephant, a bull, a horse and a lion — are seen in motion. These four animals symbolise the gods, Indra, Śiva, Sūrya, and Durgā. These are known as 'Noble beasts' and are the *vāhana*s of the gods and goddesses. These four animals are seen also on moonstones in Sri Lanka. Lion capital is the supreme religious symbolism.

> The Dharma *cakra,* the four lions and the figures on the round abacus are eloquent expression of personal ideas and ideals of Asoka.[14]

14. Agrawala, V.S., *Studies in Indian Art*, p. 70.

Of course, in his pursuit of Buddhism. The four animals symbolise four cardinal points — the elephant, the east; the horse, the south; the bull, the west; and the lion; the north. All these four directions combine to form the cosmos. Then *dhamma* was proclaimed from four sides. The animal's muscles, veins and claws are rendered in naturalistic manner and have been inspired by Greek art. V. Smith feels that treatment of the bull and elephant in the Sārnāth abacus is inspired. Actually Aśokan art does not reveal any influence from outside. It was all natural process.

> The Buddha images of Sārnāth were so beautifully carved that the sculpture did not feel like adding any ornaments. In fact, the sculptors were deeply concerned to produce pure and beautiful poems.[15]

The classic example is the well-known Buddha image in *dharmacakra-pravartana-mudrā* at Sārnāth. *Dharmacakra* is completely within the tradition of Indian art.

Sārnāth introduced refineness, a delicacy of form and a large number of sculptures illustrate this in distinctive and beautiful manner. *Dharmacakra-mudrā* is the gesture of preaching carved in chunar sandstone. Buddha is here seated in *vajra-prayaṅka* with hands in this particular *mudrā*. Mathurā and Sārnāth idioms signify collectively the Gupta classical tradition. Rene Grousset feels that the sculptures made at Sārnāth are inspired by intellectualism as to be the direct expression of the soul through purely ideal beauty of form. Sārnāth Gupta style is in the treatment of the drapery. Though fully clothed the figures are so draped that they virtually form the body contours. It will be seen that the drape covers the neck, sides and hem.

It was in the Gupta period that art enjoyed freedom and evolved in a large number of forms. Images of Buddha were installed in monasteries,

---

15. Biswas, T.A. and Jha, *Gupta Sculptures*, p. 32.

chapels, temples and even in their outer niches. Moreover, Gūpta Buddhist sculpture was dominated by images of Maitreya, Avalokitésvara and numerous deities derived from Brāhmaṇical pantheon like the goddess of fertility (Vasudharā), the goddess of plenty (Tārā and Marīcī).[16] Every branch of literature, science and art was carefully cultivated and expanded under the liberal royal patronage of the Gupta dynasty. Kālidāsa, the greatest of Indian poets, graced the Gupta court and produced masterpieces. In painting we have Ajantā, Bāgh and Sīgiriya frescoes. The style at Sārnāth is free from extravagance or monstrosity. In the words of Niharranjan Ray,

> Sarnath articulation in stone of the meditative and compassionate Buddha giving his first message of deliverance to the world.

The artist of Gupta age used their tools and skills to manifest the ideals and philosophical tradition including those of Purāṇas, myths, hence the Gupta age became rich in all fields.

SĀÑCĪ

The history of Sāñcī [*Plate XXXVII*] begins during the reign of Aśoka in the third century BC (*circa* 273-236 BC) by erecting a *stūpa* and a monolithic pillar. On the death of Emperor Aśoka in 232 BC the empire broke into pieces. But later on, Śuṅgas took initiative and erected the second and third *stūpas* but not the gateway and the Śuṅgas have also erected a monument at Besnagar which is stone column with massive abacus. Reliefs of the Śuṅga period at Sāñcī, Bhārhut and Bodh Gayā reveal the influence of hellenistic ideas.

During the Āndhra period, under the Śuṅgas dynasty Indian art achieved its zenith and four gateways of the Great *stūpa*[17] and the single

16. Khosla, Sarla, *Gupta Civilisation*, p. 163.
17. Marshall, Sir John, *A Guide to Sāñcī*, p. 13.

gateway of the third were erected. The gateways of Sāñcī are surviving. Each gateway consists of two square pillars, four lions, elephants or dwarfs. Dwarfs look ferocious, heavy and hefty, Śālabhanjikas are in a graceful and elegant mood. At the centre of the top architrave a *dharmacakra*, flanked by *cāmara* — bearing *yakṣas* and decorated with *tri-ratna* symbol the trinity of Buddhism — Buddha, Dharma and Saṁgha. The entire surface of the gateways is covered with bas-reliefs representing scenes and decorations. The subject-matter of the carvings on the gateway is: scenes from the *Jātakas*, scenes from the history of Buddhism, scenes from the life of Buddha and *bodhisattvas*. At Bhārhut, we have many *Jātakas*, i.e., importance is on *Jātaka* tales whereas at Sāñcī, the emphasis in on Buddha.

THE JĀTAKAS

The stories about the *bodhisattvas* are in the *Jātaka* tales. The *Jātaka* tales are one cf the greatest works of classical Sinhalese literature. Most of these fables including those of animals read like modern works of fiction and many of the stories including the fables are realistic. The stories expose follies and foibles, superstitious and animistic beliefs [*Plate XXXVIII*]. These are caricatures and satires full of wit and humour. People laugh at others and also laugh at themselves. Thus, the *Jātakas* stories are, as a matter of fact, a boon for the society to come up from the garb and entered in a new phase of life. The stories evince morals and responsibility towards society. The *Jātakas* respect the traditional values. The *Valahassa Jātaka* describes that the veddas were even then cannibals, it is about *yakṣas*. The *Śaṅkha Jātaka* describes the voyages from the Ganges to Suvannabhūmi. The *Sussondi Jātaka* states that merchants proceeded by water from Banāras to Nāgadīpa, i.e., northern Sri Lanka of earlier times. The *Jātaka* stories are shown on small panels and undoubtedly the viewer is able to understand the unfolding of the narrative. This aspect is the most important and one should ponder how much pains the artists took to exhibit and portray the whole story without loss of details in such a small panel [*Plate XXXIX*]. It is really surprising and is a moot point. The *Jātaka* No. 529 is illustrated in Sāñcī carvings. Horses, three or four to a chariot, are used in India. One or two horses are used for chariots in Sāñcī. The carvings at Isurumuniya indicate that the cavalry was in existence as we may see 'shining armour' or breast plate that was used. This is also seen in the *Jātaka* No. 233 and in India at Amarāvatī carvings, the horse is decorated with a high hair plume. It is also to be noted that in India in ancient times men rode without saddles. In Amarāvatī carvings there is a belt which passes round the right shoulder of the soldier. The archers formed the chief branch of the regular foot-soldiers and in Sri Lanka the veddas were the archery arm. Other foot-soldiers were spear-men. There was also an elephant corps. We find the royal stables of the third century BC referred to in the *Mahāvaṁsa*. The *Mahā Ummagga Jātaka* gives a vivid picture of regular troops of early times.

The *Jātaka*s in the panels, enabled the common people to understand the stories and practises the virtues advocated by the stories. Because these panels left a lasting impression on the public mind with their visual lessons. The people who do not know ABC of the *Jātaka*s are impressed by the pictures or paintings [*Plate XL*]. The books on *Jātaka*s give us what that author thinks or his views. But the panels give the story as it is with no addition of the artist's views. Therefore, the moral or the message is passed more conveniently through art. The stories are cumbersome to many as it has history, myths, full of epigrams, figures of speech and carry subtle meanings which are not grasped by all.

The *Chaddanta Jātaka* is on three architraves south gateway, rear side, middle architrave; west gateway front side, bottom architrave and north gateway rear side.

The *Mahākapi Jātaka* is on the top panel of the front side of the south pillar of west gateway.

The *Vessantara Jātaka* is depicted with a great wealth of decorative and picturesque details on the front and rear sides of the bottom architrave of the north gateway.

The *Alambuṣā Jātaka* is depicted at the west end of the front side of the bottom architrave of the north gateway. The same *Jātaka* top panel on the south face of the north pillar of the west gateway commemorates the story of filial love evinced by the *bodhisattvas*. The rule of the Guptas brought peace and prosperity with the result that the dormant genius of the Indian people was awakened. During the Gupta period, the sculptor and painter gave articulate expression to the then current spiritual, religious and spiritual ideas. Sublime thoughts and expressions were captured with chisel and brush and made available to the people in tranquil and picturesque surroundings so that these remained engraved in their memories. To cite one example, the Sālabhañjikās, we think are the most admirable creations in the world's art. The 'Renaissance' of India (*circa* AD 350-650) created Gupta culture which is manifest in art, literature and in many other subjects.

The Great Sāñcī *stūpa* with its hemispherical dome (*aṇḍa*), lofty terrace (*medhi*) and processional path (*pradakṣiṇā path*) is an amazing creation. Steps (*sopāna*) and then is a second processional path enclosed by balustrade (*vedikā*) of stone. This is of plain design. There are four quardrants and the cardinal points are adorned by a gateway (*toraṇa*). *Toraṇas* are enriched with reliefs on both the inner and the outer sides. The original *stūpa* was built by Aśoka. Four Buddha images were placed at the entrances of the Great *stūpa* one facing each of the four directions during the fifth century. Sāñcī and Ajantā Buddhist architecture is a combination of both Buddhist and Hindu architecture. In Sāñcī we find music, birds and animals. There are 'figures of animals, full of vigour and vitality'. Sāñcī art is mature art.[18] There are heavenly nymphs carved on

18. Bajpai, K.D., *Five Phases of Indian Art*, p. 24.

the gateways remarkable for their sensitive forms and attractive postures.[19] Lot of sensuousness is there. Sāñcī artists brought the beauty of fair sex[20] and did not conceal it.[21] the Sāñcī sculptures speak of the ideals of worldly life as conceived in Indian scriptures. There is nothing new to the nudity of the women in Sāñcī. Neither in a cosmopolitan society, or a *beau monde* society this kind of nudity is not taken as bad omen, nor in the West. The *vedikā* at Sāñcī served as entrances to the sacred compound and at Bhārhut it is adorned with monumental stone gateways, i.e., *toraṇas*. Three sites of sculpture Sāñcī, Amarāvatī and Nāgārjunikoṇḍa are important. In short, Sāñcī (third century BC to first century AD) preserved the *stūpa* form, Buddha's life and *Jātaka* tales together with decorative animals. Amarāvatī (second century BC to third century AD) and Nāgārjunikoṇḍa (second century AD to third century AD) Buddha's images generally are simple, ornate and grotesque. The railings at Sāñcī are the most impressive production in whole range of Buddhist art.[22] It is often commented upon that the sculpture portrays nude women. It is not so, they are draped in diaphanous robes which give an idea of their exquisite feminine forms. The Great *stūpa* at Sāñcī is a 'symbol of devotion to the Buddha'.[23]

At Ajantā, Buddha images are seated in *padmāsana*, or the *pralamba pādāsana*. The postures or *mudrās* are *varada*, *dharmacakrapravartana* or *abhaya*.[24] Sāñcī[25] was referred to under the name Cetiyagiri in the

---

19. Bajpai, K.D., *Five Phases of Indian Art.*
20. *Ibid.*
21. *Ibid.*
22. Percy, Brown, *Indian Architecture*, p. 14.
23. Morley, Grace, *Indian Sculpture*, p. 32.
24. Bajpai, K.D., *Five Phases of Indian Art*, p. 78.
25. Barua, D.K., *Vihāras in Ancient India*, p. 93.

Mahāvaṁsa and Chinese pilgrims were stores of information went from Sāñcī in silence.

The Sāñcī sculptors were benign and courteous. Their creative genius is seen in the workmanship. These have created and perfected by a generation of sophisticated and devoted artists. The Buddhist psychology denoted ecstasy, comparison, complete withdrawal of senses from the external world are visible in Buddha images created by them.

GUPTA

The Gupta period (fourth-sixth century AD) is known as the Golden Age of Indian History, above all, in the domain of art. Gupta art evolved classical icons and subsequently went to Sārnāth and other places. The sculpture entered on a new level of creative activity and produced a congenial atmosphere and elaborate workmanship. Gupta sculpture is a synthesis of the extreme form and hidden treasures. The sculptures at Sāñcī (AD 300-600) were supposed to be calm and most expressive of divine peace but attaining this goal they lost beauty for lack of synthesis. They are graceful and elegant, but look artificial. It is also true that the images produced during the Gupta period were marvellous and charming. They exhibited youth and images look alive. No coarseness or artificial ornamentation mars the visible life and zeal in the image. The youth is shown in a unique style which is not at all seen in other period. Even the gods and deities are shown young. No sculpture or image exhibits any infirmity or deformity. Here glory is glorified. Owing to glorification new interpretations assumed new definitions along with a new grammar of gestures [*Plate XLI*]. The gestures were shown and formulated. The gestures of hands and their poses add stress to the message. Even in dances the *mudrās*, gestures play an effective role. Movement of hands, glances, mind are intertwined with each other and mind goes, the mood follows, where mood goes there is favour. Thus, serious consideration lies behind the gesture of hand. The gestures thus became the keynote of the

Gupta period [*Plate XLII*]. The artists created supernatural qualities and superhuman beings beyond the reach of an ordinary being. Thus, the Gupta artists were regarded as having superhuman elements. Gupta sculptors made their 'deity happier'. Physical beauty and more perfection ran parallel. Beauty and purity did not mean depicting female lewdness. The women of the Gupta period had dignity and sophistication.

> Though they had ample hips and full breasts, yet 'they retained the promise of motherhood'. These females were treated in soft, subtle and sensitive modelling. . . .

Figures were heavy. Eyes indicated emotional attachment. Images are examples of perfect beauty. Sculptures or any image is the product of a relaxed moment, innocent and free. It is a delightful personal experience and expression of life and nature. Picasso says,

> Few people realise when they see a picture of mine that it is a phial of my blood which I have poured upon the canvas while painting it.

The Gupta sculptors were actually given all kinds of aid by the State in order to promote art and culture. This encouragement and the interest shown by the State gave an impetus to enhance 'beauty' in all their arts. The splendour of the paintings of Ajantā has overshadowed the elegance and serene dignity of the sculptures. Ajantā sculpture under the aegis of the Guptas and Vākāṭakas gave fillip to the artists to decorate the architrave with sculptured panels. All the *vihāra*s of Ajantā have a *garbha-gṛha* to enshrine a colossal figure of Buddha. Cave 1 has a scultpure depicting Buddha in *dharmacakrapravartana-mudrā*, there is a wheel of law. In Cave 19, we can see wealth of sculpture on the slightly ornate facade of the *caitya-gṛha*. Cave 24 has *yakṣa*s and *yakṣī*s like in Bhārhut and Sāñcī. In the world of Ajantā, the celestial mingle with human beings.

The Great *stūpa* (*mahā-caitya*) of Amarāvatī is recognised as the peak of Buddhist art in South India.[26] The Buddhist never worshipped the bull or other animals like others. But there is an evidence where bull representing Buddha was worshipped or in some variety of the 'disc-and-crescent'. Such symbols are of equal sanctity to the Buddhists as they have to *cakra*. *Bhagavato* or *Bhagvato* occurs at Sāñcī and also at Bhārhut. Professor Wilson points on the *Bhāgavata* from the dissyllable *bhaga* which means power, dominion, glory, wisdom, splendour. In Sanskrit *bhaga* means lord, wealth, sun, moon, happiness, beauty and majesty. According to Purāṇas, the three syllables *bha*, *ga* and *va* apply to the Supreme Vāsudeva or Viṣṇu. These monuments at Sāñcī bear the testimony of the same and of the symbols of Buddhist art.[27] Sāñcī influenced Thuparama *dagaba*,[28] Ambasthala *dagaba* at Mihintale[29] and Lankarama, built by Tissa who succeeded Dutthagamani and was similar to Sāñcī.[30]

In Sāñcī, we can see contemporary life of mid-India, pageantry and grandeur, beauty and peace, idyllic romanticism and violent struggle.[31] There is 'spirit of lively naturalism'. The elephants, deer and antelopes, the lotus creepers, the *pīpal* and a lot of other trees, fruit laden, are presented in richness. Reliefs of Sāñcī belong to this creative impulse, and livelier movements.[32] Ray says,

> Sanchi [sic] brings gaiety, emotion and vivacity born of a fuller acceptance of life and of its spontaneous joys and movements.

---

26. Morley, Grace, *Indian Sculpture*, p. 36.
27. Nandadeva, Wijesekera, "Buddhist Art Painting and Sculpture" (pp. 14-17) in All Ceylon Buddhist Congress Diamond Jubilee (2462-2522).
28. Nell, Andreas, "The Influence of Indian Art in Ceylon", pp. 197-206 in *The Influence of Indian Art*.
29. *Ibid.*
30. *Ibid.*
31. Ray, Niharranjan, *Maurya and Post Maurya Art*, p. 79.
32. *Ibid.*

GAYĀ

Gayā reliefs show representation of various *rāśis* and these are seen on the sandstone railings — *vṛṣabha, mithuna, siṁha, kanyā, tulā* and *dhanu*. The most notable act of this centre are the relief sculptures datable to the first century BC which have been found over the sandstone railings enclosing the Mahābodhi temple. The carvings in the reliefs represented mainly the events connected with the life of Buddha and Jātaka stories. There are various scenes showing tree nymph, winged animals, fish tailed human beings, love scenes, etc.

Flying movements portraitures in Mathurā sculptures and Amarāvatī sculpture are prominent. Kapila Vatsyayan feels that

> Back leg extensions are seen in Mathura, Nagarjunikonda and Amaravati. There are a variety of ways in which this is presented on the toranas and arches of the slabs and pillars.

Sculpture of Buddha show Maitreya that the bird will be born in human form. Avalokiteśvara was a devotee of Buddha Vairocana. His abode is Patalaka. In the fourth century Avalokiteśvara was glorified as a titulary deity of Tibet. Tārā is a Buddhist goddess and is worshipped in Nepal. The painter and the sculptor tried to paint and sculpt the images of Buddha in imitation of life. The ceremony 'painting of the eyes'[33] is always observed as a solemn Buddhist festival.

Kramrisch Stella says that in Indian sculpture and painting the majority of the figures are based on the human body [*Plate XLIII*]. Coomaraswamy says,

> that in the art of India, every form is the symbol of a clear and conscious thought and of consciously directed feeling. Nothing is arbitrary or peculiar, nothing is vague or mysterious for the very

33. *Mahāvaṁsa*, Ch. LXXII.

> *raison d'être* of all the imagery is to present concrete ideas in comprehensible and easily apprehended forms. [*Plate XLIV*]

This is true in the sculptures. Randhawa feels that sex is the fount of beauty. Sculptures of Bhāṛhut, Kuṣāṇa, Mathurā are symbols of maternity. The beauty of a woman is the major theme of Buddhist sculptures. It is true for Sāñcī also. Meyer observes:

> The enjoyment of woman is countless times in Indian literature, praised as the most glorious thing in heaven and on earth, as the one meaning and end of living, or anyhow of the years of youth. The ascetic, too, often sees the love of man and lovely women, shining before him as the goal and reward in the world beyond, or in a future incarnation.

Santayana also agrees that the works of art, whether painting or sculptures reflect the beauty of women. In fact, they are pleasurable only when they do so. It is the mathematical and mechanical laws which create the logic of form and that create emotion of beauty. The curve, the circle and the sphere are beautiful. The rhythmical beauty of flowing curves is an important element in feminine beauty.

Buddhism provided the inspiration for the development of one of the great art traditions of the world. It was Aśoka who introduced stone sculpture into India and his son Mahinda brought to Sri Lanka Aśoka's religion, *dagaba* and stone sculpture. Because of the great impact of early Indian Buddhist art, Sri Lanka art was produced. In the third century BC the creation of sculpture[34] in stone and architecture in stone was a consequence of the visit of Mahinda on his Buddhist mission. This historical setting was significant. Sculptured scenes from the life of the Buddha are

---

34. Nell, Andreas, "The Influence of Indian Art in Ceylon", p. 197 in *The Influence of Indian Art*.

rare.[35] There are a few on the pillars of Anurādhapura. One of them is the great miracle at Śrāvastī. The dream of queen Māyā carved on a stone is now in Colombo Museum.[36]

Anurādhapura

Buddha images abound in Anurādhapura and many of them belong to the Anurādhapura period only. The history of Anurādhapura period occurred in the reigns of Aggabodhi I (AD 571-604) and Aggabodhi II (AD 604-614). The sitting Buddha images of India are in cross-legged posture called *padmāsana*. It is a posture in which the right foot is placed on the left thigh and the left one on the right thigh. The Indian represents posture rightly. But the stone images of the seated Buddha in Anurādhapura and Polonnaruwa represent postures other than *padmāsana*. The Sri Lankan images are called 'cross-legged Buddhas'. It is not correct to call 'cross-legged Buddhas' because the images of Sri Lanka are not at all in *padmāsana*. Therefore, there the analogy is different. However, the Sri Lankan images can be called *vīrāsana* as these are in heroic postures. It is perfectly true when Professor James Haughten Woods says,

> A man settled down rests one foot on the ground and the other is placed over the partially contracted knee-hero posture.

It is also called *pallaṅka* posture. The Anurādhapura image belongs to this category.

The earliest Buddha image found at Mahaillupalama is a standing Buddha image in marble about six feet high and it is generally believed that it was carved in the Vengi country in India in first century AD. There are many seated postures reminiscent of the Mathurā school. During the

---

35. Nandadeva, Wijesekera, "Buddhist Art Painting and Sculpture" (pp. 14-17) in All Ceylon Buddhist Congress Diamond Jubilee (2462-2522).

36. *Ibid.*

process Sinhalese sculptures developed their own distinctive styles of carving and sculpting Buddha images [*Plate XLV*]. The seated Buddha images at Anurādhapura on the outer circular road gives an impression of peace and serenity. The groups of four seated Buddhas in the Vata-da-ge at Madirigiriya have been ascribed to the time of Aggabodhi IV (AD 667-83).

Martin Wickramasinghe, an ace writer on Sri Lanka culture and art feels that the sculpture can be read and interpreted with the help of gesture of hands, head, eyes and figures. The Buddhist sculptures were inspired by the Buddhist monks and they developed their own idiom and expression. The human figures in early sculpture of Anurādhapura are naturalistic and in Theravāda Buddhism there are gods and goddesses. The fine specimen which represents the naturalistic tendency of early sculpture is the famous bas-relief at Isurmuniya in Sri Lanka. Amarāvatī bas-beliefs are of high quality and is a happy blending of Indian, Iraninan and Hellisic factors. The illustration of Buddha images in the works of Havell, Coomaraswamy, Kramrisch, Smith and Foucher do not have a Buddha image in the sitting posture similar to Sri Lanka. According to Bhattacharya, *dhyānī* Buddha represents *vīrāsana* which is peculiar to Sri Lanka.

> Both in terms of variety and artistic achievement, the sculpture of the Anuradhapura kingdom is as rich and impressive as its architecture.[37]

When Buddha images were enshrined in Sri Lanka, the moonstone was a central theme of worship.

> There are six moonstones at Anuradhapura each one a masterpiece.[38]

37. De Silva, K.M., *A History of Sri Lanka*, p. 54.

38. *Op. cit.*, p. 55.

Buddha images were probably introduced from Amarāvatī in the first century AD and the kind of image of 6 ft high is at Maha Illupalam in Anurādhapura. The Amarāvatī style was further developed and matured with the peculiar charactertistics of Sri Lanka. Images of colossal proportions and gigantic ones like at Avukane in Sri Lanka of 42 ft high is not to be seen in India. The influence of Amarāvatī school could also be visualised on images of *dvārapālas* (guardian of the four directions usually in the form of a *nāga* king in human form but with seven-headed cobras).

Isurumuniya

The rock at Isurumuniya *vihāra* at Anurādhapura [*Plate XLVI*] is

> renowned for its sculptural embellishment; the most celebrated of which are two reliefs carved on rock outcrops: the lovers — a young warrior on a stone seat with a young woman in his lap — and the man seated in royal ease with the head of a horse behind him.[39]

Isurumuniya is a quaint name. Isuru is *īśvara*, God and *muniya* is *muni* or *ṛṣi*. Sinhalisation made it Isurumuniya. This reminds one of the name Munneswaram, temple of God, Śiva at Chilaw. The Isurumuniya is not Buddhist and it could be that this place was the abode of Hindu gods and goddesses. Another group 'man and horse' has horseman sitting at ease on a horse in 'Maharaja *līla*' pose. The pose is *sukhāsana* and sitting gracefully by his side is Goddess Pārvatī.

There is a group of lovers on a granite slab at Isurumuniya *vihāra* at Anurādhapura which displays conspicuously *śṛṅgāra* motif, picturing in stone the romance of a pair of lovers. The male figure is coarse and robust, expressive of rough vigour and the female figure in full of grace with a well proportional body, flexible limbs and a bashful face — a maiden in all her charms. The panel is strongly expressive of decorative art. The

---

39. Silva, K.M. De, *A History of Sri Lanka*, p. 56.

sculpture is at the same time reminiscent of 'harmony, serenity and balance, the key note of the Gupta art'.

Another Isurumuniya sculpture shows a group of elephants emerging out of a cleft in the rock on either side of it. On the right is an elephant in low relief in the act of pouring water on its back. The signs of Pallava art are there and the sporting of elephants must be a familiar motif in Sri Lanka and they are decorating the 'King's Bath' at Anurādhapura. Elephants must have been used because elephants are found in Sri Lanka even today. Isurumuniya retains the rural atmosphere of a village which has been lived in since civilisation began in these parts. "Of all the pretty corners of Anurādhapura", writes John Still "this little group of black rocks is the most picturesque." Rock inscriptions of the first century AD refer to the place at 'Isiramanne' a name which, according to Paranavitana means Hermit's Delight.

Paranavitana thinks that 'The Lovers' on a panel to the left of the front terrace at Isurumuniya is a fluent piece of work. He thinks that may be a Hindu god and his consort; but also thinks that they represent either a couple probably, or Prince Saliya Dutthagamani's son, who renounced his throne for his wife Aśokamālā, a low born maid. In the same rock are also carved elephants. A feature of early Sinhalese art depicting dwarfs is also amusing.

Comments

The Adam's Peak has for many centuries been one of the most noted places for art historians in the whole of Asia on account of its traditional association with the life of Buddha. Actually it is a pilgrimage centre for the Hindus, the Buddhist, the Muslims and the Christians. Hence, no archaeological evidence has been found. But this is one of the three places in Sri Lanka which Buddha is believed to have visited. That is why it is called the 'footprint' of Buddha. The Hindu tradition is based on a belief that Śiva in one of his manifestations retired to this mountain for the purpose of devotional austerities and to mark the event he left his footprint. The Hindus call this place Śivan-Olipadam (the sacred footprint of Śiva). The Hindu beliefs are not accepted because no Purāṇas contain this reference. Hence all these are mythological beliefs. To the Muslims, the peak is sacred because they believe that Adam after being banished from the garden of Eden, set foot on the peak. Thus, these are claims of every religious sect. Undoubtedly it appears to be the foot of Buddha's. Adam's Peak now known as Śrī Pada has fascinated the travellers instead of art historians. The reason is simple because it is very difficult to prove that the footprint is of the Master. Presently the study being conducted to ascertain whether the prints are of Buddha is merely based on myths, legends and memoirs of the tourists.

Fa-Hien's memoirs have attracted great interest among scholars and have been translated into many languages. He was a saintly man and was referred to as 'Śākyaputra', a keen observer, and has a vivid style and wrote usually of things as he saw with his own eyes. He also speaks of Adam's Peak. Marco Polo writes that the body of the Śākya Muni was buried in the mountain and because of this belief people flock to the mountain to pay their homage. It is absurd to lend credence to this statement of Marco Polo. However, as he says that some of his hair or teeth may be here. This may also arouse doubts and suspicions about the *stūpas*; however, Marco Polo's travelogue is not taken seriously. Marco Polo was a traveller whereas Fa-Hien came with other travellers to learn about Hīnayāna Buddhism and to copy such of the sacred writings as they did not have in their own land. Therefore, the experiences and the impressions of Fa-Hien are more valid than those of Marco Polo.

Thus, sculpture in general seeks to communicate universal living spirit of movement. Dance is in sculpture. It is a composition of form which is at once sensuous and spiritual and this form is in sculpture and in dance. The sculpture manifest to the people through a varierty of permutation and combinations of a single unit in an aesthetic configuration in a manner similar to that of a musician. Therefore, every piece of sculpture is analysed in terms of the position of the head [*Plates XLVII, XLVIII, XLIX*] the arms, the torso, the deflexion of the hip, movement of the knees or the waist.

The Indian sculptures at Mathurā are encompassed with birds, animals, plants, etc. These are friends of man and the friendship 'in birds and animals have formed the theme of delightful fables in which India is rich'. Mathurā sculptures of the Kuṣāṇa period, Bārhut *Jātaka* stories like *Latuva Jātaka*, *Bhaisa Jātaka* and very many others have birds and animals. All these birds and animals found in the Buddhist art symbolise their existence or are symbols representing a particular theme or period.

The bird a *haṁsa* standing on a pillar at Mihintale personifies the importance of birds and animals. An elephant, or a horse a humped bull and a lion are on stelae at Anurādhapura. Similarly, these animals are found in India. Actually the function of these animals has not been explained aptly. These may probably be as guardians or could act as decorative ones. These are similar to those of the processions on 'moonstones' in Sinhalese. It is Irahandagala — Sun and Moon stone. These are generally at the entrances of the religious buildings. *Haṁsa* which is identified as Sun in the *Ṛgveda* are also carved on the moonstone and *haṁsa*s, lions, horned lions and elephants are carved on the pillars around *dagaba*s. The *Mahāvaṁsa* states that

> rows of animals and *hamsa*s were painted in the Ruwanwaeli [sic] relic chamber, along with representations of the eight auspicious objects.

The Archaeological Survey Annual Report for 1895 states that a dog and a ram were also found on the moonstone. The lotus is also often found in moonstone. The railings have flowers, human beings, birds and animals. These things carved on the railings are personification of the symbolic attitudes. These are puns in sculpture and the creation of a pun has passed on from generation to generation and this has become a superb creation. The same is true in Sri Lanka — moonstone, *vahalkada* and *vatadage*. These have added a new theory of aesthetics which will be an indelible mark in the history of art. These are the creations of Sri Lankan sculptors. This has enhanced the study of Buddhist Art.

5

Symbolism

Symbols cannot be studied apart from the references which they symbolise.

— Ogden and Richards, *The Meaning of Meaning*

SYMBOLS are indispensable. Without symbols, art and literature would hardly be able to convey their message. It is, therefore, necessary that symbols be understood properly. A symbol with the help of a mark or a sign passes on to men, women, children, some suggestions which tend to make their lives meaningful. The symbol is a shape or design used to present some well-known concept and symbolism is the use of symbols.

In Buddhist art, we come across symbols that could be classified under the two categories, i.e., conventional and religious (sacred). Among the religious symbols, we have such sacred objects as the Bodhi tree, the dhamma-cakka, the footprints, the asana (throne), the 'pillar of fire', the 'triratna', the vardhamana, the srivatsa — all representing the Buddha, and as such were worshipped by the Buddhists of the early period with the same devotion and veneration as for the Buddha Himself.[1]

There are thirty-two major signs (*lakṣaṇa*) and eighty minor *lakṣaṇas* on Buddha. Because of this minor and major *lakṣaṇas*, Buddha is called *cakravartī, mahāpuruṣa*. These signs indicate the stature of the master. The Sri Lankan Buddhist in particular and the Buddhists in general all over the world venerate these symbols and signs. The Buddhists have the highest esteem for Buddha as they think of the master as the parasol which shall protect them from all evils. The Buddhist art itself gives more prominence to religious aspect than others.

India and Sri Lanka, both have close alliance and hence a system of common symbols are used to convey the sayings of Buddha. All works of art are actually meant to convey with precision and accuracy the complex philosophy of Buddhism. Each prop or an object in a particular position has a definite symbolic value. Buddha image [*Plate L*] is made in a variety of poses or *mudrās* giving hints about its own particular meaning. It was by such symbols that the message of the Master was conveyed. Some major *mudrās* known as *divya-kriyā* (divine actions) are —

Abhinaya darpaṇa gesture (movement) of right hand of the female, bending the third finger and the thumb inwards and stretching the other fingers.

Añcita mudrā gesture of the head, neck is slightly bent to one side.

Nimitilita mudrā half-closed and half-opened eyes.

Mayūra mudrā By spelling three fingers and joining the tips of the third finger and the thumb.

Nihañcita mudrā wiping away of tears.

Śṛṅgāra mudrā love gesture, born of great joy.

1. Senadeera, K. Gunapala, *Buddhist Symbolism of Wish Fulfilment*, p. 4.

Apart from *mudrās* and gestures, we have auspicious symbols [*Plate LI* & *LII*] such as *śrīvasta*, *svastika*, *padma*, *ghaṭa*, etc.

Animals signify different phases and modes and various incidents. The four chief animals in Buddhist art are: bull, horse, elephant and lion. Minor ones are deer, rhino, snakes, fish, tortoise, peacock, *garuḍa*, and with these the landscape becomes more beautiful with flora, hills, rivers, ponds, trees, creepers and flowers.

Nāgas and Cobras are most important in the Buddhist art because they not only beautify the parapets, but also serve as symbols of guardians [*Plate LIII*] and at times of evil spirits. These are ancient symbols and the onus of creating conflict between gods and demons lies with them.

> To the average Buddhists of any Buddhist country in South and South-East Asia [particularly in India and Sri Lanka], the Nāga has been a friend and protector of his faith, presiding over at the same time over his own destiny.

Bhārhut and Sāñcī have *nāga* with natural growth of reptile body. This may be not palatable to a few art historians and critics, but the argument is valid.

The gods, goddesses are worshipped and are always shown with patience, serenity, with auspicious gestures and always in a gay mood; whereas the demons or the devils are shown in the opposite fashion.

Thus, symbolism is a method of representation of persons, things, events, thoughts, feelings, ideas, creeds, or experiences by symbols, emblems or signs, gestures. The monuments of Bhārhut as a whole are nothing but a grand symbolic expression of Buddhist devotional piety. The aim of this symbol is to invoke in the viewer a feeling of piety which in turn will inspire him to the worship of a supreme personality, both human and divine, empirical and transcendental. It is also the worship of all beings, either connected with or referable to that personality. This personality in the purely historical aspect is represented by Buddha Śākyamuni; as he is called in the label attached to the Bo-tree under which he attained Buddhahood or enlightenment. Throughout his last existence, he is venerated in the label as Bhagava, the Divine Master.[2]

Lotus

Every symbol is multivalent and every myth is recounted in several texts in various designs.

> The Lotus is by far the most ubiquitous symbol in Indian art. By the second century BC the lotus was not only the support of the goddess Sri Lakshmi [sic] but it was also her principal attribute. By the second century AD the lotus had become a seat for the image of the Buddha. His hagiographers inform us that as soon as the Buddha was born, he took seven steps to announce his spiritual sovereignty over the earth. The seven steps are represented in art by seven lotuses. By the Gupta period, the lotus had become the principal support for most deities of all three religious system.[3]

Lotus is a metaphor of purity and blooms with the rising sun and closes its petals each evening. Lotus is the symbol of the Buddha's spiritual purity or divinity.[4] The lotus symbolises the faith itself and in

> later Buddhist iconography the lotus certainly is often used as a support for other emblems such as the thunderbolt or book, while the most widely uttered incantation associated with Avalokiteśvara is *om mani padme hum* meaning 'om the jewel in the lotus hum'.

Lotus is another symbol representing purity and beauty. It is 'majestic in

---

2. Barua, B.M., *Bharhut Book III*, p. 39.
3. Pal, Pratapaditya, *Indian Sculpture*, Vol. I, p. 39.
4. Coomaraswamy, A.K., *Buddha and the Gospel of Buddhism*, p. 331.

the whole of nature and sentient creation'. The lotus is a symbol for gradual development, evolution and creation. Lotus is earth. Lotus also means lily flower in water. It means water, flower and leaf. The whole symbolism of Bhārhut sculptures can be comprehended and characterised as the symbolism of the lotus. The lotus appears often on moonstone and is attributed a protective function. In Egypt, lotus is the Sun god. Lotus appears at the entrance of *dagaba*s either in a decorative or a protective character but symbolically it is the Sun. The lotus also represents virility, forcefulness and health. The lotus represents 'tree of life'. The lotus is prominently to Śrī Lakṣmī from second century BC and is 'Vedic' style. Lotus is the first member of Hindu Trinity and Brahmā is seated on a lotus. Sinhala people in Sri Lanka tried to establish a trinity of 'one language, one religion and one nation'. Buddhist literature speaks of three main varieties of lotus (*padma*, *utpala*s and *puṇḍarika*s). These are white and pink.

There are other symbols to denote the strong and weak which are all subservient to the symbolism of the lotus. Among these symbols, the first and the foremost is that of the elephant-and-scroll on the coping. The significance of this symbolism lies in the representation of the course of evolution of the *bodhisattva* from the moment of *praṇidhāna* to the attainment of Buddhahood and promulgation of Buddhism.[5]

A distinguished and celebrated writer of Sri Lanka writes:

> Hindu artists had to create symbols for expressing the creative activities of gods, their superhuman powers, the romantic stories of their exploits. So they created weird figures with numerous arms and heads and violent gestures.[6]

---

5. Barua, B.M., *Book III*, p. 40.

6. Wickramasinghe, Martin, *Buddhism and Art*, p. 12.

Sri Lankans did the same things but in a manner different from the Indian artists and called it as indigenous. But the Sri Lankan symbols also match with those of the Indians. Sri Lankan also feel that lacuna is there as very many Indians are not aware fully about Sri Lankan art and culture.

Sri Lankan devil masks

"The Sinhalese peasant believes in devils but not in the existence of a particular kind of devil." For instance, we can see usually tusks and half a dozen cobras on his head and neck. The mythology of devils is an inherited tradition in Sri Lanka. Artists who design masks generally believe and follow this tradition. Indians and Sri Lankans believe in ghosts, evil spirits and are generally superstitious. The chronicles *Mahāvaṁsa* and *Culavaṁsa* refer to these beliefs. Devil masks are also used in dances and ceremonies.

> Devil masks and human-shaped ones are used by the Sinhalese in ceremonial dance. These ceremonial dances are not always of magical significance.[7]

Characteristics of Sri Lankan masks

The masks of the Sinhalese are a peculiar contribution to their culture. Aesthetic quality of the best of them 'can only please us but not stir'. The Sinhalese masks do not represent primitive art. They are the works of semi-cultured peasants and may be some peculiar creations of primitive artists. As we see, the mask is terrifying and sarcastic caricature of some race or people. Sometime masks are also used for entertainment and sometime for magical charms. Some masks used in South India resemble the Sinhalese masks. The same mask may be used to serve as a symbol at one place, while at another place, it may depict realism. It is more apt to state that masks are of local inspiration rather than of foreign — European

7. Wickramasinghe, Martin, *Aspects of Sinhalese Culture*, p. 81.

influence. No doubt, the foreign influence is there but as caricatures of the Europeans. In the majority of cases this is a regular source of entertainment. The sarcastic humour mingled with malice makes the rural artist deliberately give his mask an animal shape and dandy appearance. The blank idiotic face represents lunacy. The mask showing deafness has no ears. That is the peasants artist's symbolic representation of deafness in man. In place of the right ear on the mask, there is a hooded cobra. Thus, a mask representing deafness may be simple or complex with magical and abstract symbolism. The unique creation of the rural artist is the grotesque mask of the warrior; this shows his contempt for war and subtle advocacy for peace.

Masks also depict humour, sarcasm and sometimes hurt the susceptibilities of sensitive folk. But folk tales also reflect the ways of our living and thinking in the same way as do the masks. Folk tales are purely based on myths and legends.

Myths and myths in symbolic form

"Myths are more real in moulding the lives of men than other worldly things."[8] This is true not only in history but also in real life. Lots of stories are narrated to the children, to young ones and to the old people and on listening to them, they are deeply and indelibly impressed. Unfortunately, myths sometimes also bring ill effects because of beliefs and wrong notions and opinions. The ancient myths of the conflict between the Gods and the demons assumes new forms in the life of Buddha. Myths are stories that people have made up in the past in order to explain how the world and mankind evolved or to justify religious beliefs and social customs. There are figures, images of Buddha and *bodhisattvas* portraying various myths and symbols.

---

8. Agrawala, V.S., *Studies in Indian Art*, p. 5.

Religious symbols

Religious symbols like *stūpa*, footprint, *dharmacakra*, wheel, etc., represent Buddha. Panels depicting *Jātaka* scenes, railings (*vedika*) which was originally meant to enclose *stūpa*s or *vṛkṣa* (Bo-tree) are included among the symbols of that period. Today, the symbols are mentioned in the foregoing line have become universal and valid without any variation in their meaning. The full vase is a symbol of spirituality and it is also called *pūrṇa kalaśa*. With this we are familiar since *Ṛgveda*.

Symbols in art and literature

Symbols add not only beauty to works of art but also enrich literature. Many poets have used symbols in their verses and became pioneers in creating new symbols and inventing new meanings to old symbols. Symbols are mysterious also. In Buddhist works the *yakṣa*s are sometimes represented as teachers of good morals and as guardian spirits.[9] The growth of symbols in Sri Lanka owes much to Indian influence. It goes without saying that Indian art being spiritual and religious had to depend upon symbols, which in turn was incorporated in the Buddhist art. Most of the *Jātaka*s depict individual characters embodying individual experiences of life. Sometimes these experiences are in an exaggerated form but we have to accept them for the sake of grasping their significance and appreciating the narratives and anecdotes. Almost all the symbols were earlier specific and of special context and slowly and slowly became universal.

> The Buddhist temple, the Buddha statue and the bodhi tree are aesthetic symbols.[10]

These are not only aesthetic but also permeates religious feelings in the

9. Coomaraswamy, A.K., *Yakṣas*, p. 13.
10. Wickramansinghe, Martin, *Buddhism and Culture*, p. 9.

heart of worshippers and this feeling is always transcient. Symbols are powerful and strong and they create emotions and feelings when we watch them. It is also a fact that in every religion the adherents tend to venerate the symbols, honour and cherish them. No instance of any religious symbols being dishonoured by its followers is known. All people honour holy shrines irrespective of their personal religious feelings. It may be because of the fact that India and Sri Lanka have been religiously connected and the gap has been filled by the Buddhism. Thus, the people of both the countries offer obeisance to both religions. We can see that the people of both countries respect places of worship. Such places become the holiest places for the pilgrims.

> After the Buddha's death, religious symbols such as the stupa, the Bo-tree, the Buddha image and other icons and sites connected with the worship of these symbols created a religious atmosphere in the temple, which led to the idea of the holy in the hearts of worshippers.[11]

The Wheel

The Wheel is described as a circle without beginning or end. Wheel is modes of advancement, preaching or 'turning the wheel of law'. Wheel is law or 'doctrine' (*bodhi*). It is also called praying wheel. Wheel is *cakravarti* and *dharma-cakra* and the disc-and-crescent symbol. The content of the wheel symbolism is extraordinarily rich and its dimensions are indefinite. A.K. Coomaraswamy says that

> its radius the variable distance between an undimensional (*amatra*) point and an immesurable (*asankhya*) circumference; there is in 'middle space' (*antariksa*, *akasa*) between the "I" and "not-I", essence and nature, lie procession and recession (*pravrtti*, *nivrtti*),

---

11. Wickramasinghe, Martin, *Buddhism and Culture*, p. 12.

> there are good and evil (*dharmadharmau*), joy and sorrow (*sukha, dukha*), light and shade (*chayatapa*), birth and death,

thus we find symbols too delineate various forms. India being a multi-ethnic religious community had primitive savagery background. It is also true that the Buddhists were not aware of the *Atharvaveda* and Purāṇas. Thus, the Gandharvas, Nāgas, Kuberas, half men, half birds, became a work of forgotten powers. *Vessavana-Kuvera* is on Bhārhut railings. *Sirima Devatā* is seated on lotus at Sāñcī.

Decorative motif

The cave temples involved no principles of architecture but we find window shape entrance and this became an ornamental and decorative motif in Buddhist architecture. A motif is a design which is used as a decoration [*Plate LIV-LV*] or as a part of an artistic pattern. Hence, in all works of art, decorative motifs are part and parcel of a figure. The decorative motif is one of the symbols and without this the piece of art may look abstract. Abstract art is a style of art which uses shapes and patterns to represent things, people and ideas rather than showing people or things as they actually look. Thus, decorative motif is an essential ingredient to develop art so that it looks more attractive and minute details are visible. Motif is intended to look pretty. It is *avant garde* in ancient coins and sealings.[12] We find flora and fauna which constitute a decorative motif.

Anurādhapura is the holiest city of Sri Lanka. Buddhists from all walks of life gather here to pay their respect to Śrī Mahā Bodhi and other holy objects. This ruined city has witnessed many upheavals but despite these even today the city retains its ancient cultural heritage. Since the city is full of *dagabas* [*Plates LVI-LVII*], the *nāga* and *nāgin* motifs figure prominently in the sculptures. The *nāga* motif is seen also in Mathurā, Sāñcī, Amarāvatī; actually in Buddhist art, the *nāgas* have a specific role to

12. Bajpai, K.D., *Five Phases of Indian Art*, p. 51.

play. The *nāga* stands for good things as well as for evil things. These also act as decorative motif. It is not necessary that *nāgas*, *nāgins*, *yakṣas* or *rākṣasa* always represent evil. They do belong to a class of beings who hail from a place where they have not done any harm; they became evil spirit because they caused harm to others or they were arrogant and they were not wise to foresee the result. It is also observed that the *nāga* images serve as decorative pieces of art in ancient palaces and shrines. In modern times, these figures are noticed in mansions, at dining halls and private buildings. It may also be pertinent to add here that people who have faith in the necromancy or in black magic do keep and worship these evil spirits to eschew evil spirit from themselves and from others. In South India these practices are still in vogue. There are many tribes who believe in these things. The Vedas of Sri Lanka do observe this practice.

In short, the *yakkhas*, *nāgas*, etc., are seen in almost in all the sculptures as decorative motifs. Then the decoration also depends on the period and its society and the rituals and customs prevailing in that period. The society of that period when symbols of these evil spirit were prominent had a totally different view about life. Today, these symbols are not at all visible. Hence time-period is also responsible in motivating ideas. Symbols of animals especially the four nobles ones, i.e., bull, elephant, lion and horse make the symbols more decorative. Their noble mien, their majestic look, their characteristics and obedience to their masters, references about them from the time of Vedas and association with Buddha have assured these animals immortality in art. All the four are very beneficial to mankind.

Decorative motif is not only for decoration but is also part of a society. They are natural, no ornamentation. Let us take motif of a cloud and pouring of rain in Bhārhut. It is a natural process. Clouds are formed with water vapour and help in producing rain. It is a natural process which helps in our daily needs. Landscapes are thus formed, the rivers, water falls, high and low mountains and people reaping their harvest and sowing fresh harvest is a process which will never be discontinued. These scenes are portrayed in the paintings and other pieces of art. What is it? It is nothing but a natural phenomenon. The poet starts writing verses. Kālidāsa has described nature extensively in his famous poems so his poetry became richest. It has become the universal history of nature. All these related things are depicted as decorative motifs. Footprints of Buddha are semi-iconic and these are shown in reliefs of Bo-trees, *garuḍas*, snakes, lions, rams. Four lions are also noticed in Bhārhut gateway pillars as shown in Aśoka's Sārnāth pillars.

The motifs indicate different versions of concepts, events and incidents. According to the Buddhist legend, the Lord came down laden with God. Brahmā, Śakra and this incident is popular motif in Buddhist art.

> The makara-torana was a well-known ornamental motif in Sri Lanka from early times. As in India, it was used as a decoration to frame Buddha images.[13]

Ornamental imagery is linked with the Waters of Cosmology.[14]

> This is expressed in various motifs notably the lotus, flowers and foliage overflowing from a jar of water, trees and vegetation in which sap the essence of water flows, and creatures such a fish, crocodiles, makaras, elephants, snakes and other aquatic creatures that live in or near water. Whatever evokes the productive or the source of life is held sacred, auspicious, and conducive to well-being and by that token, is considered beautiful as well. It is this belief that accounts for the representation of the amorous couple, the search for the continuity of human life, in every period of Indian art.[15]

---

13. Sirisena, W.N., *Sri Lanka and South East Asia*, p. 131.
14. Chandra, Pramod, *The Sculpture of India (3000 BC-AD 1300)*, p. 25.
15. *Ibid.*

Nāgapuṣpa [*Plate LVIII*] or honey-suckle is the most dominant motif in sculptures. This has a very powerful appearance. It looks as if cobras with their hood spread are hovering. Perhaps it is the most unique motif.

Śṛṅgāra motif picturing a group of lovers at Isurumuniya (Sri Lanka) is strongly expressive of the decorative motif in the early religious art of India — the *mithuna* figures in temple art. Lotus petals moulding decorate the steps, and always support the structure on their little heads. Figures of *makaras*, the composite water-animal of Hindu tradition, ornamented the balustrades.

Tree

> In both Pali and Sanskrit 'Bodhi' signifies not only a 'Buddha' himself, the embodiment of light and intelligence, but also, his sacred tree: and the doctrine of law (Dharmma) which he preached: the function of which (Sangha) constituted the 'three precious ones', or 'three precious gems' or Buddhism, as now known to us. In the earlier cult, which preceded Sakyas system and was adopted in it, the conjunction (Sangha) or 'Buddha' and 'Dharma' that is of the Sun and Moon; mind and matter; the all-creating spirit, and passive matter of concrete nature; produced the fine elements and mankind formed out of these elements.

In the *Jātaka* tales, the *bodhisattva* is shown as a *devatā* in order to deliver or indicate moral teaching. The *Matakabhatta Jātaka* and the *Ayacitabhatta Jātaka*, the *bodhisattva* has taken the birth of a tree spirit (*rukkha/devatā*) and

> delivers a moral lesson against the taking of lives to make offerings to the tree god himself. This is a standard didactic mode to be found in the Jātaka tales.

Coomaraswamy feels that in many Jātakas *yakkhas* are shown as deities and live in trees.

Tree is a very much decorative motif in Buddhist art. Tree is procreative. There are many trees found in connection with Buddha. The Aśoka (*Jonesia* Asoka) tree is a tree under which Queen Māyā Devī gave birth to Buddha. It is on a lotus that *bodhisattva* is said to have stood soon after his birth at Lumbinī. It was on 'world lotus' Buddha performed the great miracle *yamaka-mahā-pratihārīya* (the miracle of double appearances at Śrāvastī). The Jambū (*Eugema Jambu*) — under this tree Prince Siddhārtha after one of the four excursions which led to his becoming Buddha. The *Pīppala* (*Ficus religiosa*) or *pīpal* tree under this tree Śākya sat for six years in penance and attained 'the third contemplation'. The *ām* or Mango (*Mangifera indica*) tree is venerated at Sāñcī. The So-lo-Sala or *śāl* (*Shorea robutsa*) — Śākya Buddha attained *nirvāṇa* between these trees.

> The tree of knowledge (Bodhidruma) which stood at this place over the diamond throne is a pipolo (Pippala, *ficus religiosa*). At the time when Buddha lived on the earth, this tree had attained the height of many hundred feet. Although it had been cut down many times, it was still forty to fifty feet high. Since Buddha obtained complete knowledge (Samyak-Sambodhi) while seated under this tree, it is called Bodhi. Its trunk is of a yellowish white colour, and its branches and leaves are blackish green. In winter and in summer its leaves remain fresh and lustrous, without undergoing any change. But when the day of Tathagata's Nirvana arrived, they all fell and little by little the tree again attained its former condition.[16]

But the *pīpal* tree *aśvattha*[17] seen now is not the original one; it was revived

16. Mitra, R., *Buddha Gaya*, p. 95.
17. *Ibid.*, p. 61.

through grafts and seeds.[18] Sri Lanka has a special link with the Bo-tree, *pīpal* tree, this was planted at Anurādhapura during the reign of Aśoka. The tree is a powerful decorative motif. Arboreal imagery plays an important role in various stages of Buddha's career. The beautiful grove and various types of tree make the picture more interesting. The trees are depicted in a range on surviving railings and *toraṇa*s of the *stūpa* of Bhārhut (184-72 BC).

Yakkhas also live in trees and in the *Jātaka* tales they are referred to as *devatā*s and never as a *yakkha*. The *aśoka* tree has earlier been mentioned as procreative and symbolised fertility and it always looks like nubile. The green colour further illustrates this aspect. The tree has a legendary reputation for not blooming until it is touched by a nubile woman. The term for this motif is *śālabhañjikā*. This is particularly mentioned for graceful girls. This is mentioned in Kālidāsa's play *Mālavikāgnimitram*. Sometimes it is also referred to *apsarā*s or *yakṣī*s. This kind of motif is beautifully represented on railings pillars at Sāñcī and Bhārhut.

Śālabhañjikā

The term *śālabhañjikā* means a woman who breaks the *śāla* tree. But in art the *śālabhañjikā* are shown neither breaking a tree nor the tree is *śāla*; she only holds a branch of a flowering tree, *aśoka* or *kadamba* or *campaka* or *āmra*.

Śālabhañjikā is not only Buddhist motif but has a long history in India and is mentioned in all the religions.

In the *Mahāvaṁsa*, *śālabhañjikā* is called *puṣpa-sakha-dhāra*; one who holds a branch of tree full with flowers. *Śālabhañjikā* are in the art of Sanghol, Gāndhāra, Mathurā, Sārnāth and Bhārhut. The *śālabhañjikā*

---

18. Mitra, R., *Buddha Gaya*, p. 61.

were first found at Bhārhut in second century BC.

Sivaramamurti says,

> To understand the beauty of the *torana* adorned by a *salabhanjika* and the importance of this motif of the *torana* itself there is the description given by Asvaghosa in his Buddhacarita which is almost a contemporary work just posterior by a litter over a century. The term *salabhanjika* was used to connote the game of gathering *sala* flowers as given by Panini. He has given other examples like *Uddalakapushpabhanjika* and *asokapuspaprachayika* all of which connote games by girls gathering different flowers from the trees.[19]

The *śālabhañjikā* or the motif of the damsel gathering flowers under the *śāla* tree is very prominent. The *śālabhañjikā* in her typical *tribhaṅga* pose is the most attractive feature of this motif. We can see this in Mathurā and in some of the Kuṣāṇa *toraṇas*.[20] The *śālabhañjikā* motif is seen in eastern and northern gateways of Sāñcī and the turbans, necklaces, earrings, have an identity with Amarāvatī too. This denotes that presenting and preserving the essence of feminine beauty was considered as great art by the artists and their patrons in that period. This is evident in the Mathurā school too.[21]

> The artist of Mathura served a different purpose through shaping their extra round breasts, heavy lips, graceful postures suggesting movements, attractive looks and inviting gestures. Numerous toilet scenes, more than thirty varieties of coiffure and about fifty kinds of ornaments speak of the gaiety and abandon of the beauties of the Kusana period. Apparently, the artist of Mathura aimed at

19. Sivaramamurti, C., *Sources of History Illumined by Literature*, p. 118.
20. *Ibid.*
21. Sharma, R.C., *Buddhist Art of Mathura*, p. 136.

> revealing the unfailing charms of female beauty through voluptuous form. This was again a unique experiment which blended the fervour of sensuous emotion with a religious and spiritual flavour.[22]

In other words, women were undoubtedly the focal point in achieving the glorious culmination in the most beautiful pieces of art. In Ajantā Caves II, XVI, XVII, certainly represent the classical peak. There are scenes showing women's apartments in Amarāvatī and Gāndhāra sculptures. Women lie on the floor in different postures[23] and the motif of two sleeping women lying in an awkward position is noteworthy. Aśvaghoṣa, the poet has given many similar analogies in his description of sleeping women.[24] Ratan Parimoo further maintains and gives importance to the sleeping women and conveys an impression that the women of that time were not pious. This, of course, is debatable. Wonder how he expects a woman fast asleep in the privacy of her own chamber to exhibit piety while deep in slumber. Nevertheless, he points out that

> reliefs depict in general the harem life of Siddhartha being entertained by the female attendants and the movement before the women feel asleep.[25]

The scene is further in progress and the atmosphere of pleasure is further enhanced when a female attendant is serving wine to the guard and her "dress is slipping to reveal her sensuous back".[26] This kind of relief is also found in Gāndhāra relief where a women is offering wine to a male

---

22. R.C. Sharma, *op. cit.*, p. 137.
23. Ratan, Parimoo, *Life of Buddha*, p. 79.
24. *Op. cit.*, p. 80.
25. *Op. cit.*, p. 81.
26. *Op. cit.*, p. 83.

companion.[27] J. Ph. Vogel has defined *śālabhañjikā* as a Sanskrit term to denote the tree-and-women motifs in Indian sculptures. The *Mahāvaṁsa* employs *puṣpa-sakhadhāra* ('holding the bunches of flowers and branches of trees') as an expression to denote such motifs that are obviously all decorative. As Grunwedel reads them, in these motifs "woman stand under a tree,[28] and raise their hands among the branches as if to pluck the blossoms."[29] While discussing *śālabhañjikā*, and about the large number of panels showing these ladies, R.C. Sharma says,

> Mathura School is known for presenting feminine form with great beauty, charm and attractiveness.[30]

There were more than thirty varieties of coiffure.[31] Coiffure is a hair style and this is one of the remarkable features. Since ancient times, ladies keep their hair immaculate. The coiffure delineates various signs and speaks of many unknown things. In the *Jātaka*s various coiffures have been mentioned. Long hair — *lamba keśa* — is referred to in *Takkariya Jātaka*. Kālidāsa has named this *keśa* as *barha-barha keśa* in his *kāvya*s. *Jaṭābhāra* is described in *Bhisa Jātaka* and this very design is seen in Bhārhut and Amarāvatī. At Sāñcī curly hair and long hair springing from the forehead are visible. Twisted hair are also very common in Bhārhut and Amarāvatī. In *Māndhātu Jātaka* there is mention of knotting hair into a bun. In Kuṣāṇa art too, we see curly hair, simple and long hair with protruded knot on the forehead, double bun and looped hair. In Vākāṭaka-Gupta period, wigs were seen. This is from Rome and this Roman influence is seen at Ajantā. Symbolism is descended from primordial tradition and

27. Ratan, Parimoo, *Life of Buddha*, p. 83.
28. Barua, B.M., *Bharhut Book III*, p. 80.
29. *Ibid.*, p. 81.
30. Sharma, R.C., *Buddhist Art of Mathura*, p. 136.
31. *Op. cit.*, p. 137.

have aniconic representations, e.g., *cakra*,[32] *pādukā*[33] *nandī pada*,[34] vegetative and human form. The tree was a symbol even before these. The tree is significant. Tree is the unique representation of Buddha. *Kalpa-vṛkṣa* — wishing tree is also seen in Indian art at Sāñcī. Symbols of pearls, *makara*, *svastika* and *śālabhañjikā*, coiffures compose the symbolism which is the sheet anchor of the Buddhist art.

Svastika

Svastika in India as well as in Sri Lanka is a holy symbol. It is found in earlier coins. *Svastika* symbol was considered useful to ward off evil spirits. In Egyptian glazed pottery, there are various forms of *svastika* and it came into vogue in 2500 BC. General Maisey says,

> Many of the relic chambers opened at Sanchi and other places were *svastika* shaped in plan, as also were the funeral chambers found in some of the Kistvaens of southern India; and in the centre of the Stupa (dagaba). . . .

The *svastika* in cross form is also seen in *dagaba* at Anurādhapura and *Atharvaveda* also has recorded cross *svastika*. It is also believed that *svastika* was developed as a magical protective image.

In symbolism, it is not necessary to depict a design in full, a portion or a single line, ray may render the exact meaning. There are different cross *svastikas* have been developed in phased manner.

---

32. Wheel.
33. Feet.
34. *Triśūla*.

Plain Cross

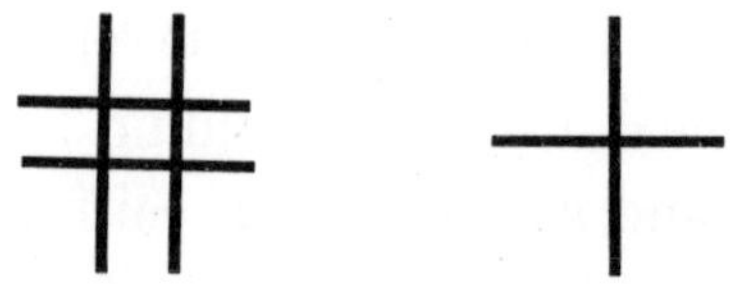

Guarded Cross

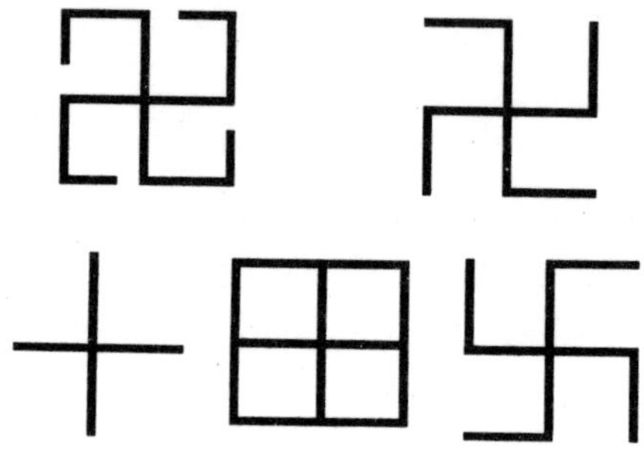

Barred Cross

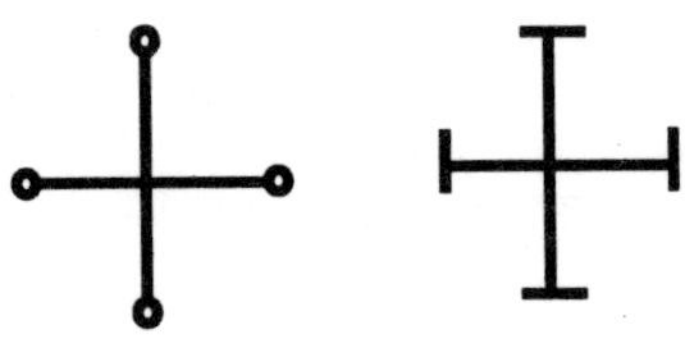

Barred *Svastika*

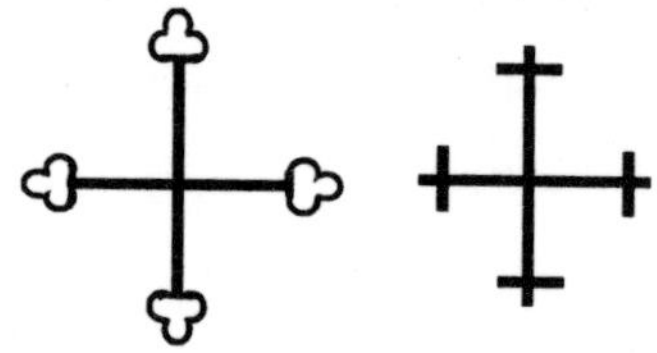

Pointed *Svastika*

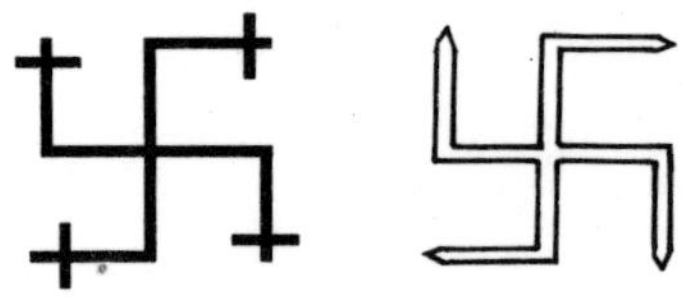

Svastikas are not straight-line figures as known to be. These are ornamental and are used by different races at different intervals of time. Many have become outdated too, traditionally some are used even today.

Senadeera K. Gunapala writes:

> The Buddhist writers who were dealing with the auspicious signs (*mangala*) accommodated with the wheel mark on the sole of the Buddha's feet enumerated them to be one hundred and eight in number. However, every sign was presented in a pair [probably due to the belief that a union of two — the mithuna (sic) — was more efficacious for producing the desired result] and as such this figure rose to two hundred and sixteen.

Aṣṭa-maṅgala have also been noticed in containers, caskets and these are popular in Sri Lanka and in India. The important and significant *aṣṭa-maṅgalas* are visible and found in all forms of Buddhist art. Brazen Palace (*Loha Maha Prasadaya*) in Anurādapura of second century BC was installed by king Dutthagāmanī and was adorned with *aṣṭa-maṅgalas*. Tortoise is known as 'former Buddha', 'man-eagle'. Garuḍa is called 'the foe of snakes'. Garuḍa is also called former incarnations of *Jātakas*. 'Bhalli' resembles the crescent-portico of the disc-and-crescent symbol.

There are many auspicious symbols (*aṣṭa-maṅgalas*):

Mānasāra	*śrīvatsa*, *pūrṇa kumbha* ('brimming pot'), *darpaṇa* (mirror), *cāmara* (fly-whisk), *dīpa* (lamp), *chatra* (umbrella), *svastika.*
Parāśara	conch-shell, *rocana* (yellow pigment), *candana* (sandlewood), pearl, *hiraṇya* (gold), umbrella, fly-whisk, *adarśa* (mirror).
Śabda-kalpadrma	swan, lion, bull, elephant, pitcher, fan, flag, drum, lamp

Nārada-saṁhitā	brāhmaṇa, cow, fire, gold, snake-king, sun, water, king.
Aupadika-sūtra	*svastika*, *sirivaccha* (*śrīvatsa*), *kalaśa* (pitcher), *maccha* (fish), *darpana* (mirror)
Sikha-valanda-vinisa	conch-shell, umbrella, pitcher, *mugma* (club), *amkubu*, flag.

The symbols were brought from Bhārhut, Bodh Gayā, Sāñcī and Amarāvatī (second century BC to third century AD) and were adopted later on in other places.

6

Conclusion

WHILE summing up, on the Study of the Buddhist Art in India and Sri Lanka we can safely affirm that the entire Buddhist Art of Sri Lanka is much more than a copy of the Buddhist Art as it has existed in India. The chronicles would have us believe that Buddhism originated in India and Gautama preached that life was suffering and suffering was caused by desire. The word *duḥkha* has no precise English equivalent. Suffering is the keynote of Buddhism. The contribution of Buddhism to art and architecture throughout is impressive. Buddhism was introduced to Sri Lanka in the reign of King Devanāmpiya Tissa (250-210 BC), a contemporary of the Indian Emperor Aśoka. Aśoka introduced food production based on Buddha's philosophy and protected natural resources.

The term Buddhist Art is a popular nomenclature like Hindu and Jain art. By Buddhist Art we mean monuments and paintings which were created solely for the purpose of edification or popularisation of Buddhism. Therefore, all or at least the principal features of Buddhism must be delineated in this art. This has been done so not only in India but in other places where the Buddhism exists.

The art of Sri Lanka has two peculiar qualities which can withstand any challenge. These are surely incontestable. Sri Lankan art reflects first, the cultural divergence of opinions and groups in diversity of India and second, the regionalism. There is a difference between the classical past and folk tradition. While talking of Sri Lanka, we have to keep in mind the background of India and it is what has been developed and researched in Sri Lanka.

History is built up from many sources. Out of these sources, two are chosen here: works of plastic art and literature. The first one includes sculpture, painting and architecture, while the second relies on epigraphy and manuscripts.

Imitation of wood carvings are at Sāncī, Bodh Gayā, Mathura and Bhārhut sculptures. Mainly spirits or human beings are seen at Bhārhut sculpture.

Early Buddha and *bodhisattva*s sculpture reveal that these are bulky, plump and corpulent. They are carved in round show *abhaya* attitude; the left hand of the image rests on the waist; some space is left between the two legs, decorated girdle or a belt is noticed on the waist and a under garment is seen fastened to the girdle. By wearing a girdle, the body appears slimmer and the sculptures of this period have more aesthetic sense than those of the later period.

The art of sculpture attained maturity in the Kuṣāṇa Age. The sculptors were inspired by the new ideals of the Mahāyāna Buddhism which concentrated on *bhakti* and the worship of Buddha as an individual and person god in the form of *bodhisattva*. The creation of the Buddha image was the greatest contribution of the Mathurā artists. They were spurred by a rare enthusiasm for creative work and new ideas. This was in the Kuṣāṇa period. The three figures, i.e., Buddha, Mahinda and Vijaya form the heroic form.

It seems that the famous Buddhist places were identified and surveyed in the reign of Kaniṣka and the statue of Buddha of the Mathurā origin was sent to various sacred places like Sārnāth, Bodh Gayā, Śrāvastī and Kuśinagara and other several places.

Mathurā was the centre of art activity even before the Christian era and Kuṣāṇas gave a favourable impetus to the stone sculpture. The Kuṣāṇa age is considered one of the formative periods of the Indian civilisation. Stone sculptures of excellence (from second-first century BC) are found in the Deccan and South. In the carvings on the gates of Sāñcī, we find natural instinct, natural manner and the total lack of inhibition.

The Sātavāhanas did much for the development of cultural activities during second century BC to second century AD. The Sāñcī art excels the Greco-Buddhist art by its deeper spiritual longings, charm, suavity and spontaneous flow of forms in an overwhelming manner. Indian art flourished during this period. Sculptures of Aśoka's reign were stylistic, full of vigour and vitality.

Bhārhut sculptures were probably the earliest to show *Jātaka* scenes; these have been interpreted in detail. Evidently, their fame spread far and wide; for, there is a reference in *Mahāvaṁsa* too. The Bhārhut sculptures served as models to all contemporary and subsequent sculptures in India and Sri Lanka. King Dutthagāmanī in the first quarter of the first century BC had built Lohapasada and the Relic Chamber of the Great *stūpa*. The sculptures mirror their age and period in which they were sculpted. They are actually focusing the interest and the importance of the rulers about their regimen. *Ācārya* Nāgārjuna who founded the School of Mahāyāna Buddhism and a University during the reign of Ikṣvākus, representing a cultural evolution from the prehistoric period to the medieval times. Hieun Tsang a Chinese traveller visited and wrote significant terms. The Ikṣvāku dynasty lost the power and their decline started. Nāgārjunikoṇḍa is a sacred place and intricate carvings in bas-reliefs bespeak the grandeur of a distant past.

The worship of *bodhi* tree was widely prevalent and there are many representations on the panels of Bhārhut, Sāñcī and Amarāvatī. Bodh Gayā and Sāñcī were the other important centres of Buddhist Art. The main interest is Great *stūpa* at Sāñcī. It was the work of the Sātavāhana King Śātakarṇi (first century BC) and the King was described as the Lord of the West. The northern Gateway is the best preserved. Buddha is here symbolically represented by symbols and motifs. The early Buddhist Art of Bhārhut, Sāñcī, Bodh Gayā and Amarāvātī show no anthropomorphic representations of Buddha. Symbols have been used to represent him.

Till today there is no inclination to explore the possibilities of using symbols for Buddha. Why so, calls for an answer. Buddha has preached many wonderful and simple ways for the welfare of humanity. He wanted every human being on this earth to prosper; he wanted people to give up all kinds of worship and sacrifices for attaining their material desires. He did that marvellous work which is to all intents and purposes, needs will and dedication to implement. Still Buddhism prevails and so too Buddhist Art. From this it is obvious that Buddhism has an inherent greatness. What is this greatness? It lies in the middle path propagated by Buddha. According to Buddhism, a man should free himself from desire by following the eightfold path — eight kinds of actions and thoughts which lead to virtuous living and which Buddha assured shall lead to a balanced life, without wanting too much of anything. Buddha also emphasised the importance of *ahiṁsā* or non-violence. He forbade the killing of animals as part of religious sacrifices. It is indeed difficult to depict these ideas in the form of a simple symbols which can be easily understood; also his *ahiṁsā* is a delicate issue. So no artist will prefer to take up such a controversial subject for portrayal in visual art.

Buddhism is an offshoot of Hinduism. Hinduism is older than Buddhism. Buddha had to become the disciple of Brāhmaṇa ascetics Alāra Kalāma and Uddaka Ramaputta and they taught him their own doctrine and discipline (*vinaya*). According to scriptures, Brahmā asked him to preach the truth. Buddha preached the truth and knowing all vices in and around him, he followed the middle path to achieve his goal. He rejected the concept of God and the theory of Brāhmaṇism. Since a kind of confusion is apparent, i.e., on one hand he seeks the help of Brāhmaṇa ascetics and accepts the instruction of the Brahamā and later rejects the existence of God. Therefore, probably to eschew all kinds of dogmatic ways, he was shown and venerated through symbols.

Later on, an original thinker Nāgārjuna rejected the Hīnayānist Buddhism and started the Mahāyānist Buddhism. A school of thought believes that Nāgārjuna was a great philosopher like Buddha. But neither Buddha nor Nāgārjuna was a philosopher. With the advent of Mahāyānism, worship of Buddha as a deity began. Thus, began making of images of Buddha in the first century AD, i.e., as a result of the growing popularity of Mahāyānist Buddhism.

Symbols were used probably not to identify himself or the emancipation of Brahmā. It is thus opined that the symbols were used in order to uplift the existence of God as well as of Buddha. The other argument put forward is that the symbols were used even for the gods and goddesses. It is not everytime that they are shown in human form. They are also identified with their *vāhana*s or flowers etc. Symbols were also used to enrich and elevate the art form. The symbols are expressive, can camouflage all fables, anecdotes and parables in lines or in a symbol. Symbols are a powerful and dominant medium to illustrate the history of the piece of art or for what it indicates and elucidates. One can talk or write by going through the symbols properly. Thus, symbols are the tools and without symbols neither art nor literature can exist. The extant classical literature is full of symbols.

Animals have been treated as the best partners in the social environment. These have been used not only by the deities but by the common people too. It is a sin to kill animals. Buddhism preached that no animal sacrifice should be made. However, it seems dogmatic from the Buddhist point of view. Almost all Buddhists are non-vegetarians. Therefore, exception appears to be the rule with regard to this teaching of Buddha. In justification of this breach, it is also said that he too ate prawn (some say in a *kheer*, prawn was found); whether this is true or not — for the answer there is no evidence. But undoubtedly there is a strong belief that Buddha did take some meat. It was placed before the *saṁgha* and a lot of deliberations were conducted and it was realised that the Buddhist were not killing the animals. Animals were being killed or slaughtered by a particular community of non-Buddhists hence the Buddhists were not at fault. They were not sacrificing animals or killing them as they were not directly involved in the act of killing.

Even today the same situation prevails. The Buddhists eat meat, fish, etc., but are not involved in killing the animals. However, the idea is not relished by many people, even by the Buddhists and the explanation given by the *saṁgha* and the monks is far from being satisfactory. The killing and eating of animals tantamounts to the same. Both actions are directly proportional to each other. It is important to remember here that Buddhist Art flourished and in this art, animals of all kinds occupy a prominent place. Therefore, it is also true the Buddhist monks earlier were not at all keen to show any kind of disrespect to animals. There is no abhorrence or degrading the animals. It is equally true also of Indian art. Indian art is full of animals and birds. Famous sculptures are seen with birds and animals playing important roles.

It is also argued here that the artists were fully aware that the laity were mostly ignorant about the Buddhist doctrines. Those in vogue at that time were not properly understood by people hence the artists resorted to well-known symbols to convey their significance. They might have pondered over the issue and did their best by using symbols to avoid any kind of misrepresentations. To the artists symbols were the surest, infallible and quickest means to get the teachings across.

We feel this argument is more valid than others. The artist, as an artist, must be content with the splendour, and through the splendour strives to convey the truth. His function is to exhort men of letters or the society of the people who can think logically to do good work, or to prove things through various symbols and artefacts. He loves beauty and then he communicates it to others; thus the vision and reproduction. It is the artist's creed. Beauty is the best interpreter of God to man; when he has got hold of beauty. He has got hold of the surest way to knowledge of God. In Buddhism no God exists, there is only Buddha, the Master. Hence, the Buddhist Art depicts Buddha instead of the deities.

Indian art is a reflection of the Religion.Which is directly exhibited in Indian art, especially the earlier art. The Buddhist Art is also in one way a replica of Indian art. The Buddhist Art is not merely a composition in line, colour and image — it is primarily rich in ideas. The Buddhist Art may not improve our mind; it may not be useful, so pleads a school of thought. But the Buddhist Art pleases. Indeed, such is the inherent delight of Buddhist Art that in it not only the ugly becomes pleasant, but even sorrow becomes a joy. This is the implicit meaning of Buddhist Art.

Buddhist Art depicts Buddhism and is the message of Buddha and this art is taken as part and parcel of Indian art. Undoubtedly, it is originated from the Indian art but now Buddhist Art is treated as a separate subject. Buddhist Art is the greatest art in the world because it is basically religious and it flourished wherever the Buddhism travelled.

The *Jātaka* stories are actually in exaggerated form but have been blended in a cohesive group and this creates a grave and sometimes grim situation. The paintings exhibiting the *Jātaka*s are result of emphatic passion. These are the tales which exhibit the cohabiting scenes, life of robbers, murderers, enceinte and especially the life of the individual's experience. That is why the literature and art of the earlier period is regarded as genius as it is in original. But later on, the originality has been missing and thus the idioms invented earlier are still used because they are not conforming with the new concept. Hence, the Buddhist artefacts were in original, independent and gradually the paintings lacked in originality and were pseudo-romantic. Some of these arts thus became indistinct. Sāñcī is 'essentially pagan', but why only Sāñcī? The Buddhist Art as a whole, may be. It may be because Buddhism entered in Indian art as it reached the people conveniently. The culmination of both arts gave rise to a new impetus in the growth of Buddhist Art.

Very many opinions, scholarly writings and debates have been held with regard to Buddhist Art in India and whether it is confined to India. The nearest neighbour Sri Lanka was bound to have reacted; for Buddhism went to Sri Lanka from India. The advent of Buddhism, strengthened the position of rulers at Anurādhapura who in turm played their parts. The city became a centre of Buddhism and Anurādhapura and Mihintale became pilgrim centres. Rulers of Anurādhapura took a special title of *devanāmpiyatissa* which are higher than Rājā, King or Ārya. Thus, the ruler at Anurādhapura of that time was re-named as Devanāmpiya Tissa. Two South Indians Sena and Guttika seized power at Anurādhapura in 145 BC. Elura, another king, seized power and ruled over Anurādhapura. The spread of Buddhism gave birth to a new culture and that was known as Sinhalese culture. Thus, the Sinhalese culture is also the creation of Buddhism which had its birth in Indian environment. No study can be complete without an understanding of Buddhism and there can be no last word on this theme.

The *Mahāvaṁsa* and the *Dīpavaṁsa* end with the reign of Mahāsena (AD 274-301). The continuation of *Mahāvaṁsa* is called the *Culavaṁsa* and *Vaṁsa* means 'lineage' as well as chronicles. Thus, sometimes the names give a different notion because very many times writers and critics have used the names of the chronicles in their own way. Actually, in many places, *Dīpavaṁsa* and *Culavaṁsa* have been interchanged which is wrong. There are also differences in the chronicles. The *Dīpavaṁsa* is the oldest extant chronicle of the country. Most scholars have expressed the view that it was written about a century or two before the coming of *Mahāvaṁsa* — the greatest chronicle of Sri Lanka. *Mahāvaṁsa* was written by Mahānāmā Mahā *thera* of the Dighasanda Sewapathi Privena in Anurādhapura during the reign of his nephew, King Dhātusena. He closed his work with 37 chapters up to the reign of King Mahāsena (AD 275-302). The chapters subsequent to chapter 37 of the *Mahāvaṁsa* are called *Culavaṁsa*, whereas actually they too form part of the *Mahāvaṁsa*. The name *Culavaṁsa* deals with ancient Buddhist history, culture and tradition. The *Dīpavaṁsa* lacks in presentation and because of its inaccurate grammar and mere repetitions and omissions it has become clumsy. According to *Dīpavaṁsa*, Buddha went to Kelaniya, Mahāmeghavanaramya and at the spot of Bodhi-Tree. But the *Mahāvaṁsa* refer to Kelaniya, Sri Pada, Divaguhawa, Dighawapi, Mahameghavanaramya, spot of Bodhi-tree, Ruwanwaeli and Thuparama. The *Dīpavaṁsa* mentions the name of *theri* Sanghamitta and other *bhikkunīs* but the *Mahāvaṁsa* has no such reference. The *Mahāvaṁsa* states that the *arhat* Mahinda is said to have questioned King Devanāmpiya Tissa to test his knowledge before preaching the *Dhamma* but in *Dīpavaṁsa*, no account of such test exists. It is thus believed that both the chronicles have varies incidents and it is therefore necessary to connect these references with historical facts. The Buddhist Art of that time, therefore, is a blended one. It is not at all correct to say that it has all Indian traits. The two chronicles have contributed a novice culture which has thus been a boon for the Sinhalese artists.

The period from (AD 67-429) was a period of peace, prosperity and the people who had come to Sri Lanka with the Bo-tree formed the Lambarkanne clan. The Sinhalese terms *lamani* means writer, scribe and this indicates their interest. Sri Lanka at that period does not appear to have had her own culture and influence of India was visible in almost all spheres.

The Buddhist way of life is to lead a life which purifies the mind and helps to attain *nirvāṇa*. Buddhists are popular because of Buddhism and Buddhism became popular because of the brāhmaṇas. They made life more religious and difficult hence the Buddhist Art and Buddhism became part and parcel of normal living. Buddha never wanted to be worshipped. It can be argued here that Buddha albeit was not at all in favour of his image or himself to be worshipped, yet this negative propaganda led the people to worship him. In Sri Lanka or in India or anywhere, people are seen worshipping his image. It is also because the ancient Indians used to worship their teachers and elders. So it might be one reason. The other reason could be that the image made earlier had deep religious feelings. It can also be argued here that because of the impressive and hefty weight, of these images the viewers are so impressed and compelled to worship them. It is also true that in Buddha's time, there was no classical Sanskrit literature and he used Prākṛt, the spoken language of the common people in order to allure them. He never wanted even his image to be worshipped. Nāgārjuna interpreted Buddha's doctrine. Full blown cheeks, tightly closed lips of Buddha are prominent features of the best classical Buddha image.

Buddha in his sermon used the language of the common people and drew his imagery and parables from the life of the common people. He drew them from Sanskrit literature and thus developed an exclusive art of a learned few. The *Jātaka* stories gave birth to verse and paintings. The Buddhist Art of India and Sri Lanka have great humanitarian tradition fostered by Buddha. This tradition has influenced the whole social environment. There was no real literature is Sinhalese before the twelfth century. Therefore, no maturity or independence, which are signs of classical literature, is not seen. Thus, they could not produce exquisite sculpture, architecture and painting. That is why Sri Lankan Buddhist art lacks originality in most of the pieces. It also lacks depth of feeling and imagination and this tradition in India is very strong at least in sculpture. This is quite evident and vivid in the Buddhist sculptural masterpieces. Buddha image in *samādhi* is beyond the creative genius of the artists. It was created and perfected by scholastic artists. The *samādhi* image is *in-communicado* because of its gravity and seriousness. It is inconspicuous because it is not easy to understand the allegorical poetry. The poetical genre of the image imply great humanitarian tradition, which is common in the people of Sri Lanka and India and because of this Buddha is highly venerated. Buddha in the mood of *samādhi* and the image of Śiva in cosmic dance are masterpieces. While comparing both the pieces of art, we find both are superpieces because of the serenity in Buddha and the vibrant energy in Śiva. Originality is seen in the Polonnaruwa images. There is a mood of spiritual serenity but a tortured expression of peace and calm. The Sinhalese artists have a gift for sculpture and an imaginative feeling. A Buddhist who enters a Buddhist temple (pansal) is first attracted by the colossal statue of sitting or standing Buddha. He first offers incense flowers and then he finds wall paintings. This has instilled in the mind of the Sinhalese, a feeling for sculpture.

Drawing their inspiration from the Buddhist lore, the sculptural pieces are decorative and allegorical. In the West, mass, solidity and roundness are taken as special features but in India and Sri Lanka rhythm, linear grace figures are taken as prominent features. Buddhist sculptures reveal abstract mystical ideas. In Anurādhapura period, after the introduction of Buddhism in the third century BC there was an uninterrupted development of Sinhalese culture which grew up to ninth to tenth century. This paved way for maturity and gradual growth of sculpture. This is attributable to Indian sculptures produced during the Gupta period. Indian sculptures right from the inception of the Buddhist Art, were produced under the influence of Hinduism and Hindu culture. During this period, a special phase sprang up, i.e., classical phase. This phase of second century BC grew under Buddhist India influence.

Once the *stūpa* came to Sri Lanka, it was developed to an extent that it never reached India. Thus, Sri Lankans developed their *stūpa* in their own way. It will be seen that the early *stūpa*s were essentially domes made in the shape of a bubble. The early *stūpa*s were smaller in size and lost their originality. The later *stūpa* had a solid cube above the dome and a conical spire *vata-de-ge* or *cetiya* house which became the creation of Sri Lankan. Another impressive feature of Sinhalese architecture is moonstone.

The moonstone is believed to be based on Amarāvatī style. This style was developed in the hands of Sri Lankans into objects of such artistic expressions which were never parallel to the style of Amarāvatī or elsewhere.

The most impressive sculptures of Anurādhapura period are Buddha images. Buddha image carved in the Vaṅga country in the first century AD was brought to Sri Lanka. The seated posture of Buddha images are reminiscent of the Mathurā School. Sri Lankans have discovered a new idea of making Buddha images of great size. It is because they wanted to have a distinctive style. We also find Buddha images in copper bronze but they are not of any significant value.

Architecture in Sri Lanka was inspired by Buddhist architecture in India. It was developed under the total stimuli of the active adherents of Buddhism. It advanced further and Sinhalese type was found which was named as 'the art of India or of Asia as a whole'. Two outstanding types of Sinhalese architecture are the *stūpa* enclosed by a circular shrine called *vatadage* and the massive brickstone with a vaulted roof, rising from a heavily moulded plinth. It has no parallel in India. The giant *stūpa*s are from third century BC to fourth century AD. The circular shrine '*vatadage*' is marked by a concentric of monolithic pillars. The circular form remained in Sri Lanka till fifteenth century but went out in India in early period. Mementos of this type in India are noticed in the bas-reliefs of Amarāvatī. The *vatadage* of Polonnaruwa and Medirigunya in Anurādhapura are well known. The main architectural features of the *stūpa* is 'Vahalkades' is often alluded to as 'frontispieces' altars at the four cardinal points. Flanking the altars are the decorated upright sculptures in low relief with various artistic motifs. The foliated scroll or palm-leaf plants with leaves and flowers rising from a vase and figures mostly of animals and birds are among the conventional motifs gracing a stele. It is reminiscent of the Buddhist Art as represented by the bas-reliefs at Bhārhut and Sāñcī.

Nāga figure in human form are yet another feature seen in southern Vahalkade of the Jetawanarama *dagaba* at Anurādhapura. Other sculptures are: a group of lovers in a granite slab at Isurumuniya *vihāra* at Anurādhapura, 'man and horse', decorative sculptures embellished flight of steps, lotus petal mouldings, dwarfs, etc.

Amarāvatī bas-reliefs are of high quality and are a happy blending of Indian, Iranian and Hellenisic factors. Horse is represented in the moonstone with a fidelity to nature. It is also surprising to know that horse is not found in Sri Lanka and is rare. Still, horse has been given an important place like lion. Lion is also not found in Sri Lanka but it has a co-relation with the National Flag and with the Sinhalese race, it assumes a grotesque conventional form.

The human figures became the main subject matter for the artist in the Gupta period and all these were in ideal forms. The image worship that was initiated in the preceding centuries received greater momentum in this phase. During the Gupta period, Buddhist Art progressed despite resurgent Brāhmaṇism and revival of the ancient Vedic sacrifical rituals. The Gupta period (fourth-sixth century AD) marks the brightest period not only in India but in Sri Lanka too. The main centres of Buddhist Art were Mathurā and Sārnāth. The mural paintings of Ajantā, Bāgh of earlier period and Sīgiriya were the representation of Buddhist Art. Sīgiriya painting women are dacked with a profusion of ornaments. In these paintings we find legs have not been drawn because of cramped space. The paintings as such are profound and speak of profundity of high society.

Thus, they are similar to Ajantā and Bāgh. The carves of Sīgiriya paintings are the most important and interesting to learn their skill. The Ajantā may be termed as frescoes like Sīgiriya frescoes. It is, in fact, a combination of tempera with fresco. All these are similar beause India and Sri Lanka were dominated by Hindu ideas and the ancient literature of India and Sri Lanka have numerous references to pictorial art. Ajantā constitutes a great gallery of Buddhist Art. The walls, pillars and ceilings illustrate the life of all sections of Indian people — rich and poor, young and old and it gives ample opportunity to understand Indian tradition. Ajantā and Bāgh are two great centres of Buddhist Art of painting in India. The Bāgh cave walls are the creation of great master craftmen. The subject matter of the Bāgh paintings and Ajantā paintings are common and the soul of these paintings have been to portray Buddha and *bodhisattavas*. The paintings display secret messages. Ajantā, Bāgh and Sīgiriya are expression of pure love. The Gupta age was very advanced. There were many new achievements which are associated with an advanced civilisation. It was economic prosperity which encouraged art and sciences. It is also true that material prosperity was used to advance knowledge of various kinds.

'Isurumuniya lovers' is a gesture of the faces and eyes and are so natural that they seem to suggest the title to the minds of the intelligent men. The sculptor with the help of the language of the gestures tries to tell the story of their reunion and depict their emotional reactions.

It is essential for the critics of the Buddhist Art to understand the religious art of India and Sri Lanka. This religious art, in spite of its sophistication and stylisation, has its roots deep into the soil. The Sri Lanka Buddhist Art in spite of all variations and mutations under Indian influence still survives as an integrated whole. Bell, Hocart and Paranavitana, Coomaraswamy, Marshall and many others have left indelible imprints and their works are the monuments for an analytical study of the Buddhist Art of both the countries. A diligent study reveals that art of both the countries owing to close proximity have many features in common and differ only in some phases because of the change of scenario in the social environment.

The Western influence has not only affected India but also Sri Lanka with the result there is a loss of cultural identity, hence the Buddhist Art is likely to fade if not properly maintained. The modern Buddhists do not agree that Buddha is the ninth incarnation of the Viṣṇu. In the second century BC there are references to coins and Kahuvanu is mentioned in the Pāli chronicles. At Mampita Vihara in Kagelle Kasepona and Kahapane are mentioned, meaning money, from third century BC to fourth century AD. Punch marked coins wre found. Some coins marked 'Buddhist Cakram type', 'Elephant and Svastika', 'Harre and Svastika', 'Lion and Svastika' and 'Tree Svastika' were in circulation from first century AD to sixth century AD. But these were not in demand and were rare. Similarly, coins minted in Rome were discovered from third century to sixth century AD in the vicinity of ancient parts. As such coins have very little to contribute to this study. To summarise the Buddhist Art in relation to Sri Lanka and India from third century BC to sixth century AD: it has left its rich heritage to Sri Lanka. The magnificent and colossal *stūpas*, the ornamental and decorative architecture of Anurādhapura, the sculptures of dwarfs and of *nāga* deities, the moonstones, the railings of Anurādhapura recall those of Sāñcī and Amarāvatī — all these and more that defy enumeration characterise the earlier Buddhist Art of Sri Lanka.

The latter part of this epoch is distinguished by influence of typical Andhra art, as seen in the Buddhist sculptures of Amarāvatī and reproduced in a number of Sri Lankans sculptures of Buddha and *bodhisattvas*. The Śuṅga Andhra epoch (second-first century BC) was one of the most creative periods of Buddhist Art. Though Śuṅga rulers were followers of Brāhmaṇical faith and Buddhism was deprived of the State patronage which it enjoyed during the reign of the Mauryan rulers like Aśoka and some of his successors, there was no setback in the propagation of the Buddhist faith. Buddhism flourished in Bodh Gayā, Bhārhut and

Sāñcī. The art of this period consists mainly in the excavation of rock cut temples or *vihāras* and erection of railings and *toraṇas* (gateways). The ancient artists had to work within fixed conventions to express their individuality and creative genius. The conventions were conditioned by the nature of the medium and the use to which it was put. In the case of the plastic medium of sculpture, when used for religious interpretation, certain conventions arose. The sculptures of Sri Lanka made use of these conventions. Therefore, the sculpture of Sri Lanka represents the phases and external features of sculpture in India.

The Buddhist Art is distinctive of the Gupta Age of India about AD 300 to AD 600. It established its tradition in the plastic and fine arts of both India and Sri Lanka. The Toluvil stone sculpture of Buddha at Anurādhapura is among the outstanding figures typical of this age. This tradition was followed in the metallic arts of Sri Lanka when the Gupta influence waned, Sri Lankan architecture was mainly influenced by that of South India beginning with the Pallavas from AD 600 — this architecture being called the Draviḍian for distinction. From the Draviḍian architecture we have four main styles — the Pallava, the early Cola, the late Cola and Vijayanagara and the modern period.

The Mauryan period is remembered for the greatness its empire which made the Buddhist Art prominent and Sri Lanka and India. The Mauryan art is West Asian according to Havel, Smith, Codrington, Coomaraswamy and Raj. But there are 'Persian' and 'Assyrian' elements and thus became indigenous. And there are references of wooden pillar in the Vedic period hence the pillars are Indian and became pillars of Buddhist Art.

The popularisation of Buddhist Art especially with reference to Sri Lanka has been mainly the work of Ananda Coomaraswamy, Marshall, Cunningham, Martin Wickramasinghe and Paranavitana. These connoisseurs of art had made their mark as researchers of high excellence in the rightest form. They wrote extensively and compared the Buddhist

Art with many countries where the art flourished. But opinions still do not hang together and there is always a point at issue. Martin Wickramasinghe, an ace writer of Sri Lanka, original thinker, having intellectual ferment to awaken the litterateurs but is treated as one who has shown prejudice against Sanskrit. He thinks that the art is borrowed from India but feels that now it is independent. Thus, it leads to different interpretations. The Buddhist Art of Sri Lanka is borrowed, adapted and readapted from Indian art.

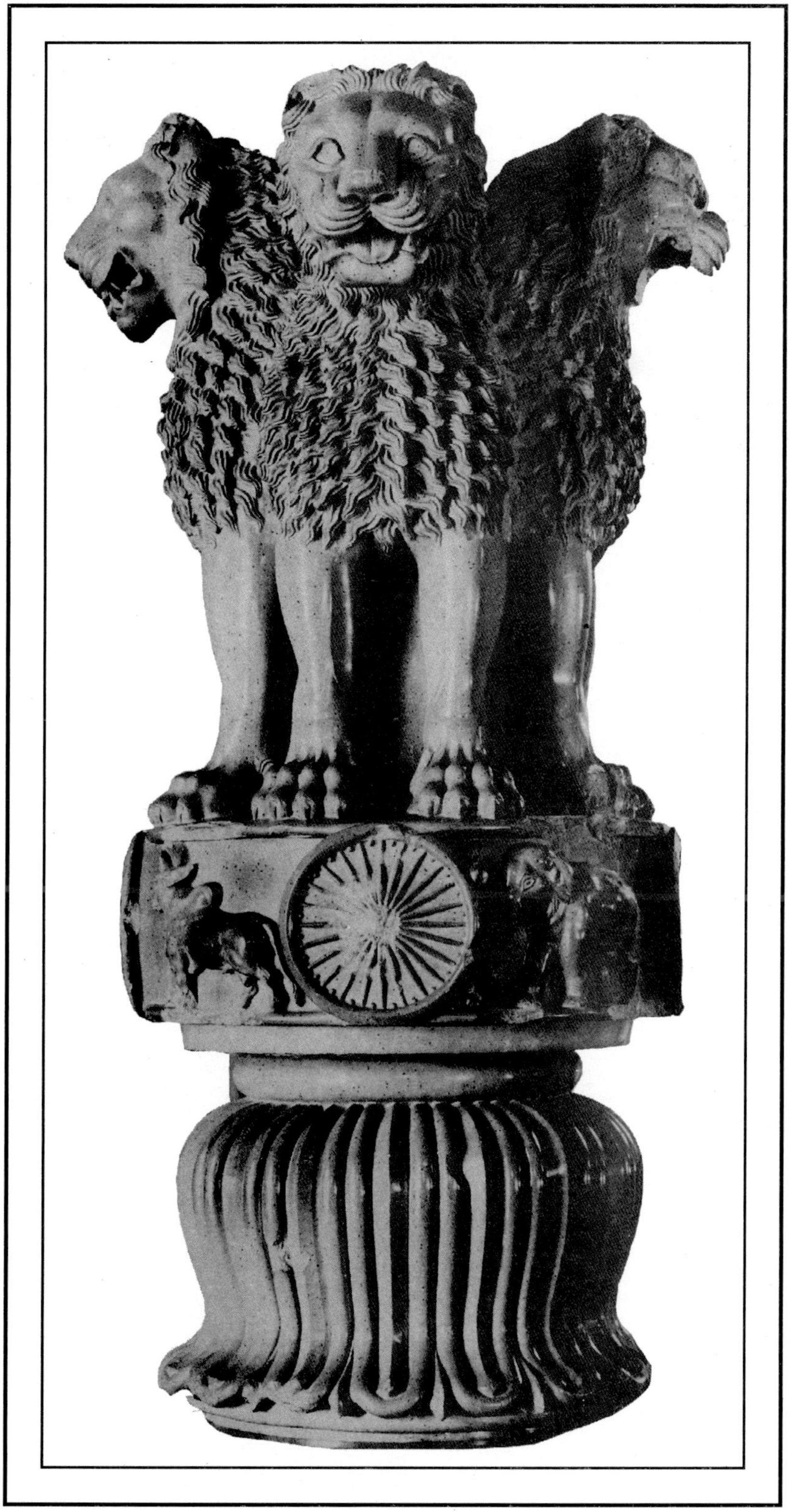

Pl. I : Sārnāth, Lion Capital.

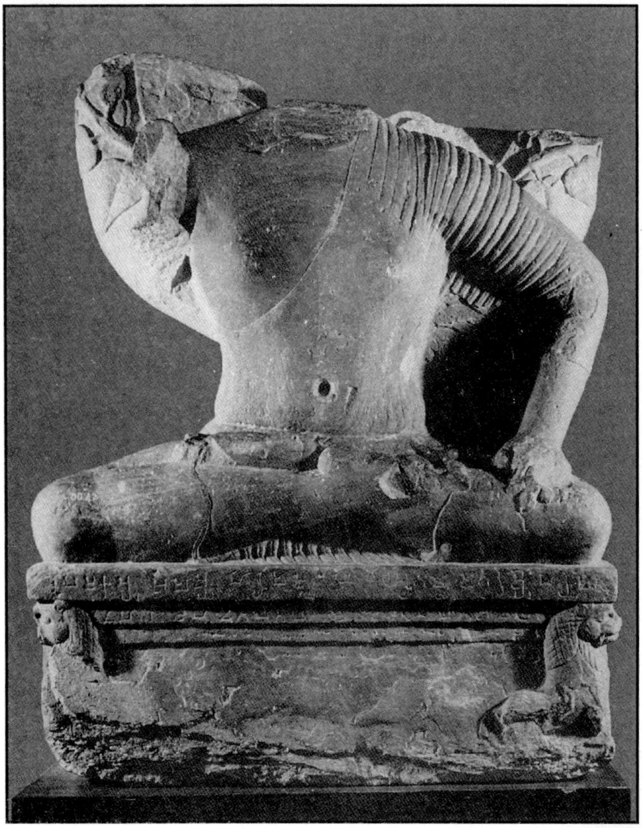

Pl. II : Inscribed Image of Buddha.

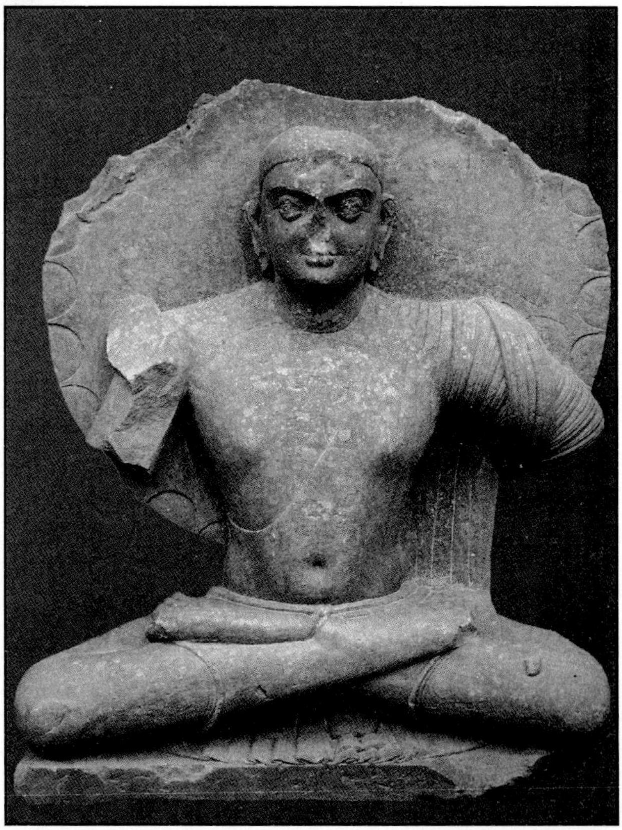

Pl. III : Buddha.

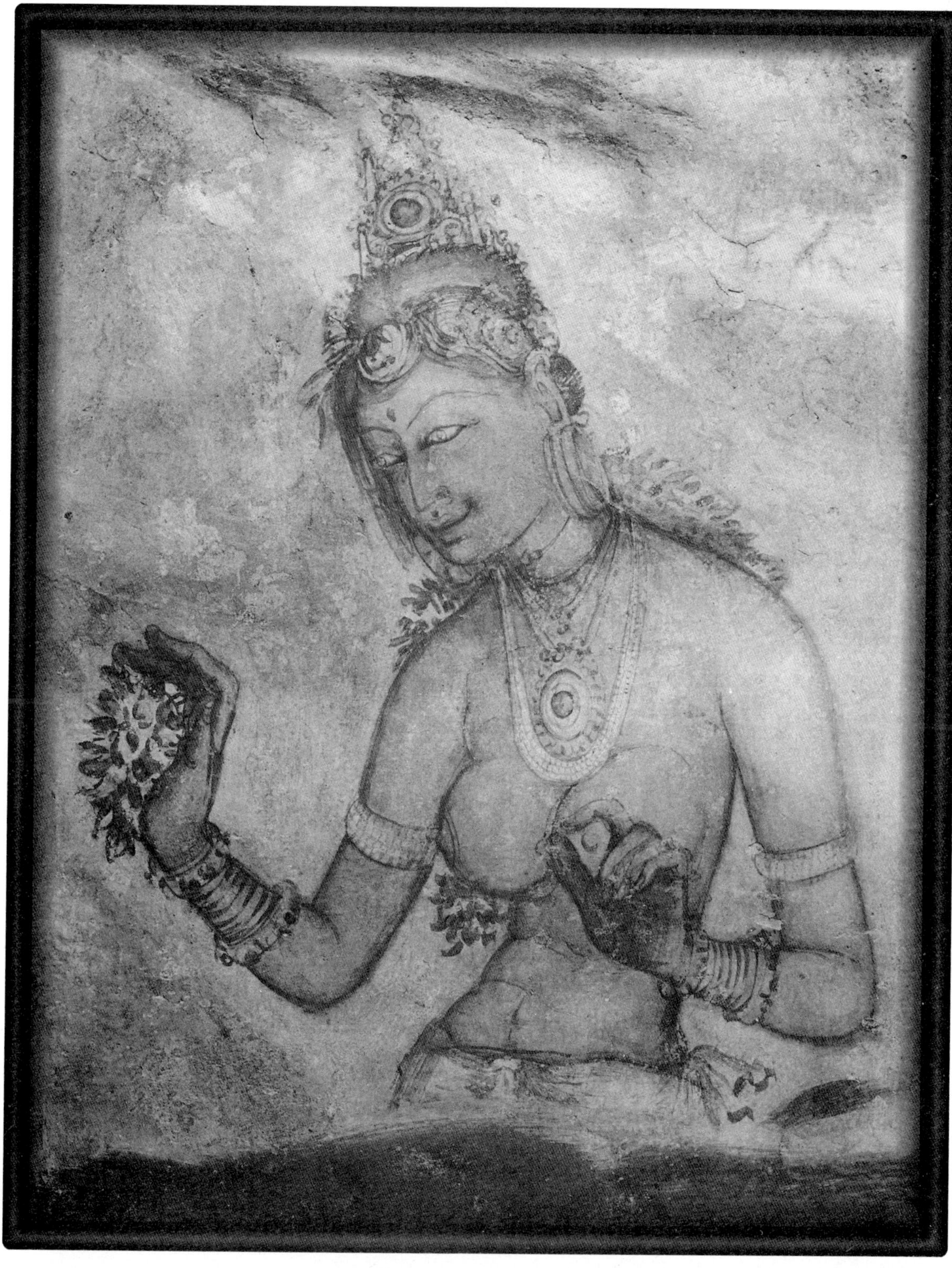

Pl. IV : Sīgiriya, Fresco on rock face.

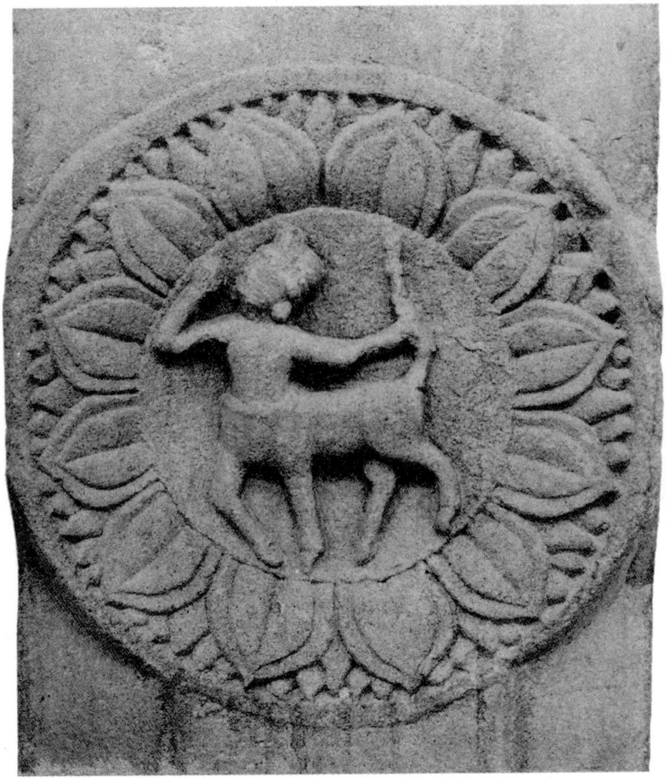

Pl. V : Bodh Gayā, Railing pillar.
A man with a body of horse in lotus medallion.

Pl. VI : Bhārhut *stūpa*. Great Railing.

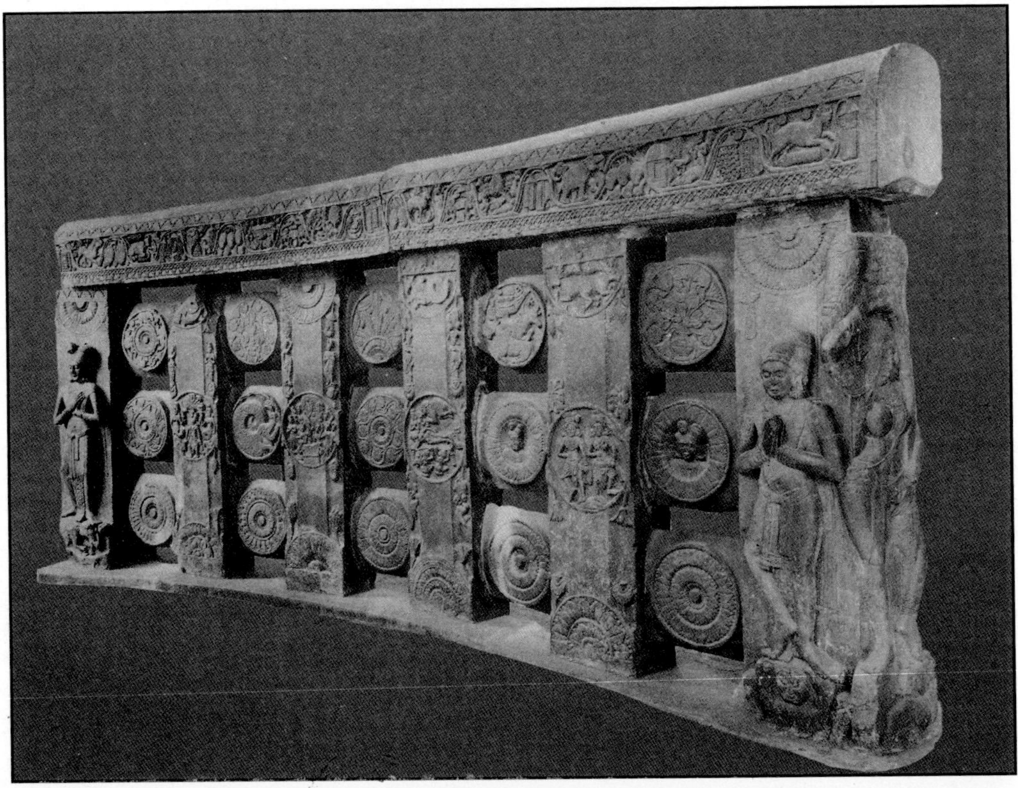

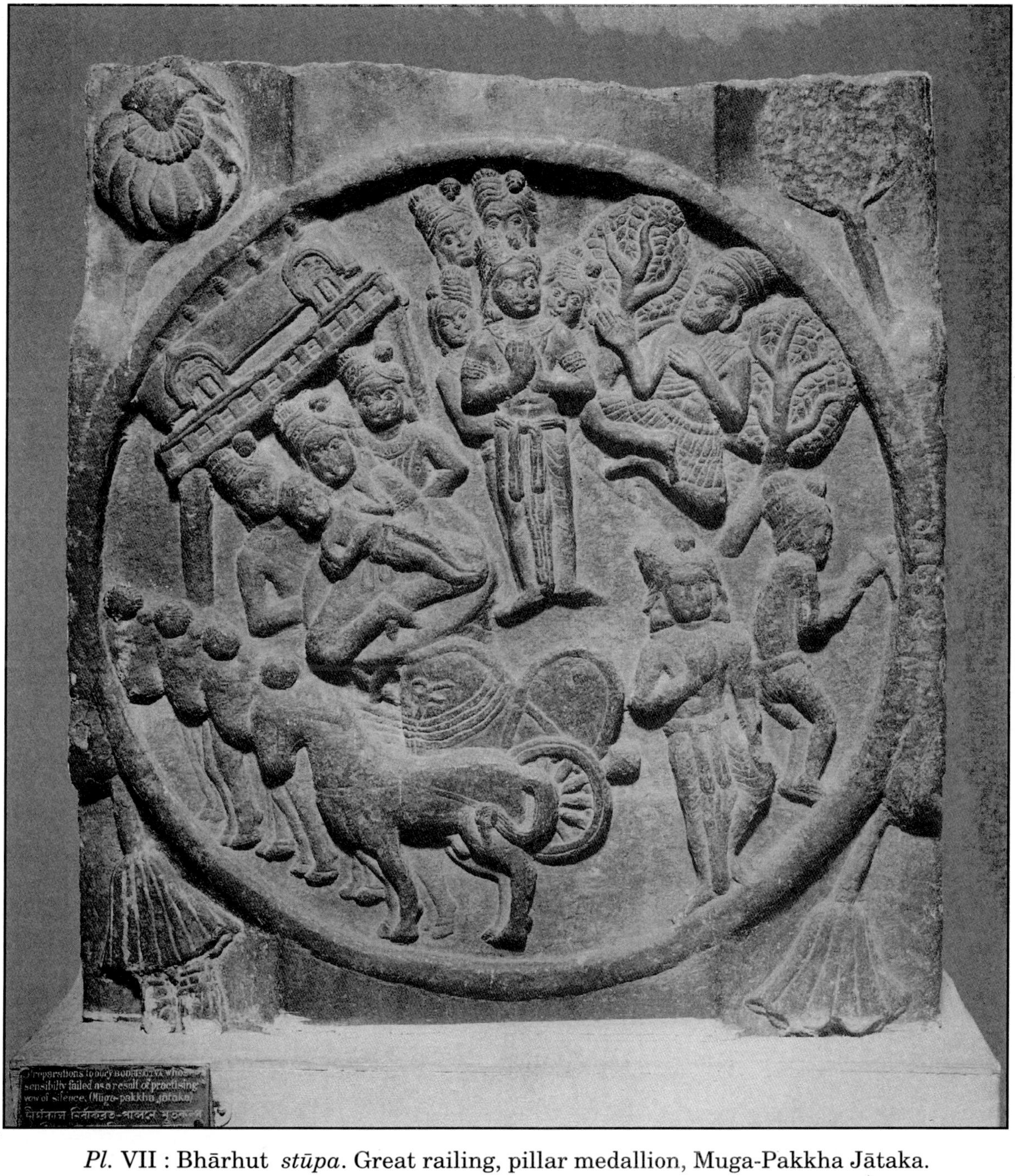

Pl. VII : Bhārhut *stūpa*. Great railing, pillar medallion, Muga-Pakkha Jātaka.

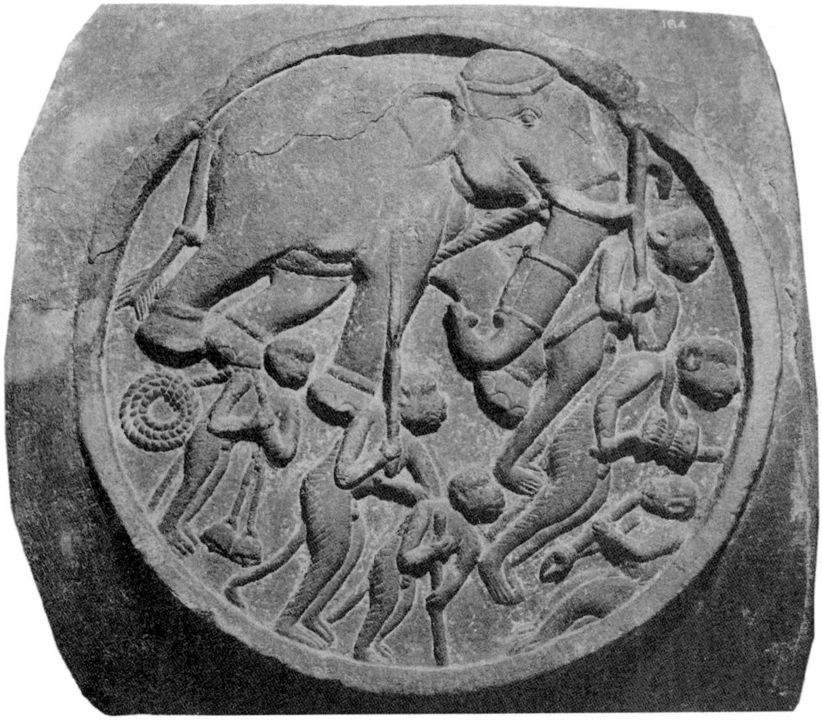

Pl. VIII : Bhārhut *stūpa*. Great railing, crossbar, medallion, monkeys leading, captive element.

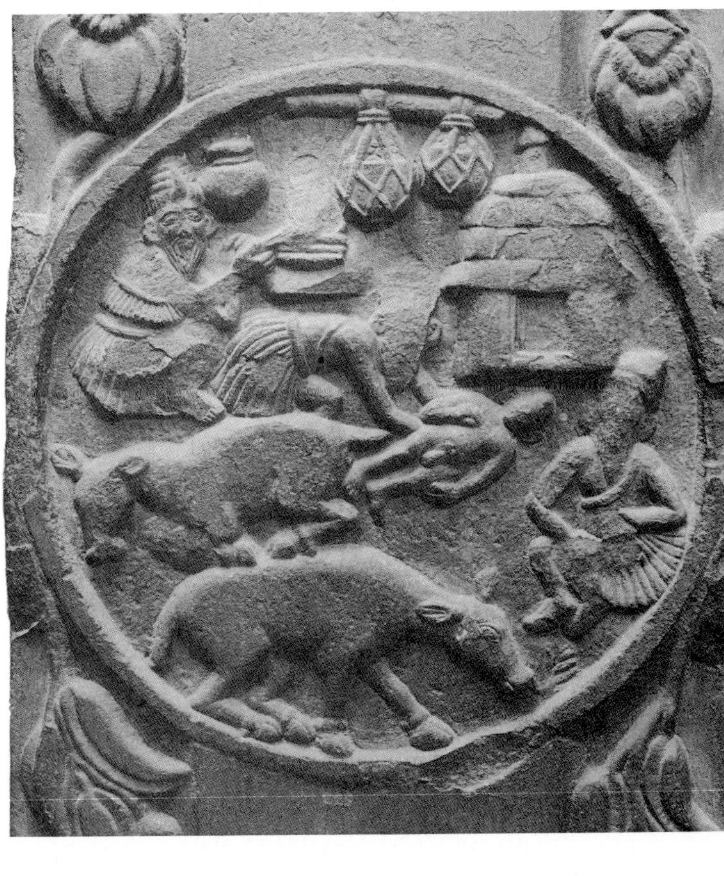

Pl. IX : Bhārhut *stūpa*. Great railing, pillar medallion showing Alambusa Jātaka.

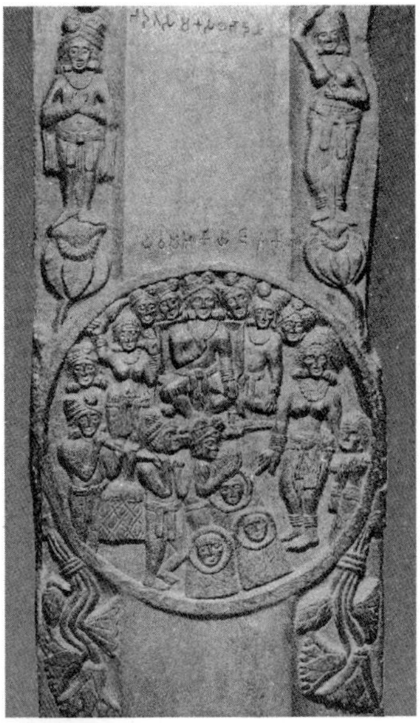

Pl. X : Bhārhut *stūpa*. Great railing, south-west quadrant pillar, medallion at centre on Yavanajhakiya Jātaka, Virtuous wife of absent *bodhisattva* producing entrapped lovers before king.

Pl. XI : Bhārhut *stūpa*. Great railing, south-west quadrant pillar, medallion at centre, expanded view. Yavanajhakiya, Jātaka [or Maha-Umagga Jātaka].

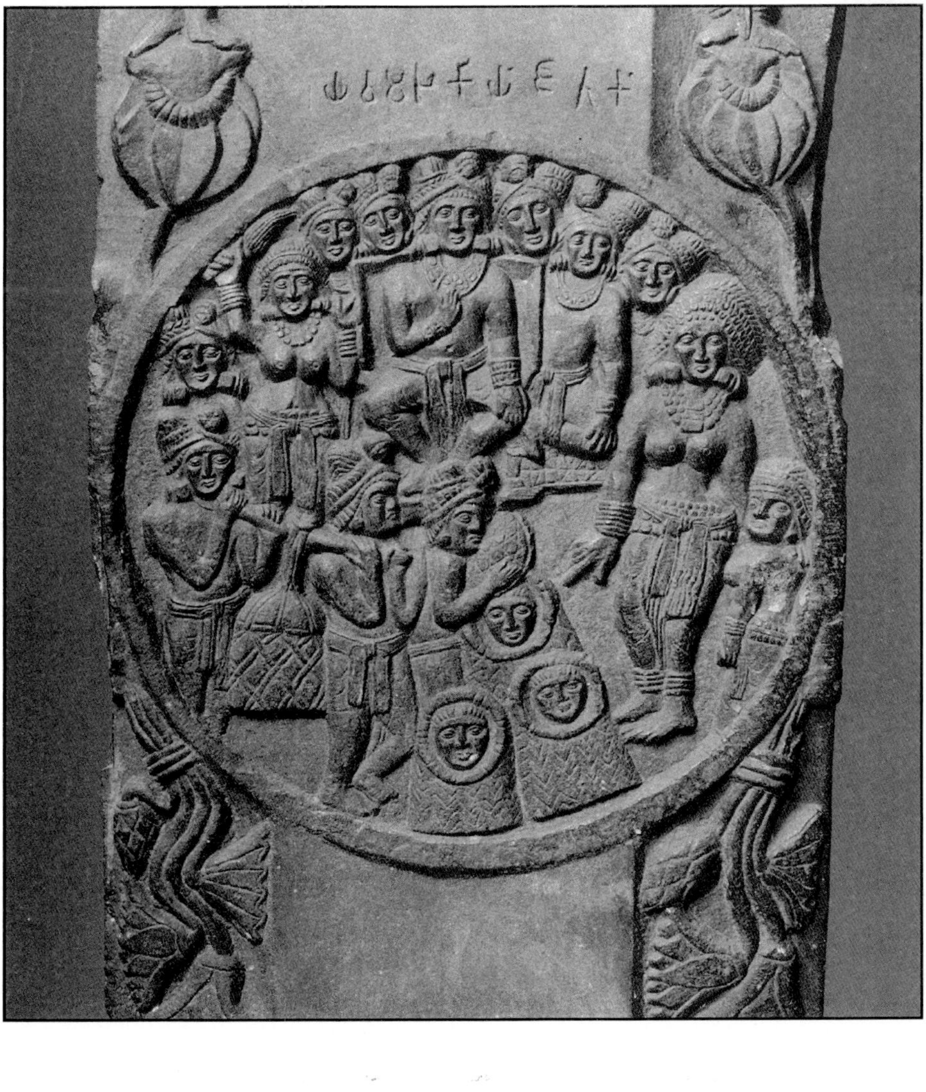

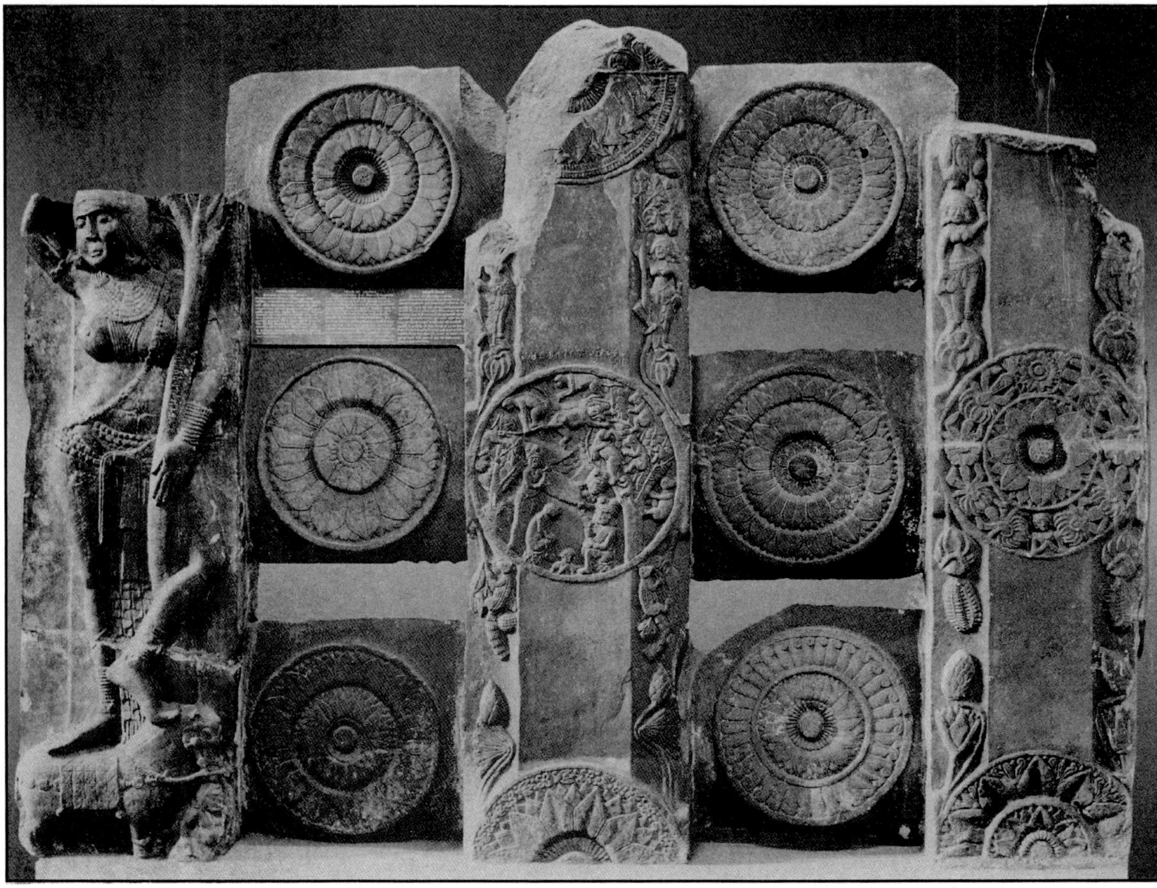

Pl. XII : Bhārhut *stūpa*. Great railing, pillars wife Yakṣī and Mahākapi Jātaka.

Pl. XIII : Bodh Gayā, Mahābodhi tree coping stone with rosette

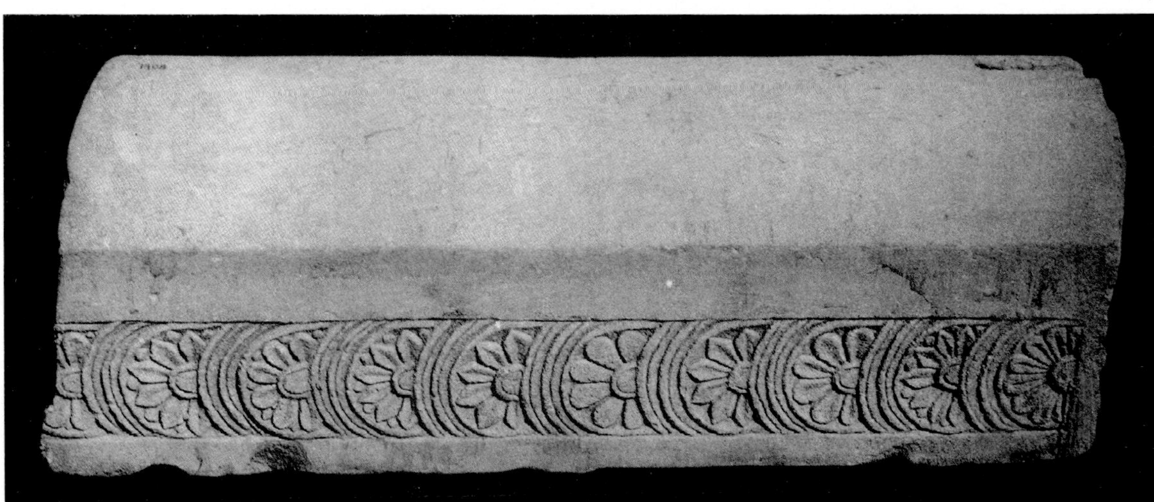

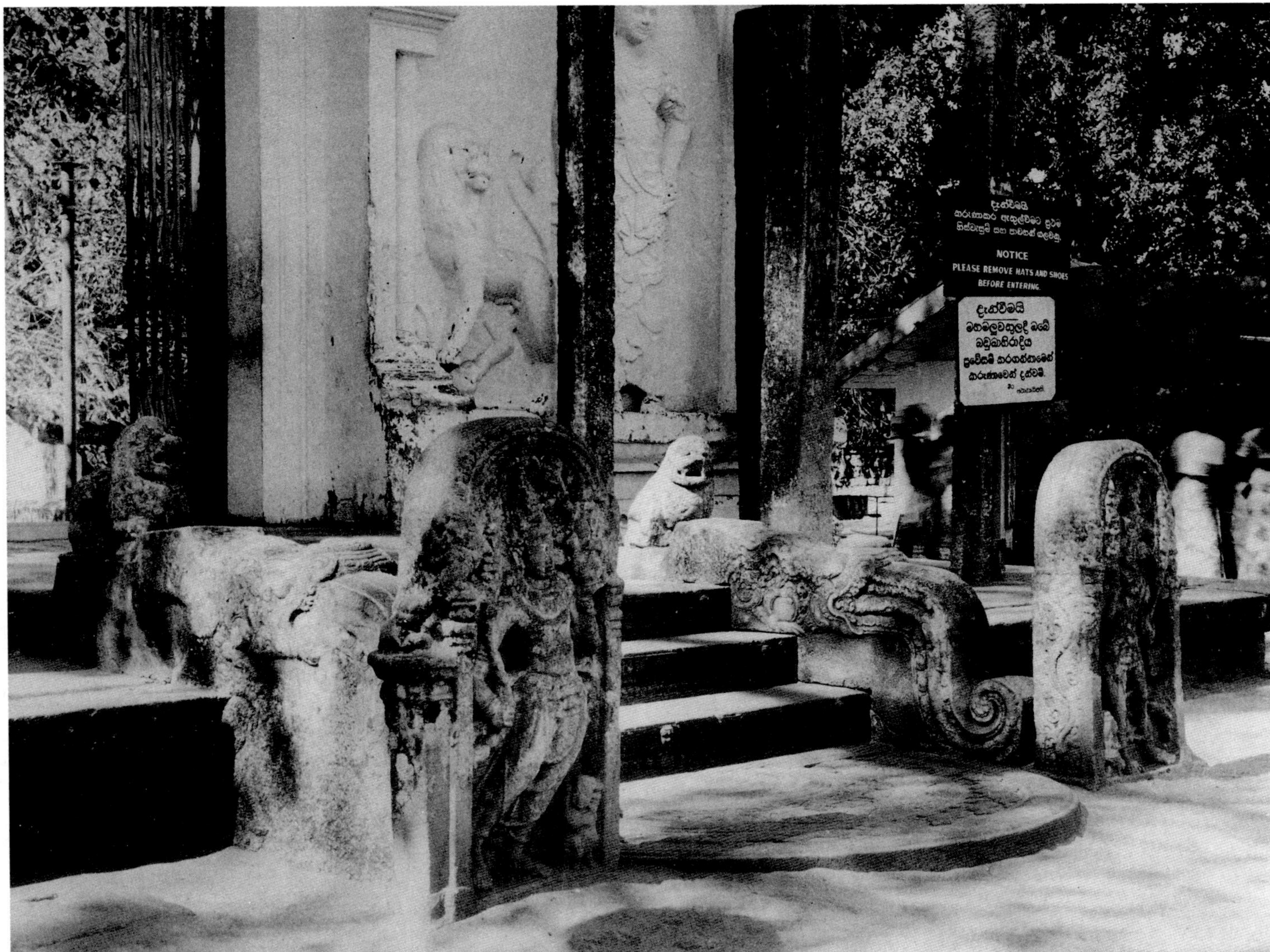

Pl. XIV: Bodhivṛkṣa Temple at Anurādhapura, Sri Lanka.

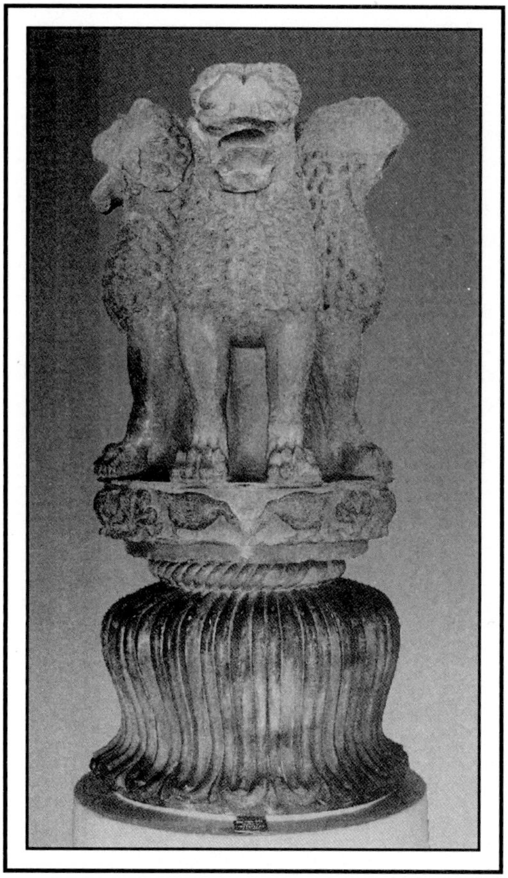

Pl. XV : Sāñcī, Capital of Aśokan pillar.

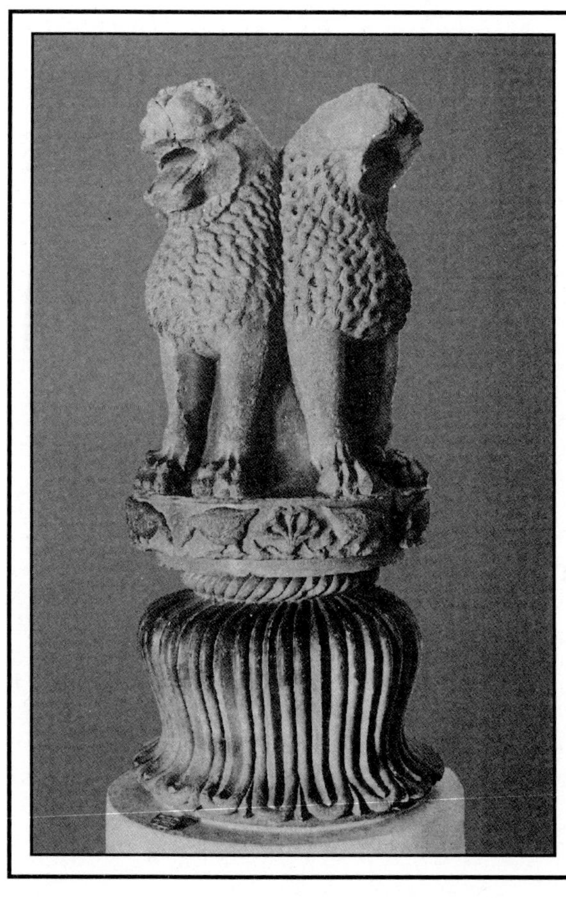

Pl. XVI : Sāñcī, Capital of Aśokan pillar.

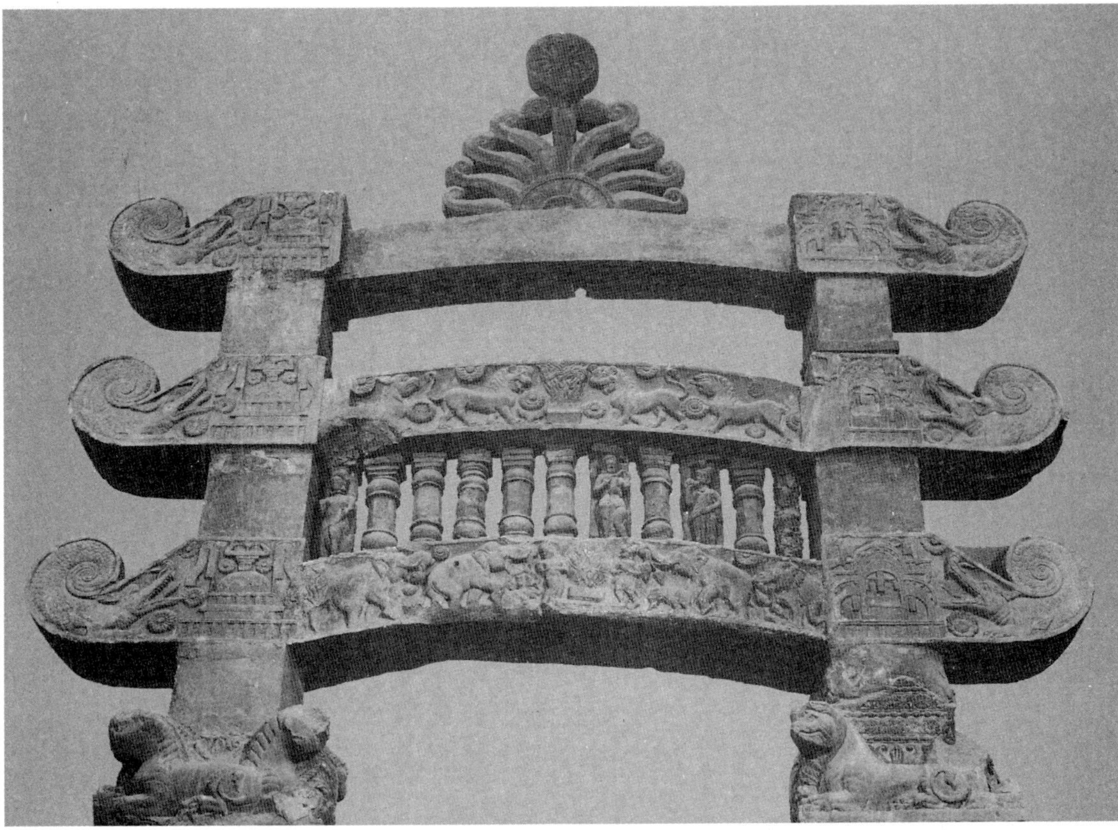

Pl. XVII : Bhārhut *stūpa*, Great railing, east gateway architraves.

Pl. XVIII : General view of Jetavana *dagaba* at Anurādhapura, Sri Lanka.

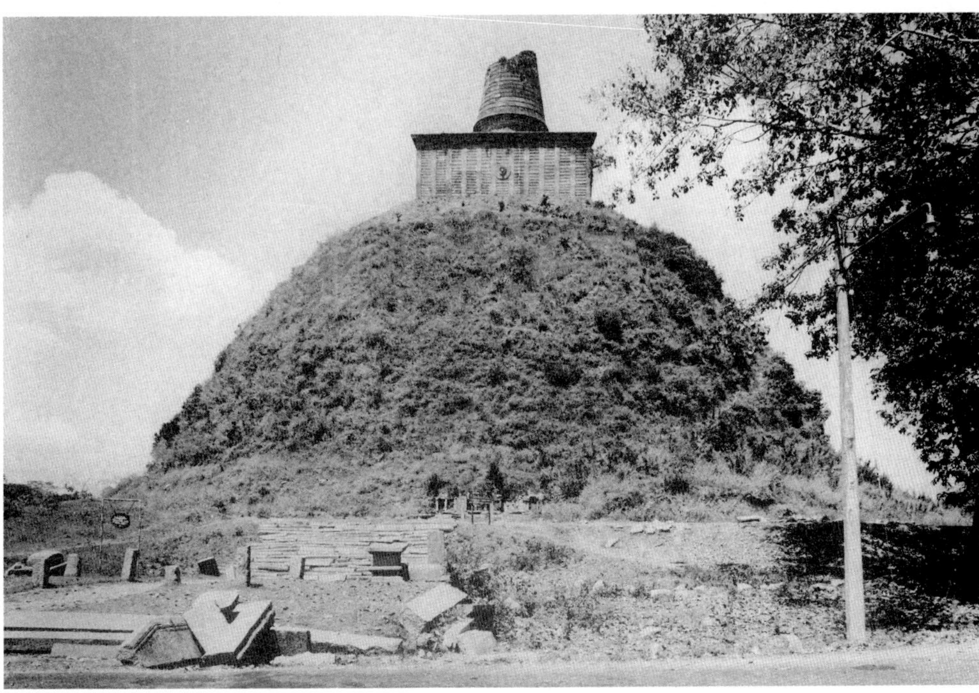

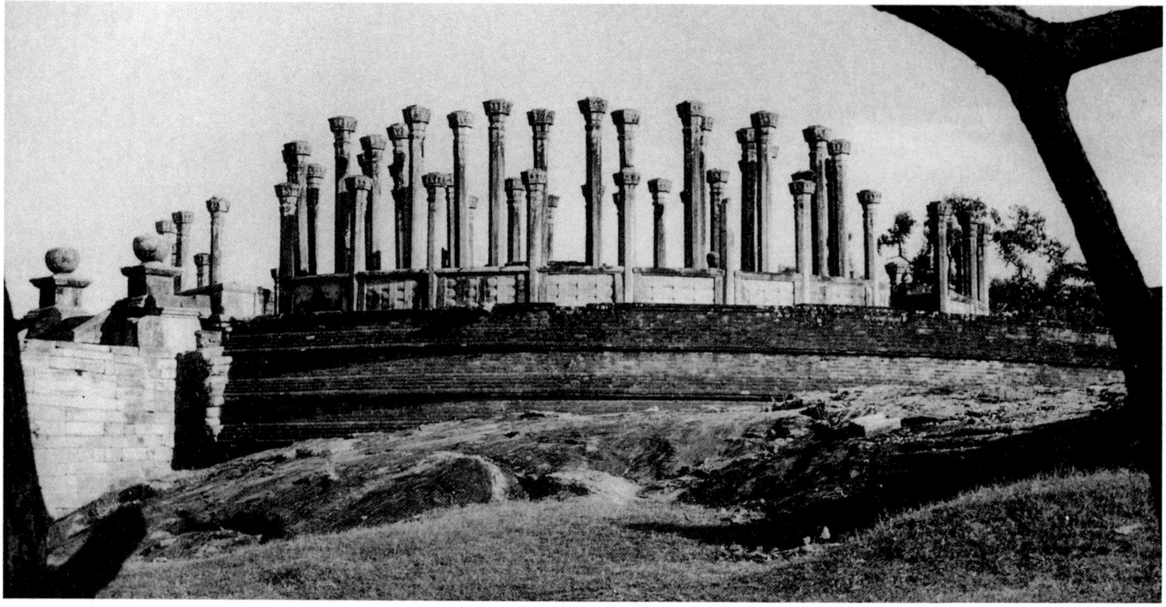

Pl. XIX : Vatadage — General View, Sri Lanka.

Pl. XX : Mihintale, Mahaseya *stūpa*, General view.

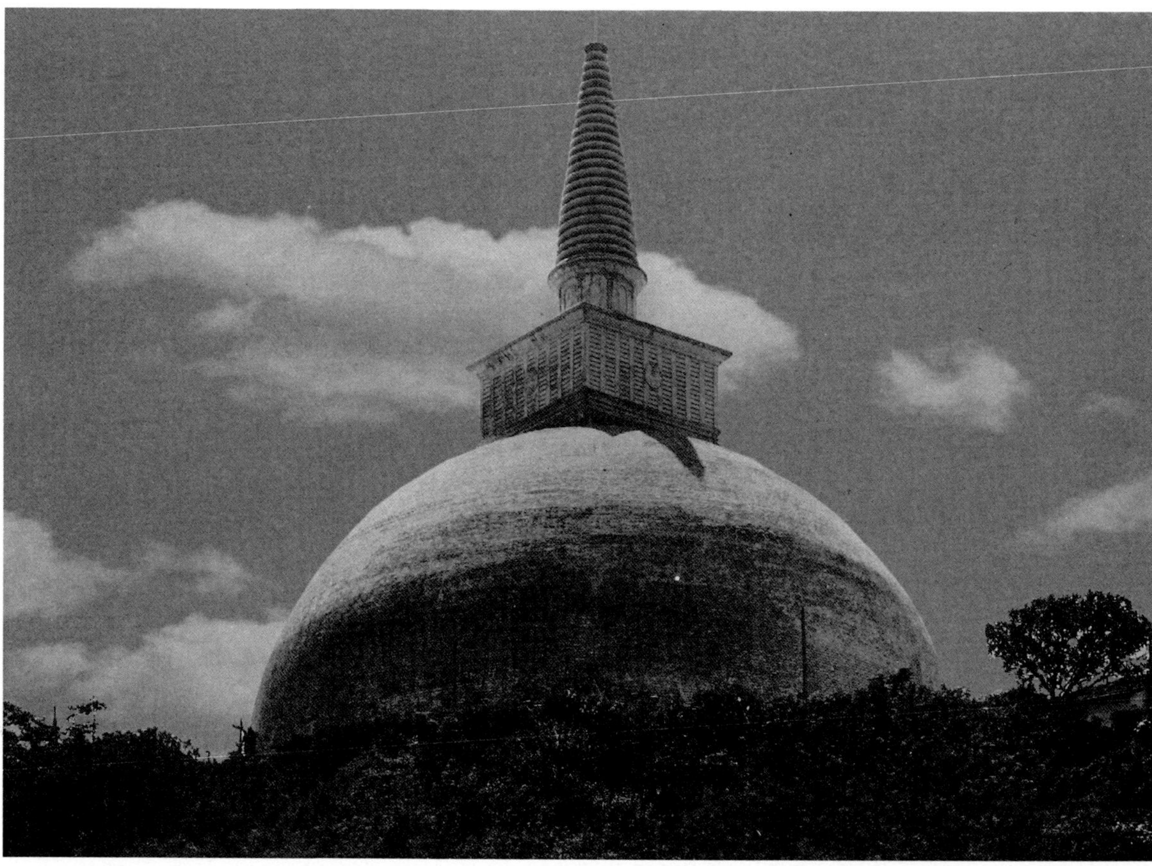

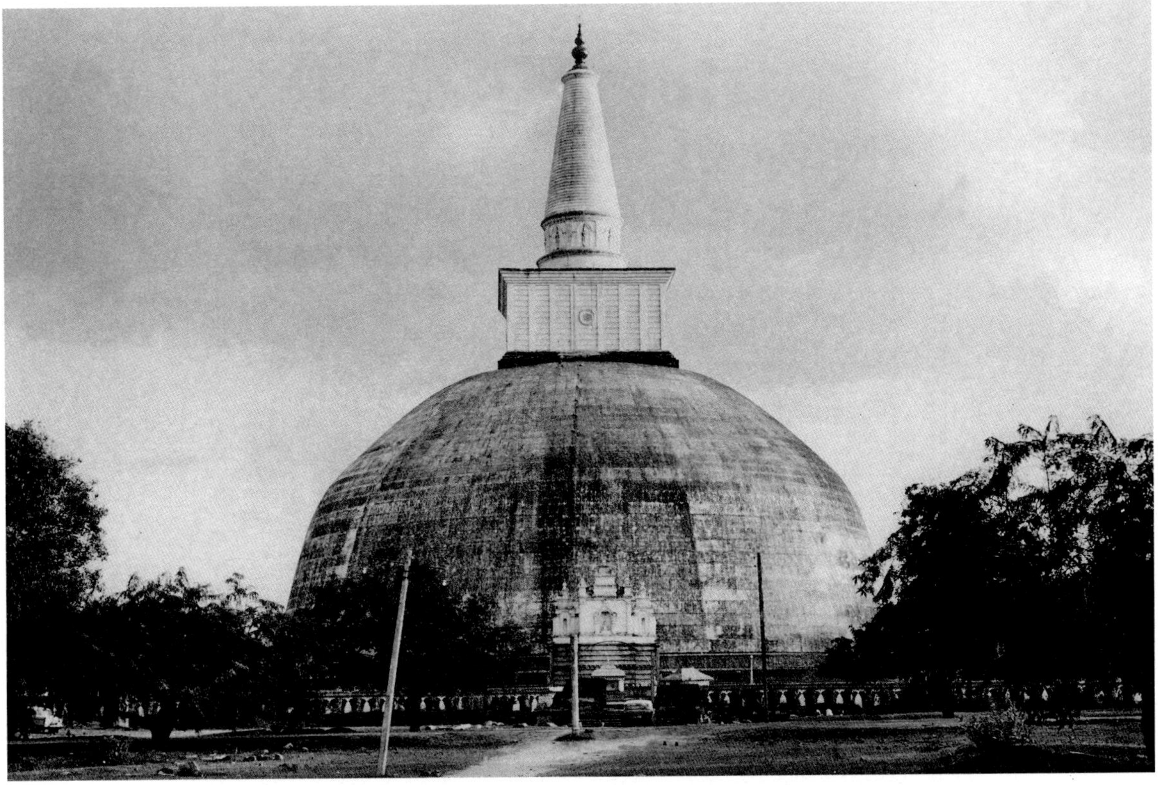

Pl. XXI : Anurādhapura, Ruwanweli Seya, General view from north.

Pl. XXII : Moonstone Sri Lanka.

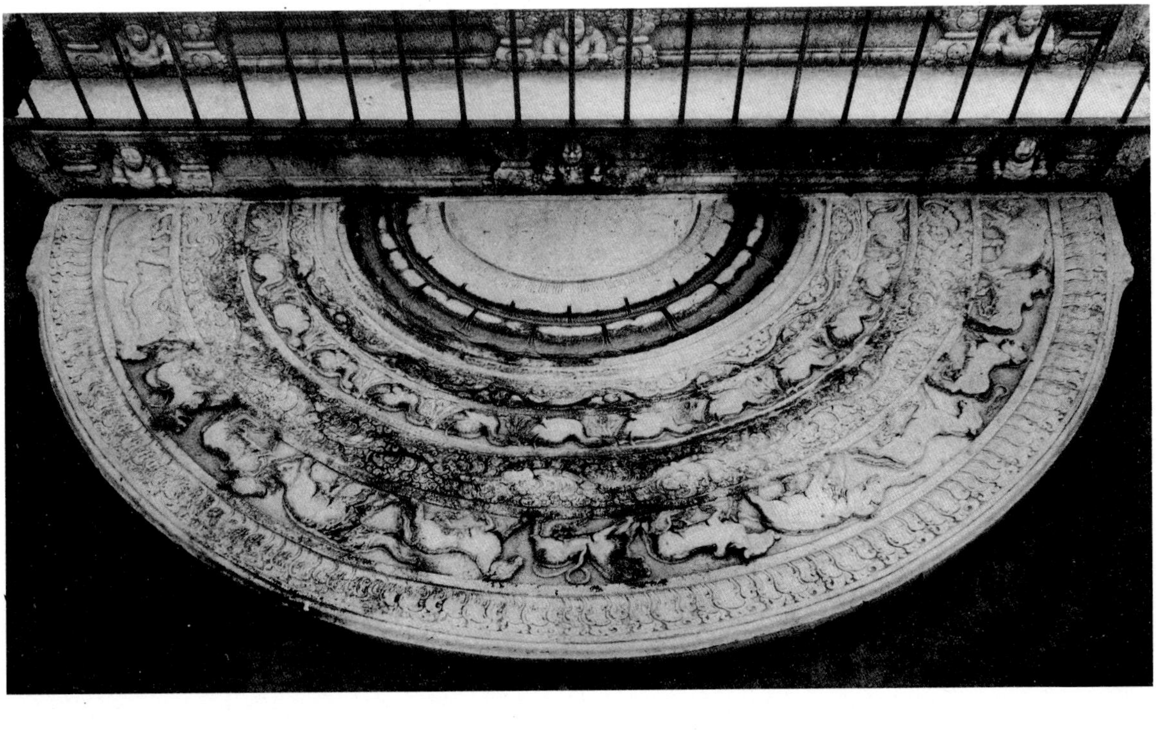

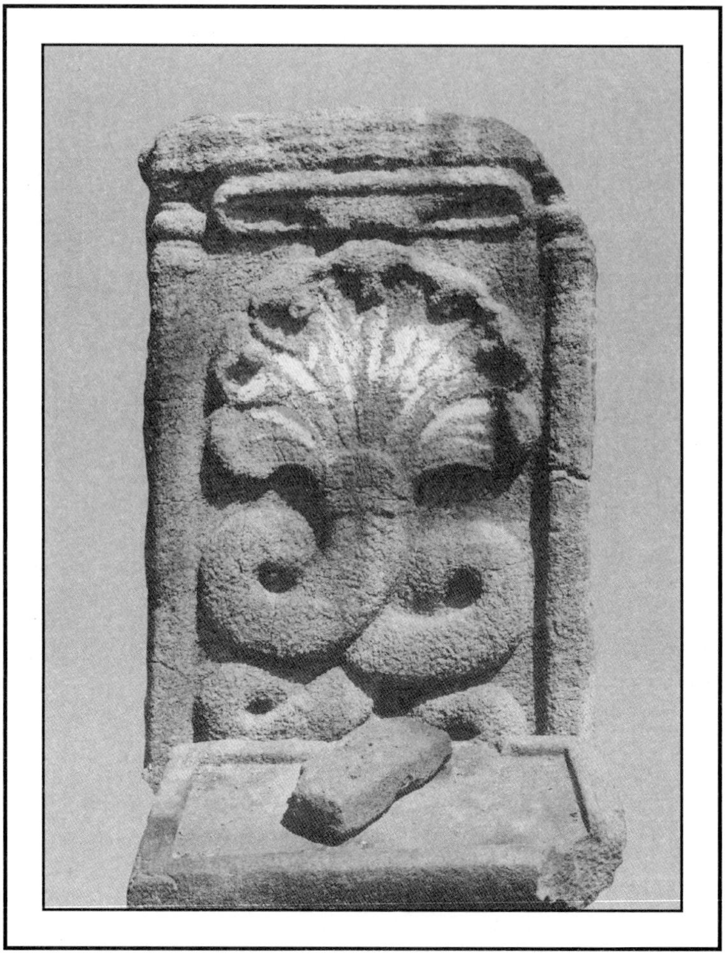

Pl. XXIII : Anurādhapura, Jetavana Dagaba, Naga stele.

Pl. XXIV : Anurādhapura, Buddhist railing south of Jatavana Dagaba.

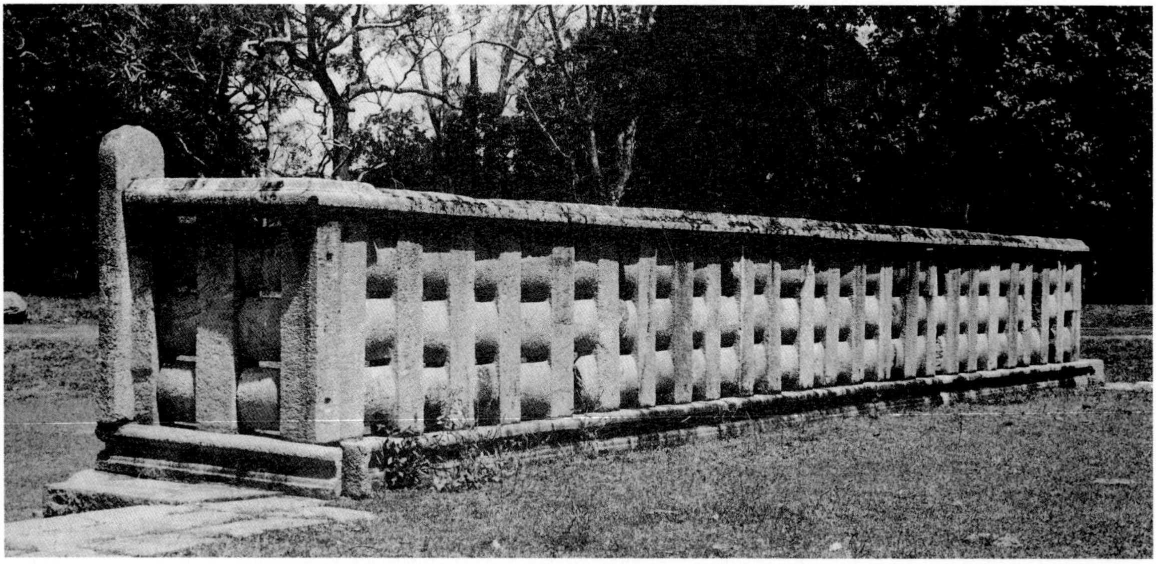

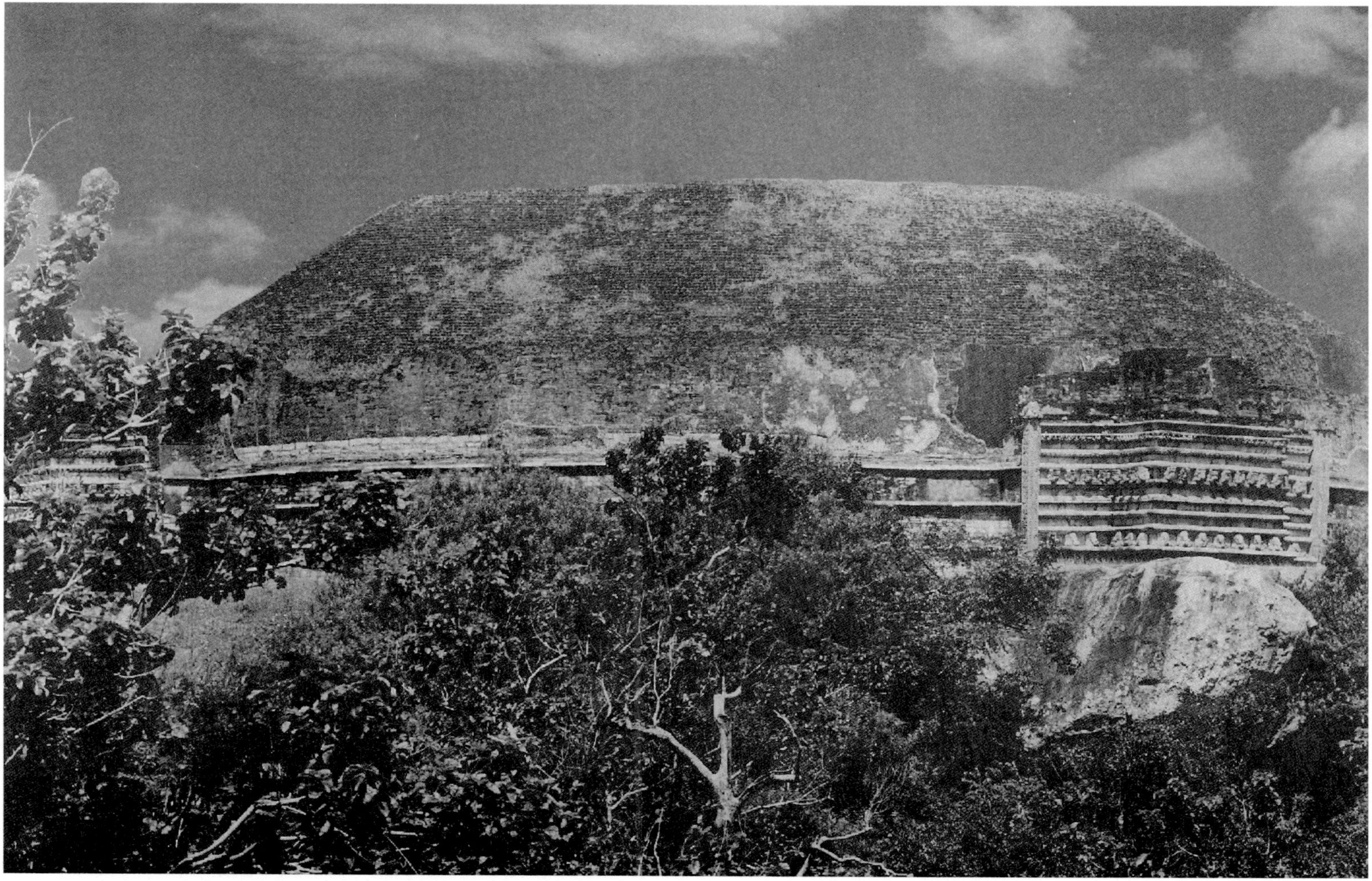

Pl. XXV : Mihintale, Kantaka *caitya* [*stūpa* of Mahinda], General view.

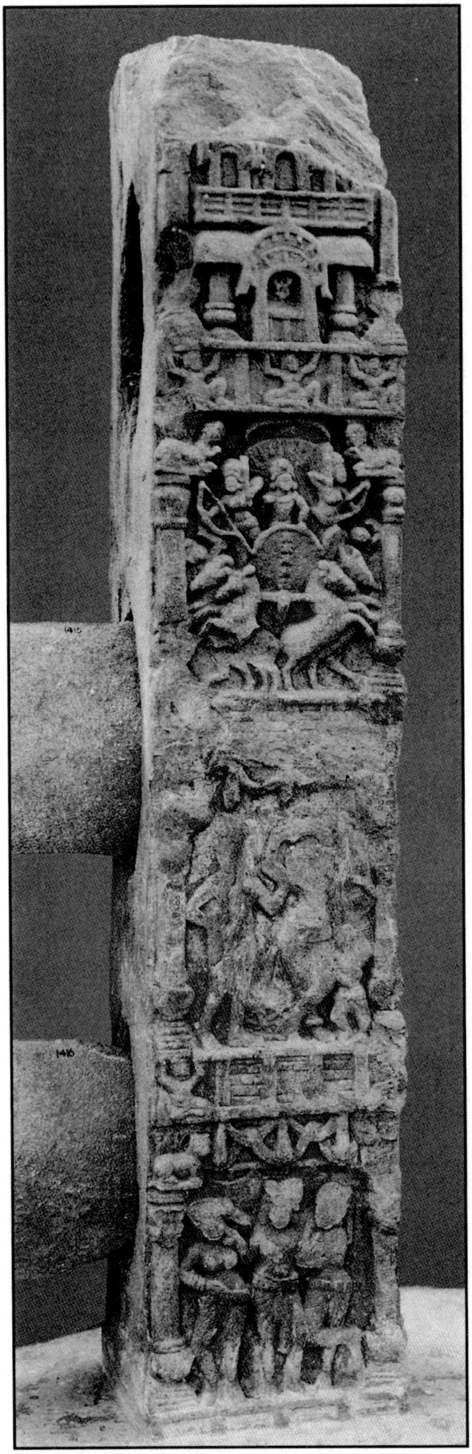

Pl. XXVI : Bodh Gayā, Railing pillar.

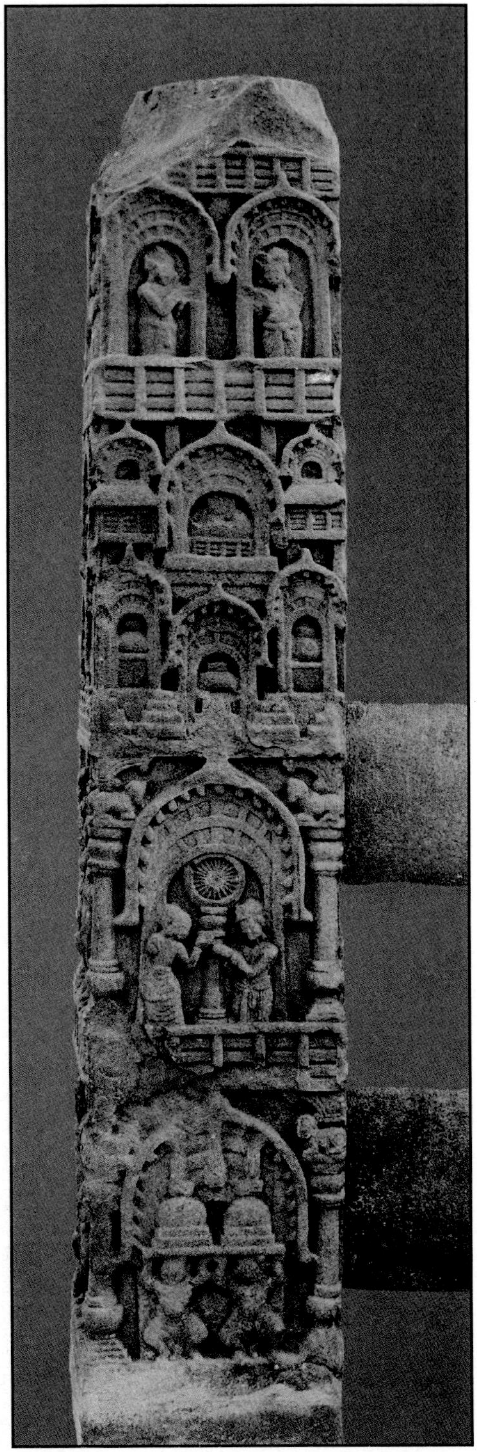

Pl. XXVII : Bodh Gayā, Railing pillar.

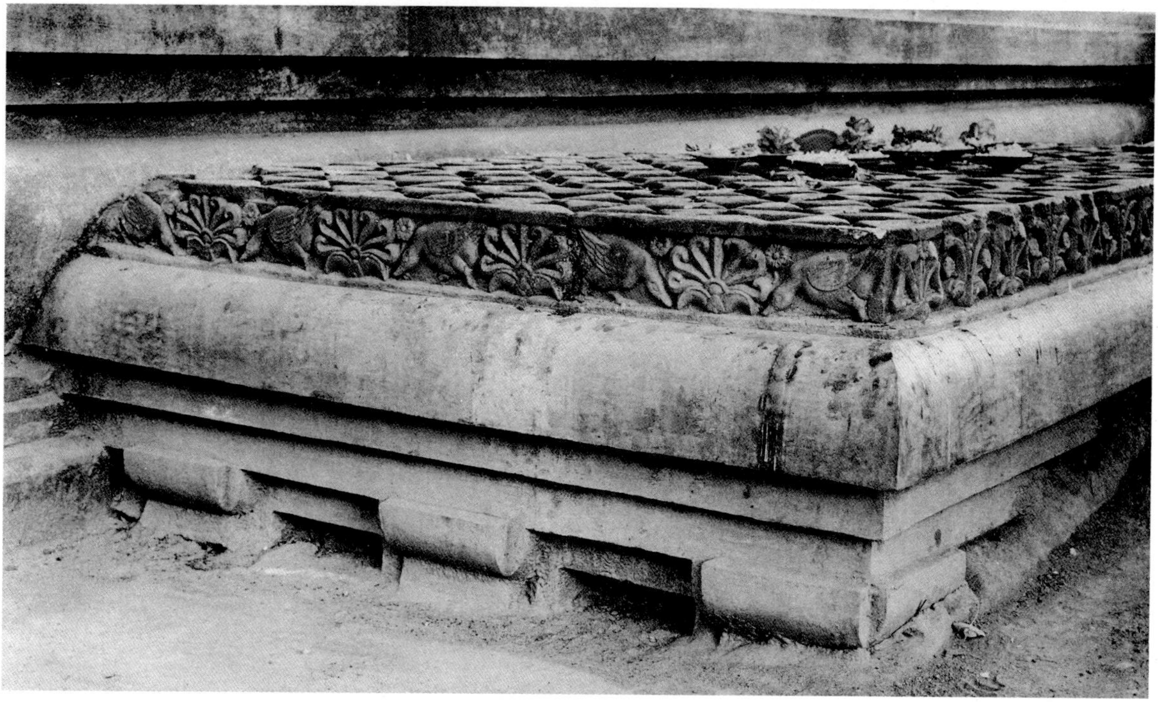

Pl. XXVIII : Bodh Gayā, Mahābodhi Temple, Vajrāsana, Under the modern Bodhi tree.

Pl. XXIX : Sīgiriya, Fresco on rock face.

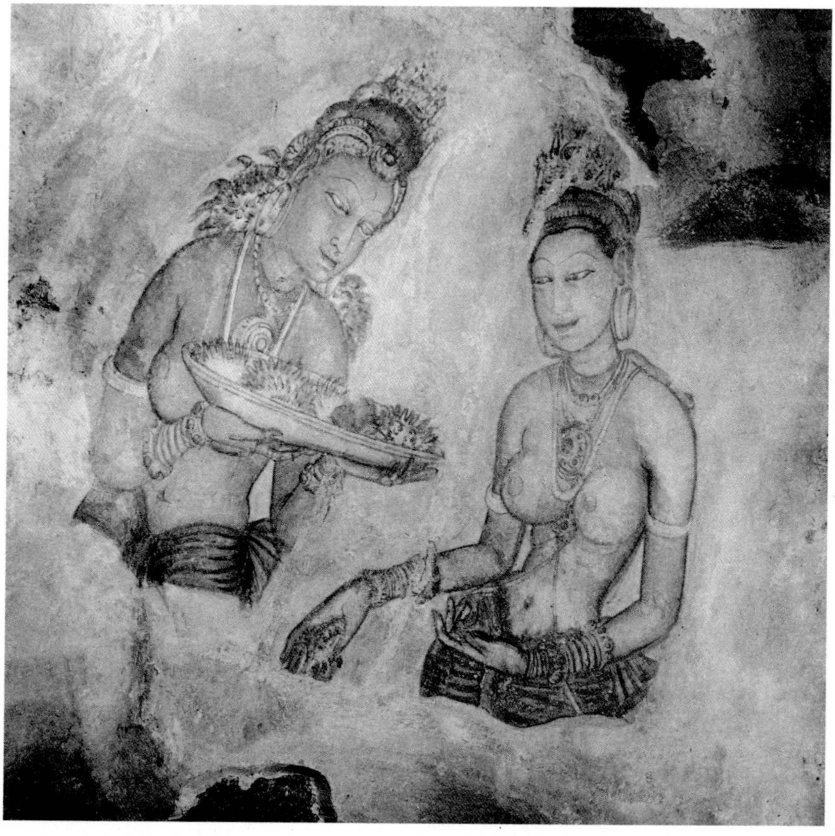

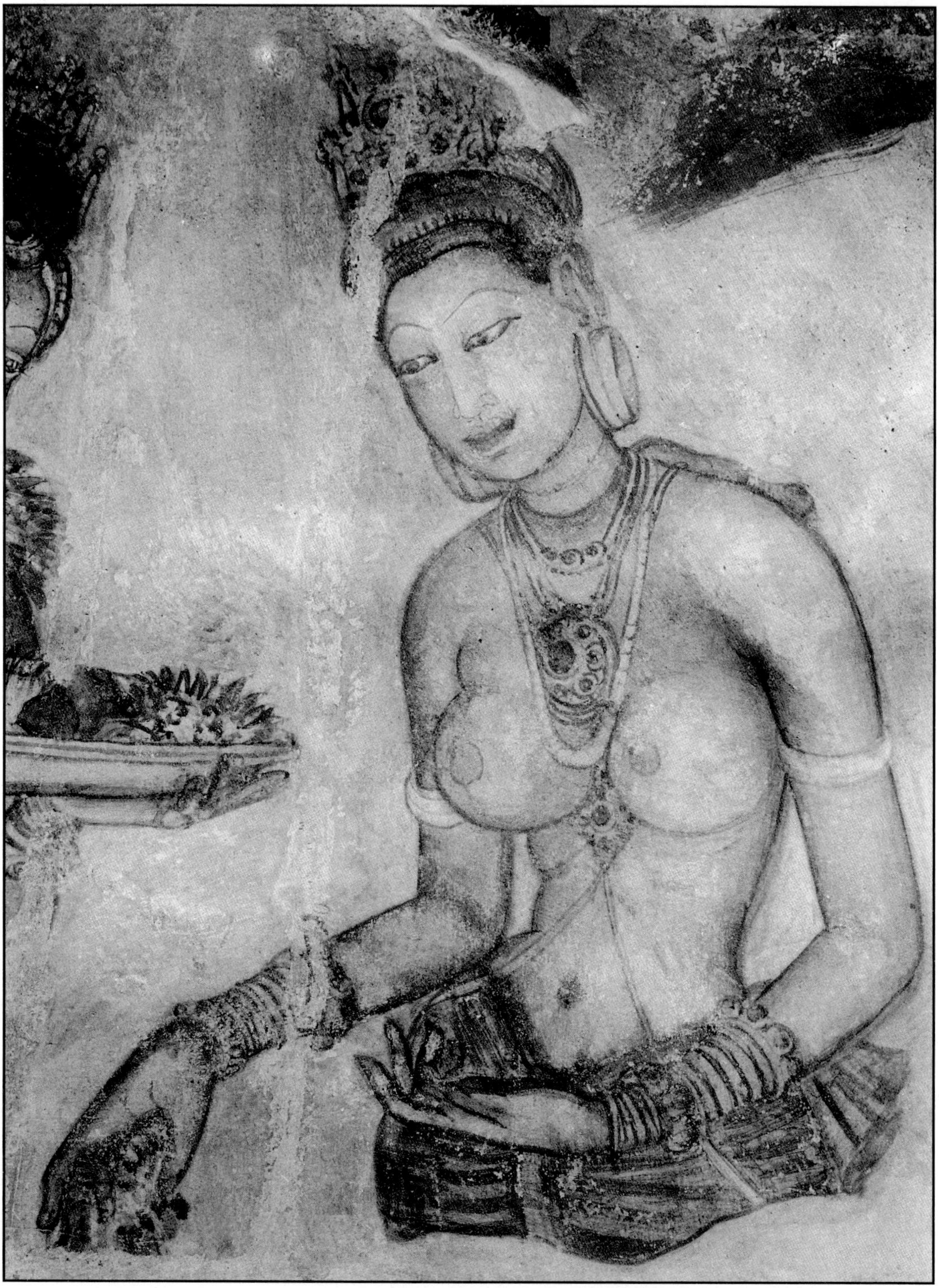

Pl. XXX : Sīgiriya, Fresco on rock face.

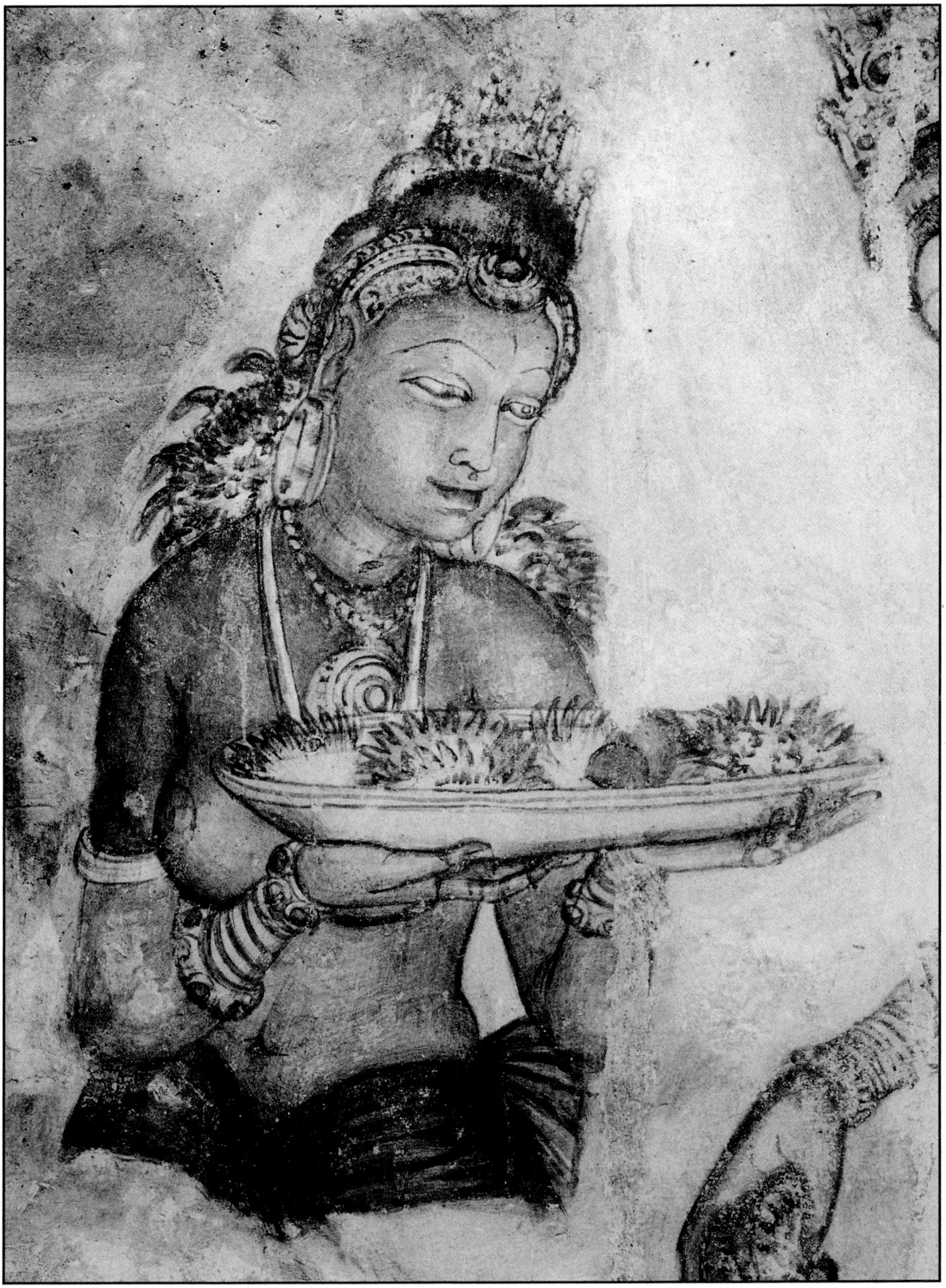

Pl. XXXI : Sīgiriya, Fresco on rock face.

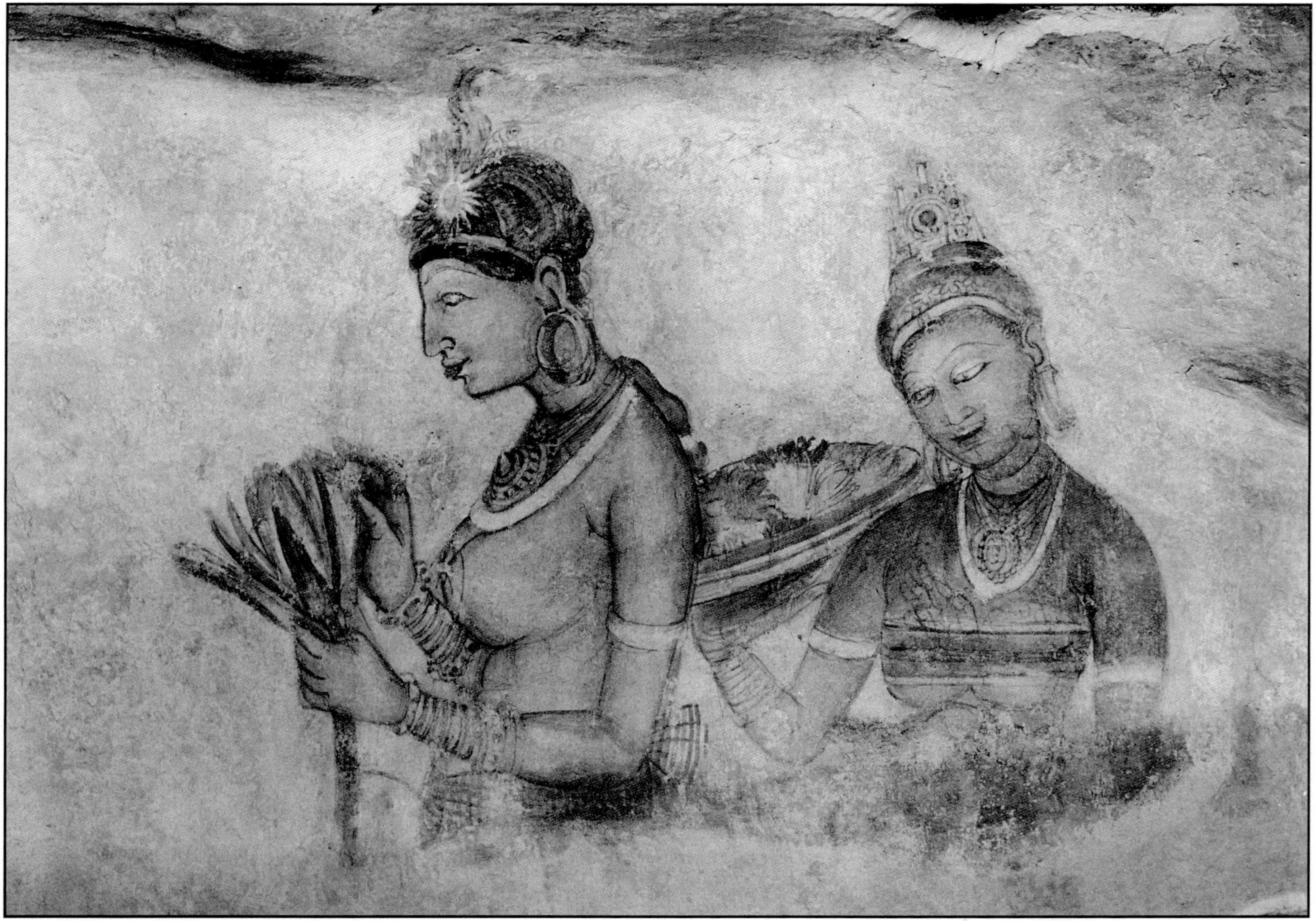

Pl. XXXII : Sīgiriya, Fresco on rock face.

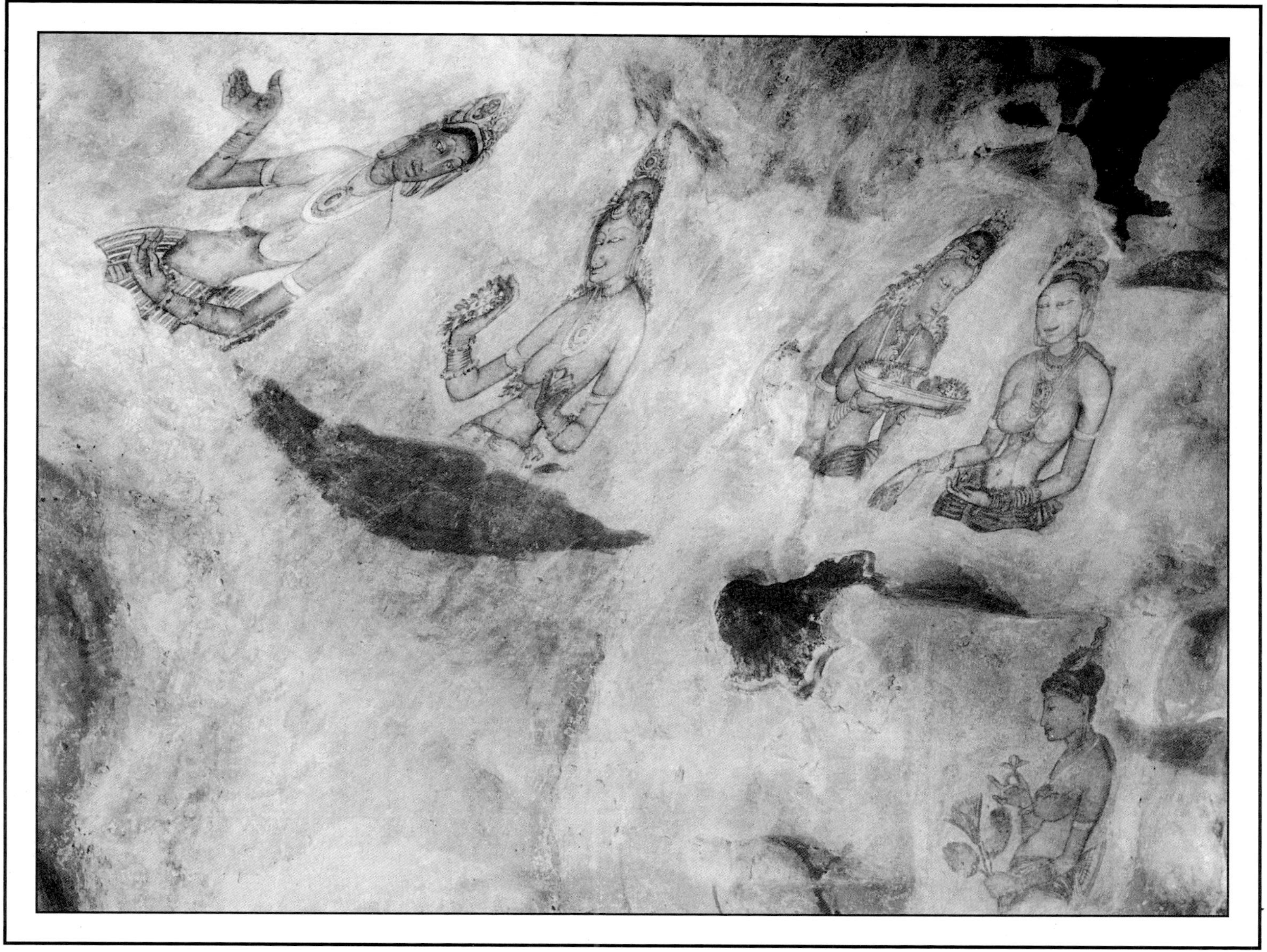

Pl. XXXIII :Sīgiriya, Fresco on rock face.

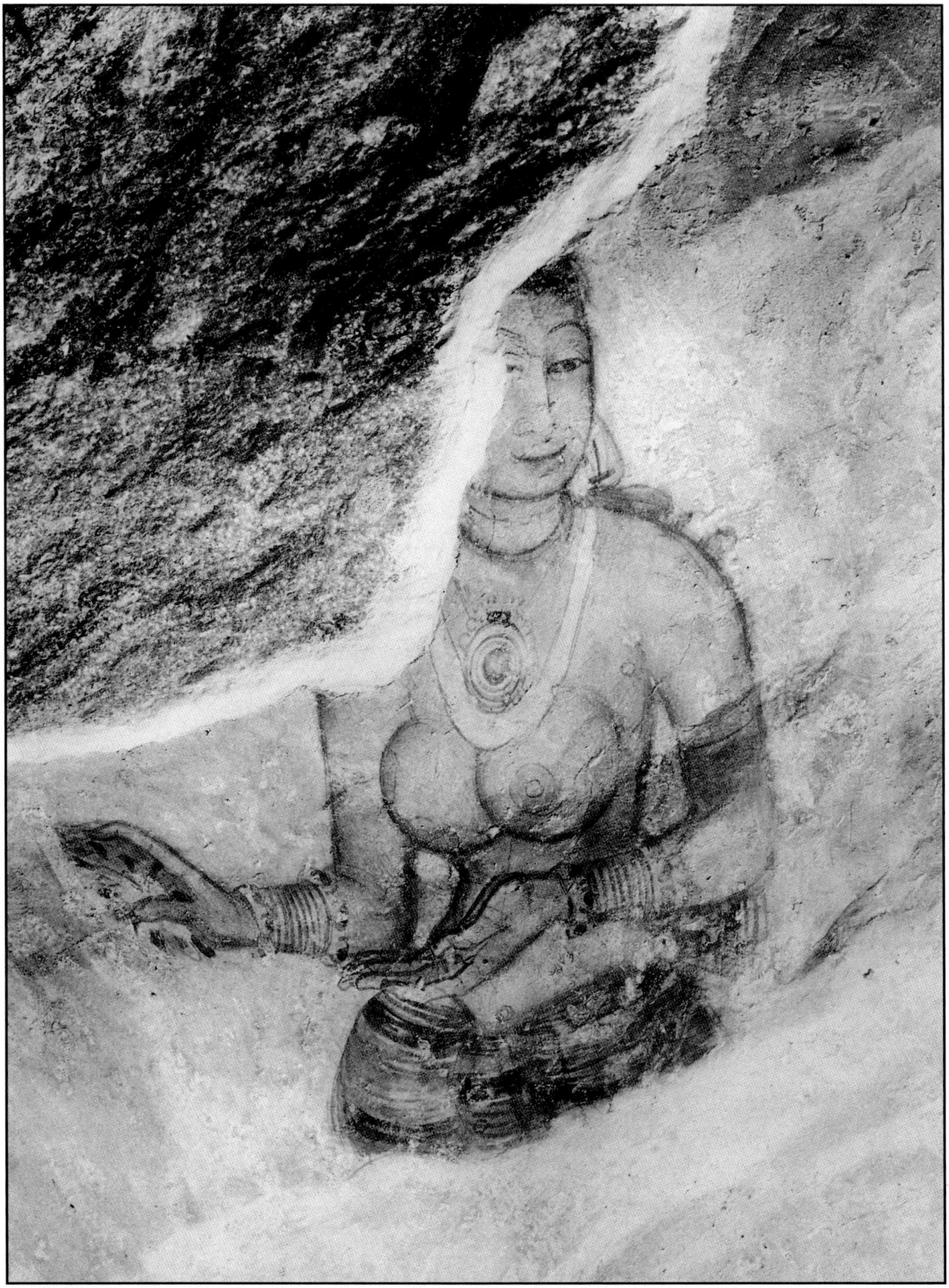

PL. XXXIV : Sīgiriya, Fresco on rock face.

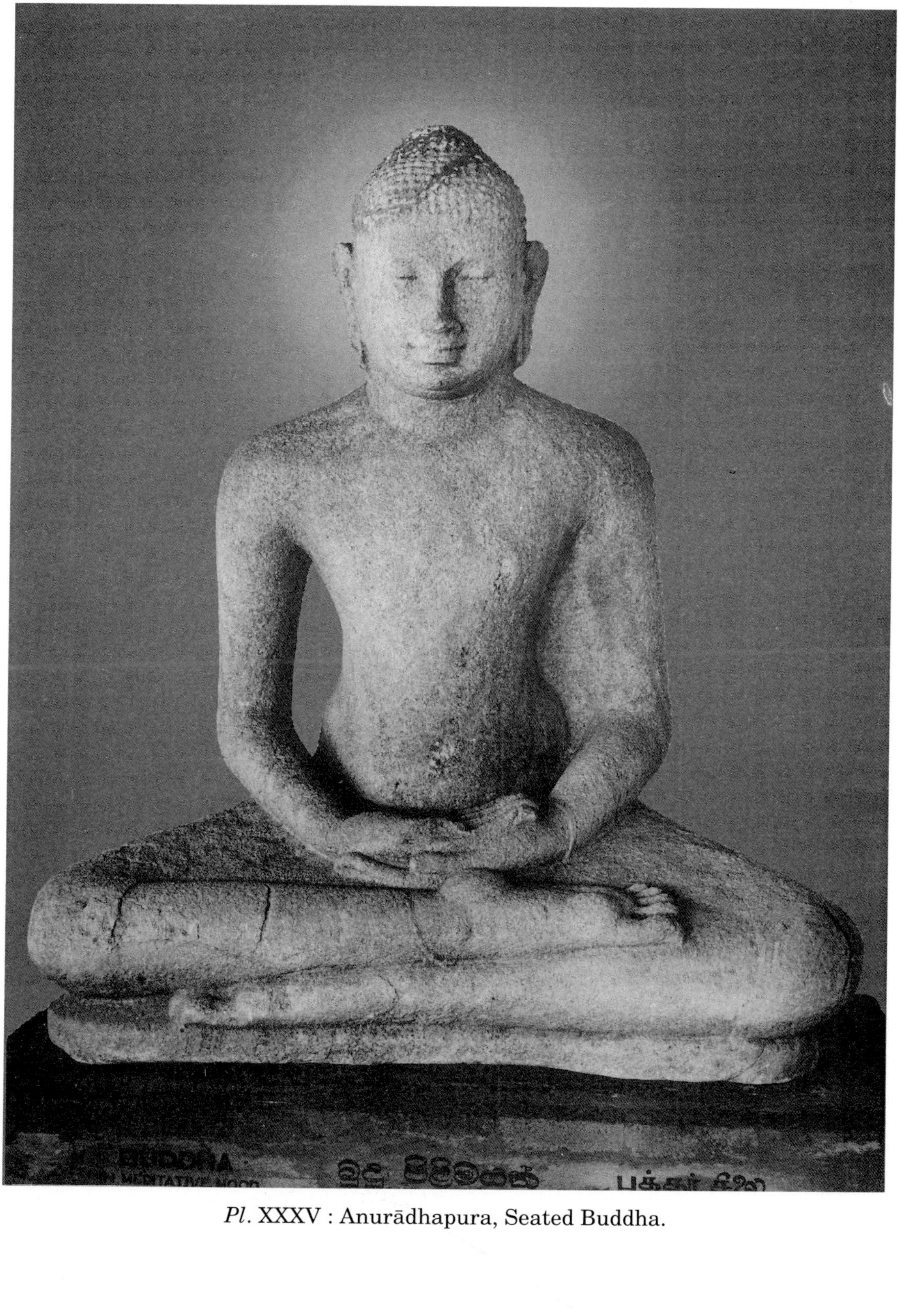

Pl. XXXV : Anurādhapura, Seated Buddha.

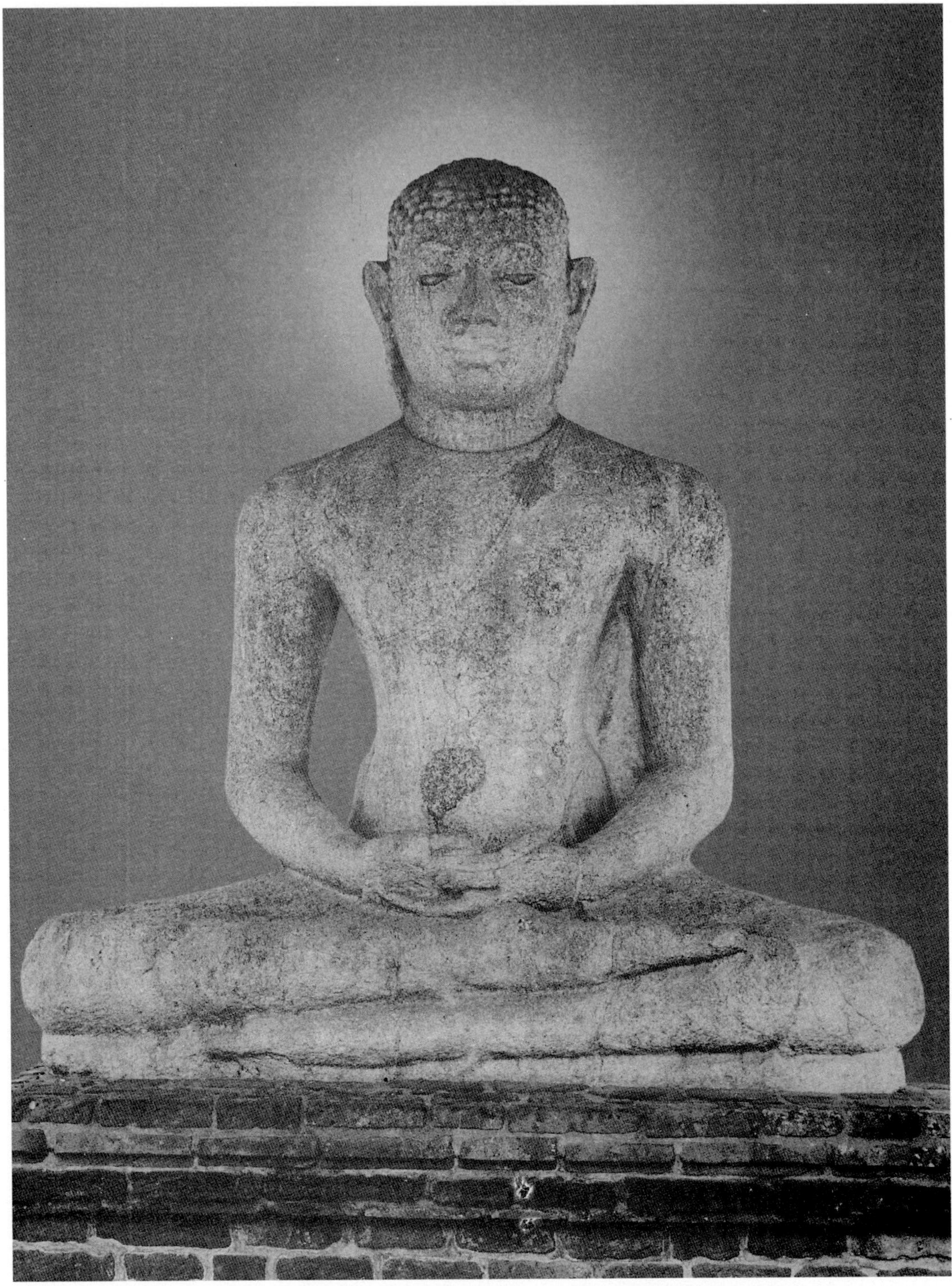

Pl. XXXVI : Anurādhapura, Samādhi Buddha on outer circular road.

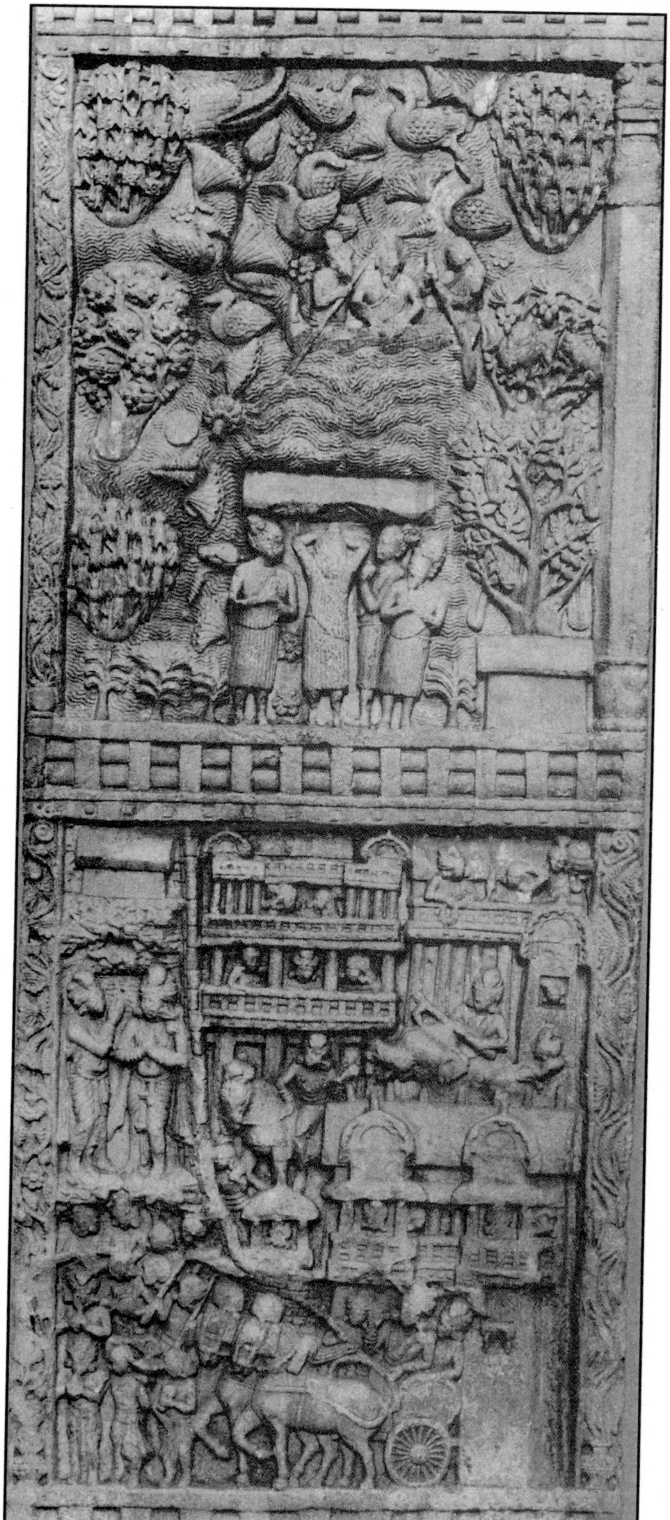

Pl. XXXVII : Sāñcī, Eastern Gateway — Buddha walking on water.

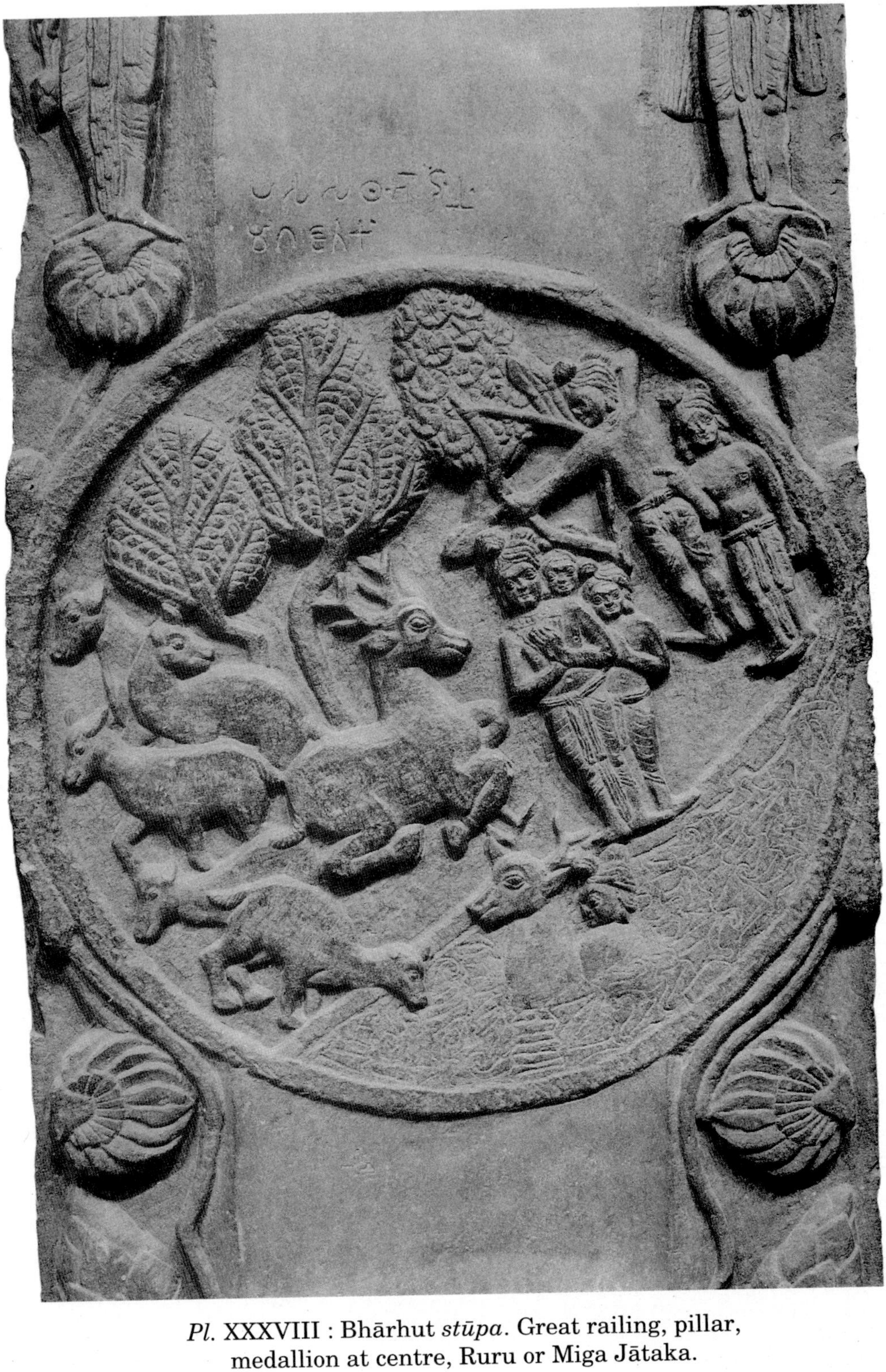

Pl. XXXVIII : Bhārhut *stūpa*. Great railing, pillar, medallion at centre, Ruru or Miga Jātaka.

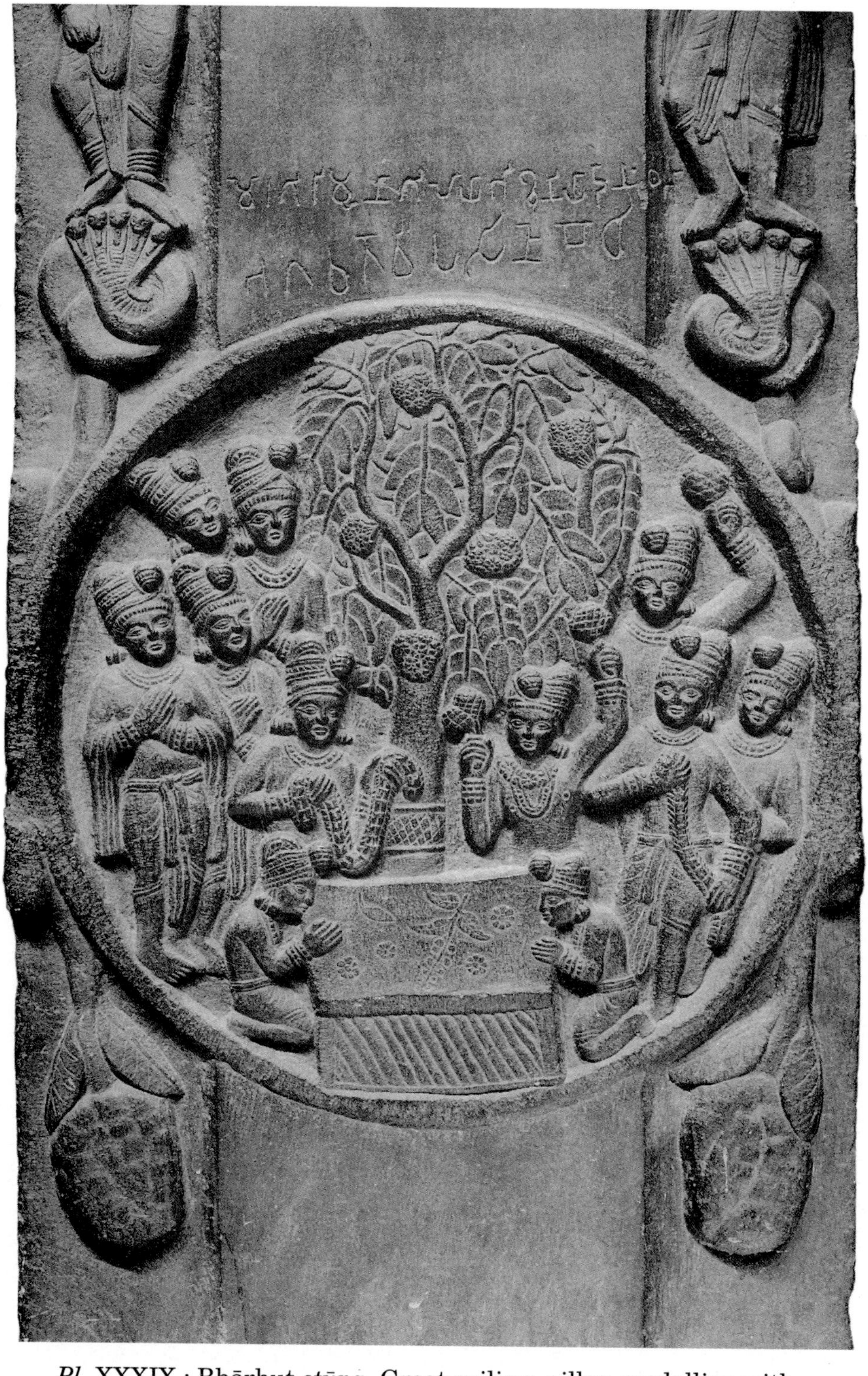

Pl. XXXIX : Bhārhut *stūpa*. Great railing, pillar, medallion with Patali tree, Bodhi tree of Buddha Vipasyan.

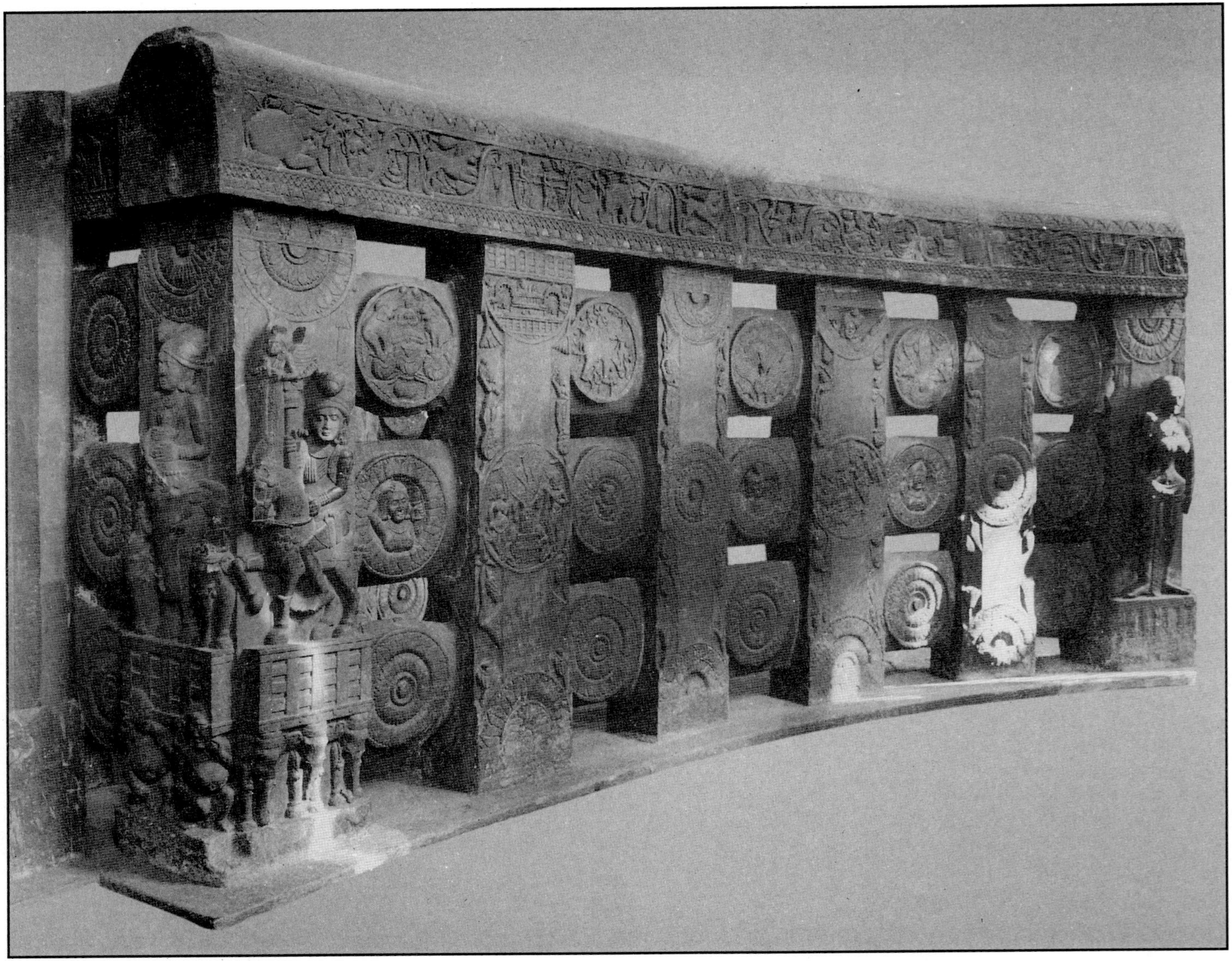

Pl. XL : Bhārhut *stūpa*. Great railing.

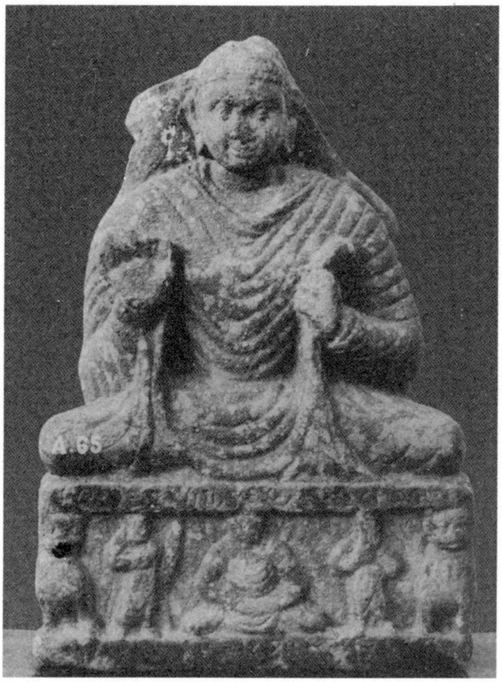

Pl. XLI : Buddha seated in *abhaya-mudrā*.

Pl. XLII : Buddhạ's bust part in Gupta era.

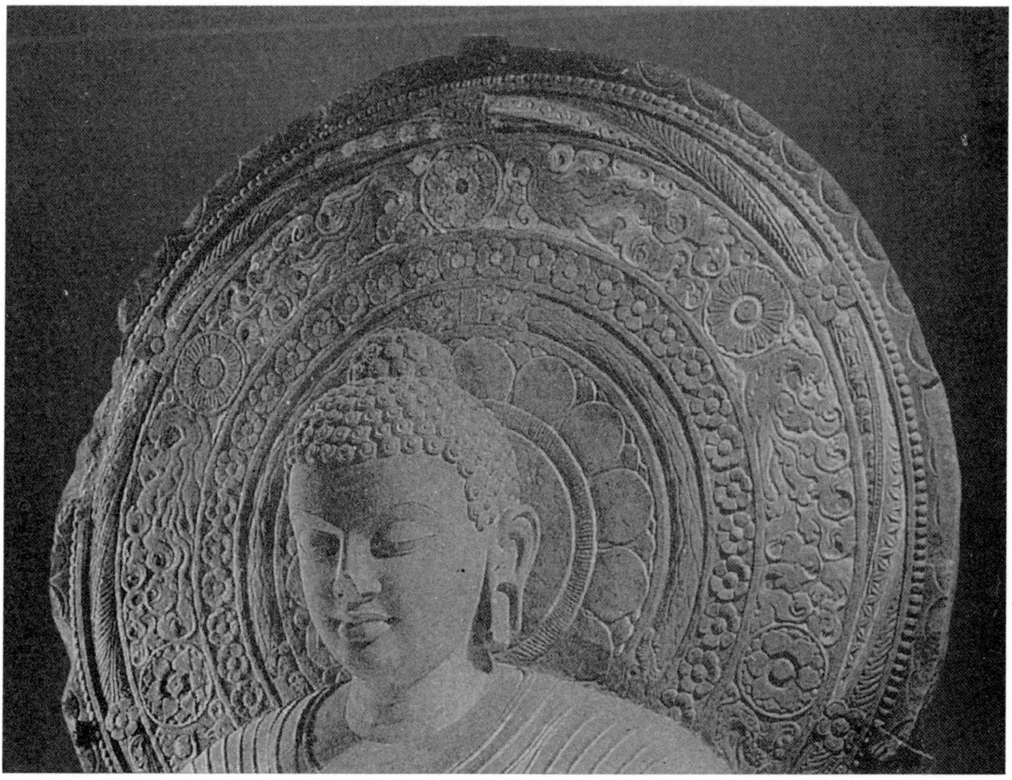

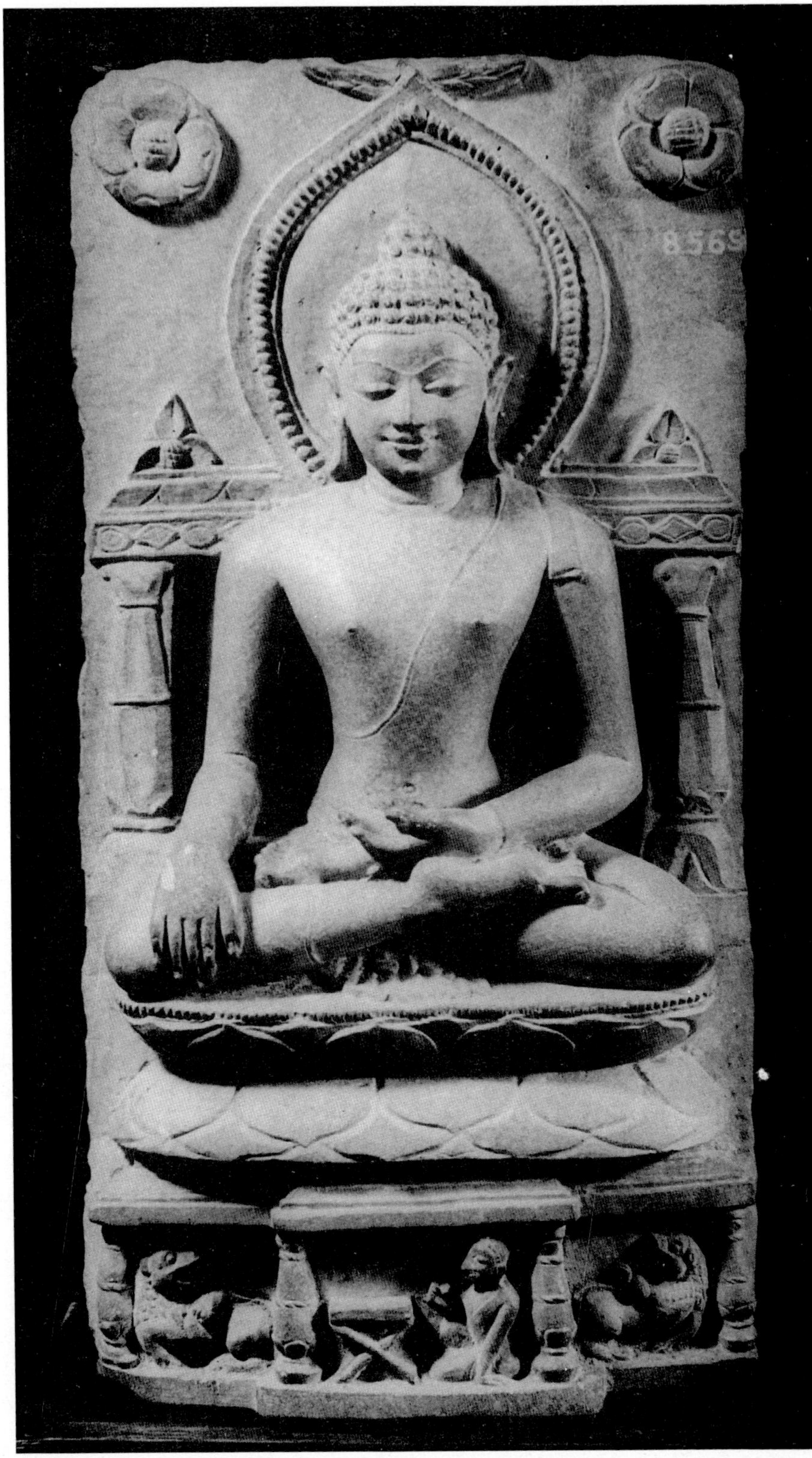

Pl. XLIII : Śākyamuni Buddha.

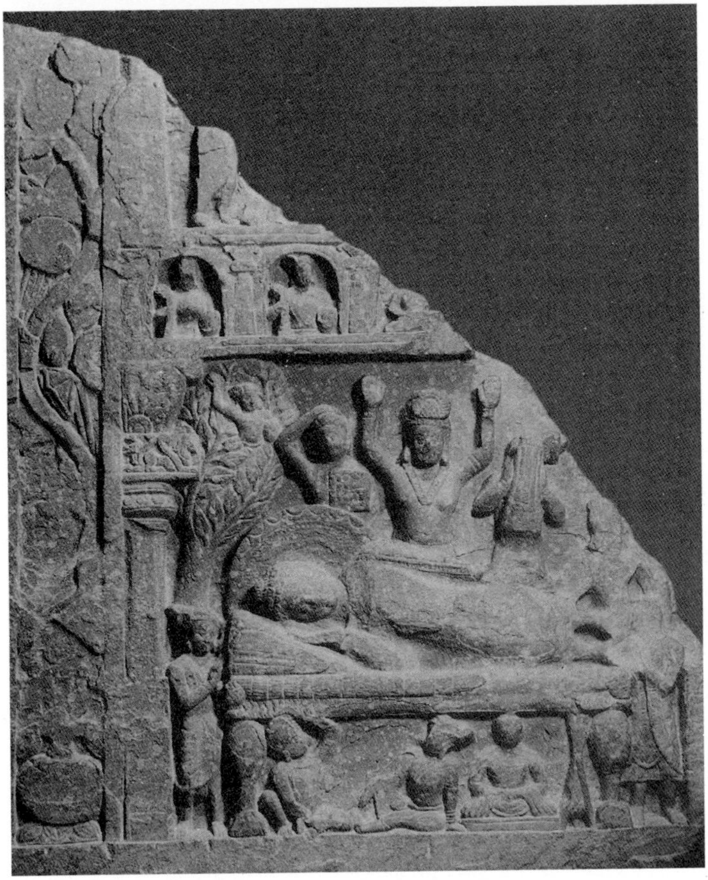

Pl. XLIV : Relief showing the exterior of Buddha.

Pl. XLV : Lion, Sri Lanka.

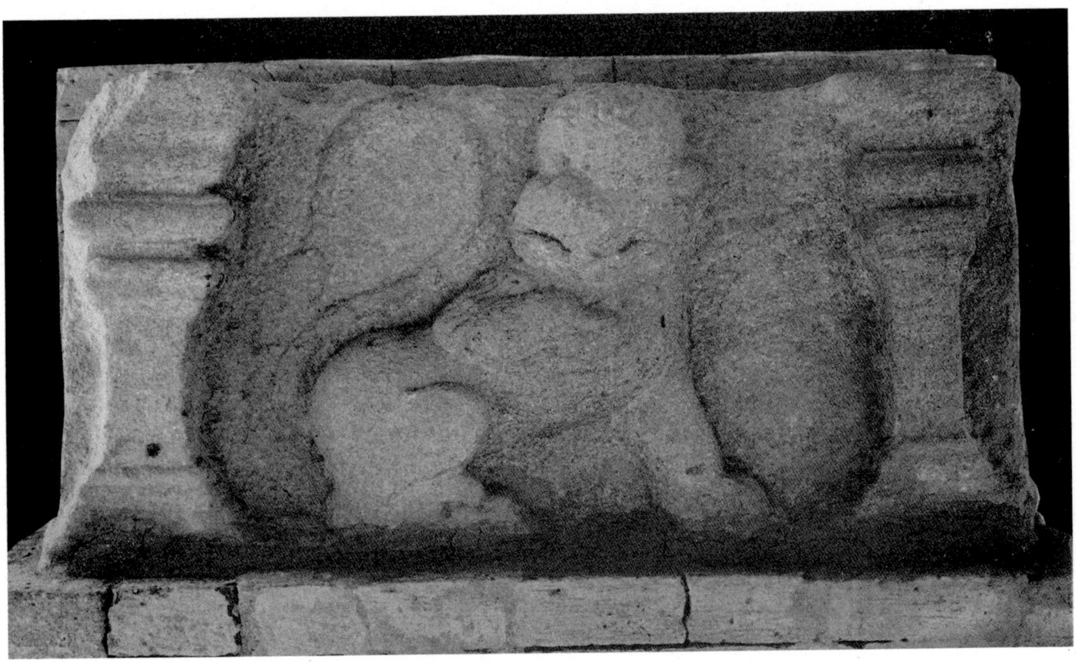

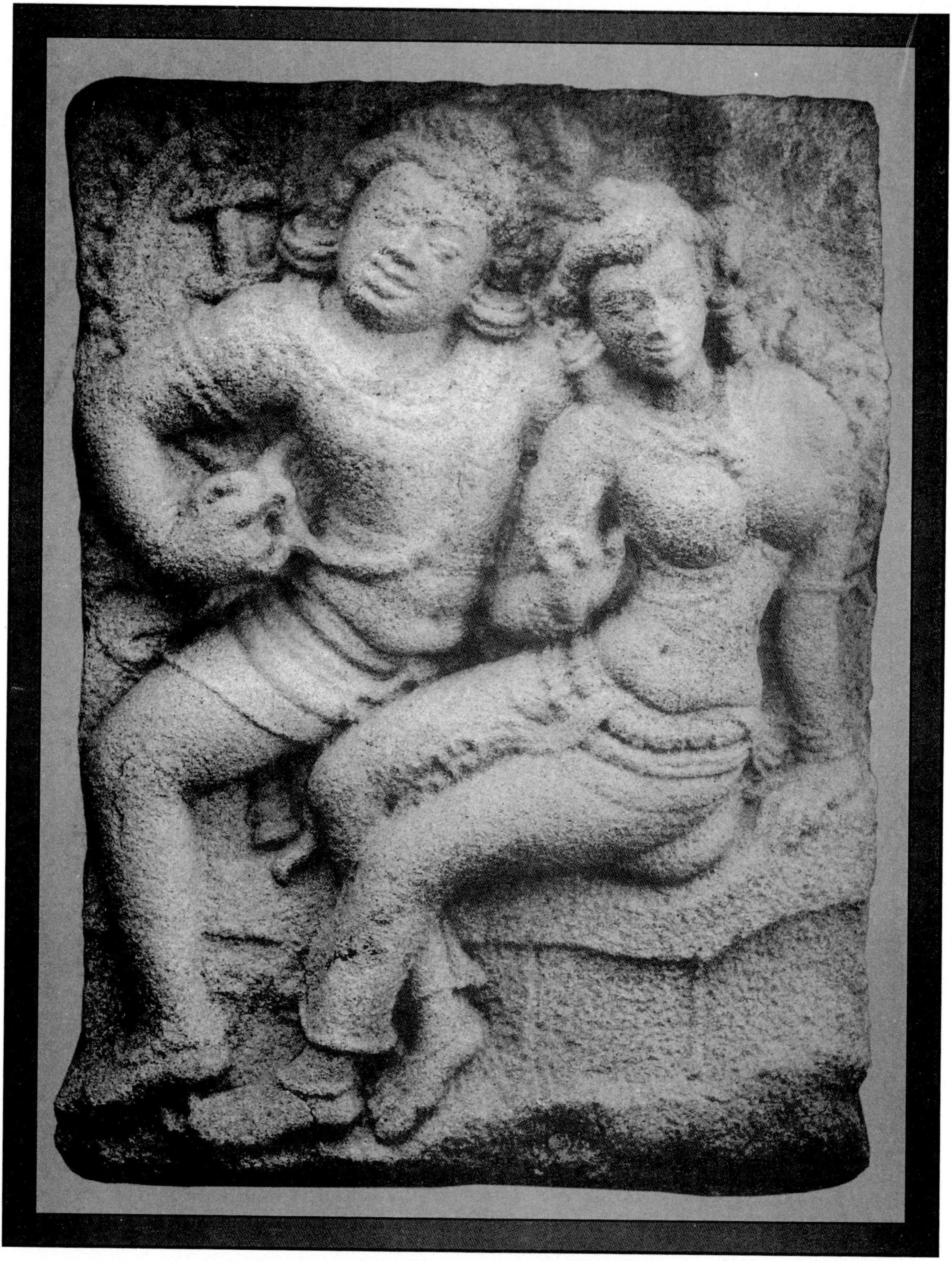

Pl. XLVI : Mithune couples at Anurādhapura, Sri Lanka.

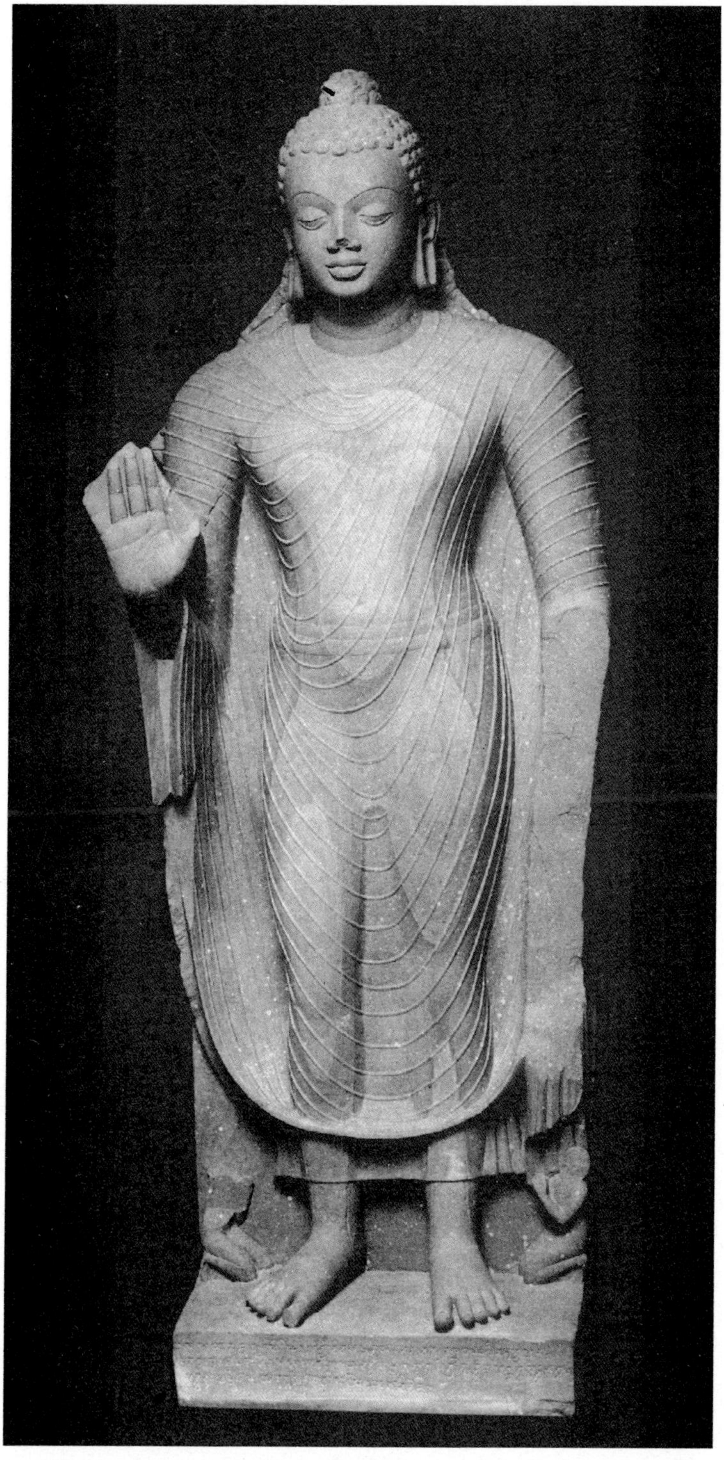

Pl. XLVII : Buddha standing.

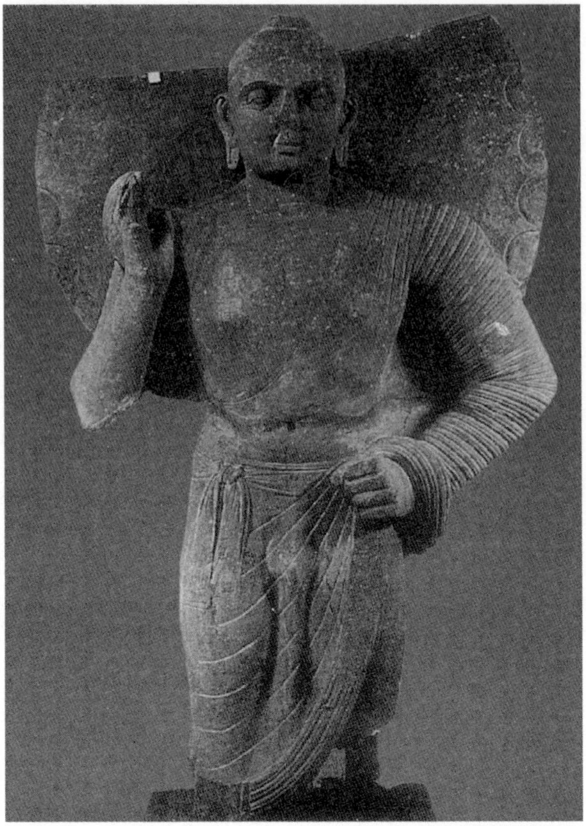

Pl. XLVIII : Standing Buddha, Kuṣāṇa.

Pl. IL : Headless Buddha seated.

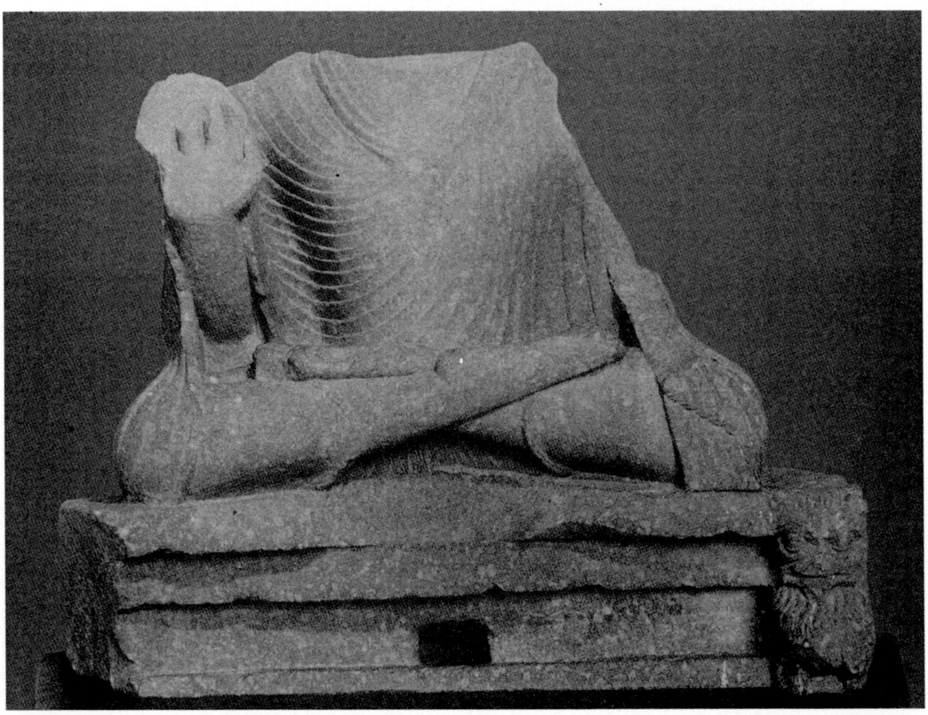

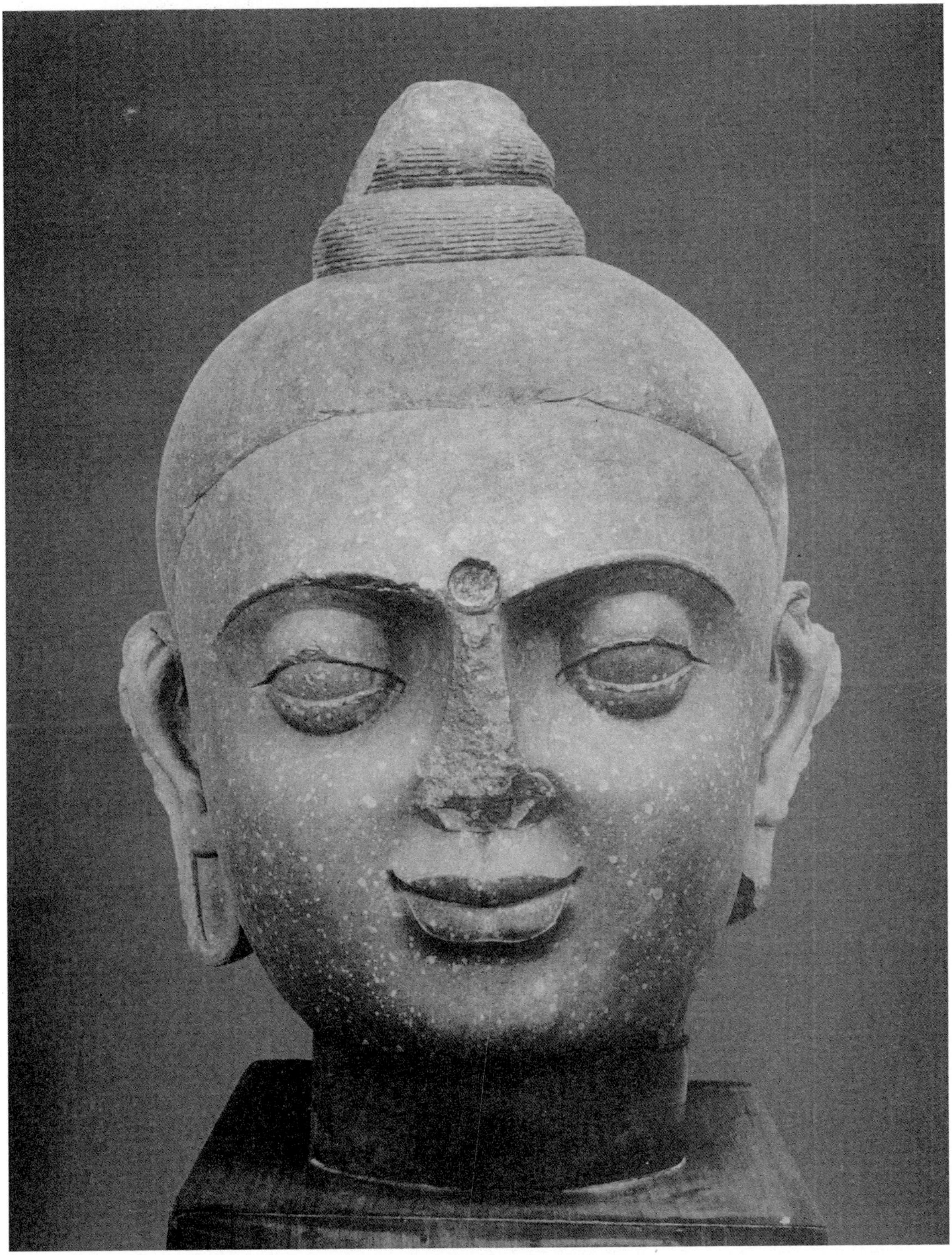

Pl. L : Colossal Buddha Head.

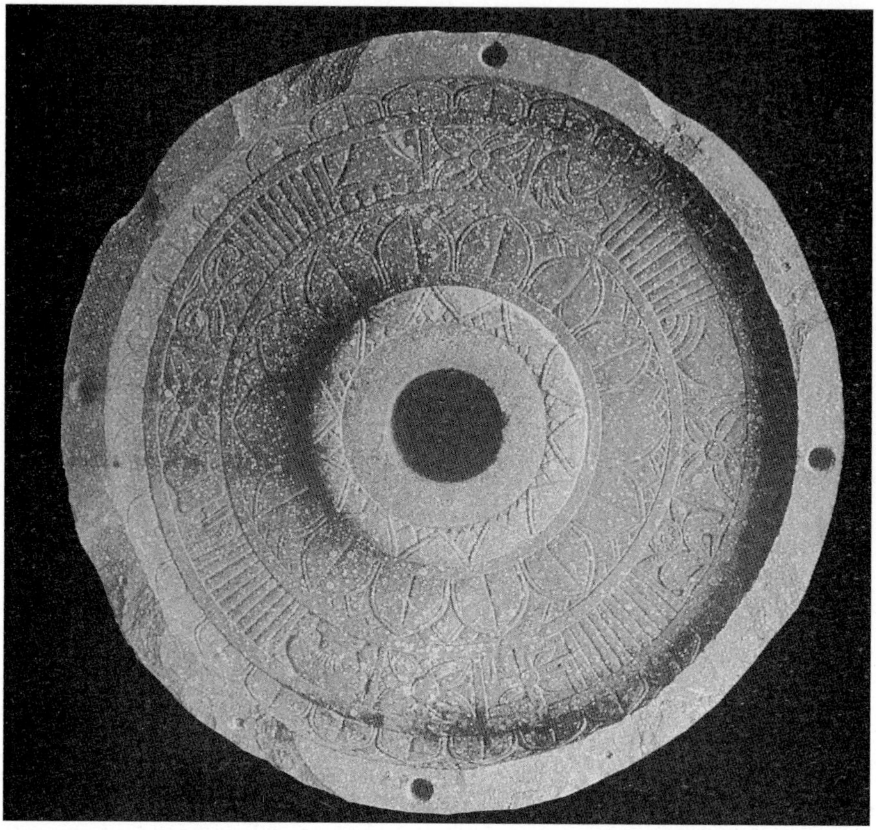

Pl. LI : Parasol with several auspicious motifs.

Pl. LII : Bowl with creeper decoration probably representing the begging bowl of Buddha.

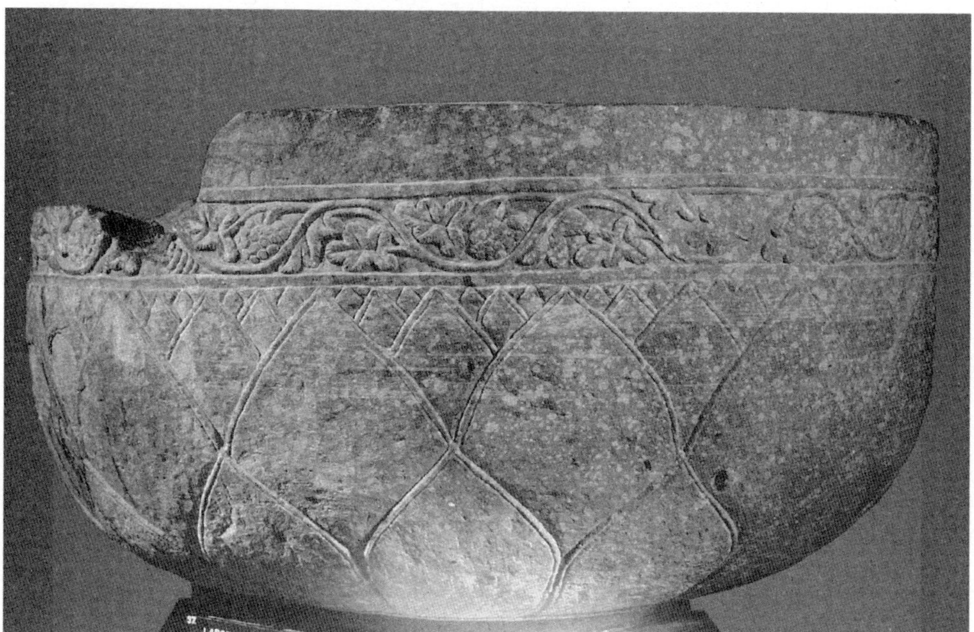

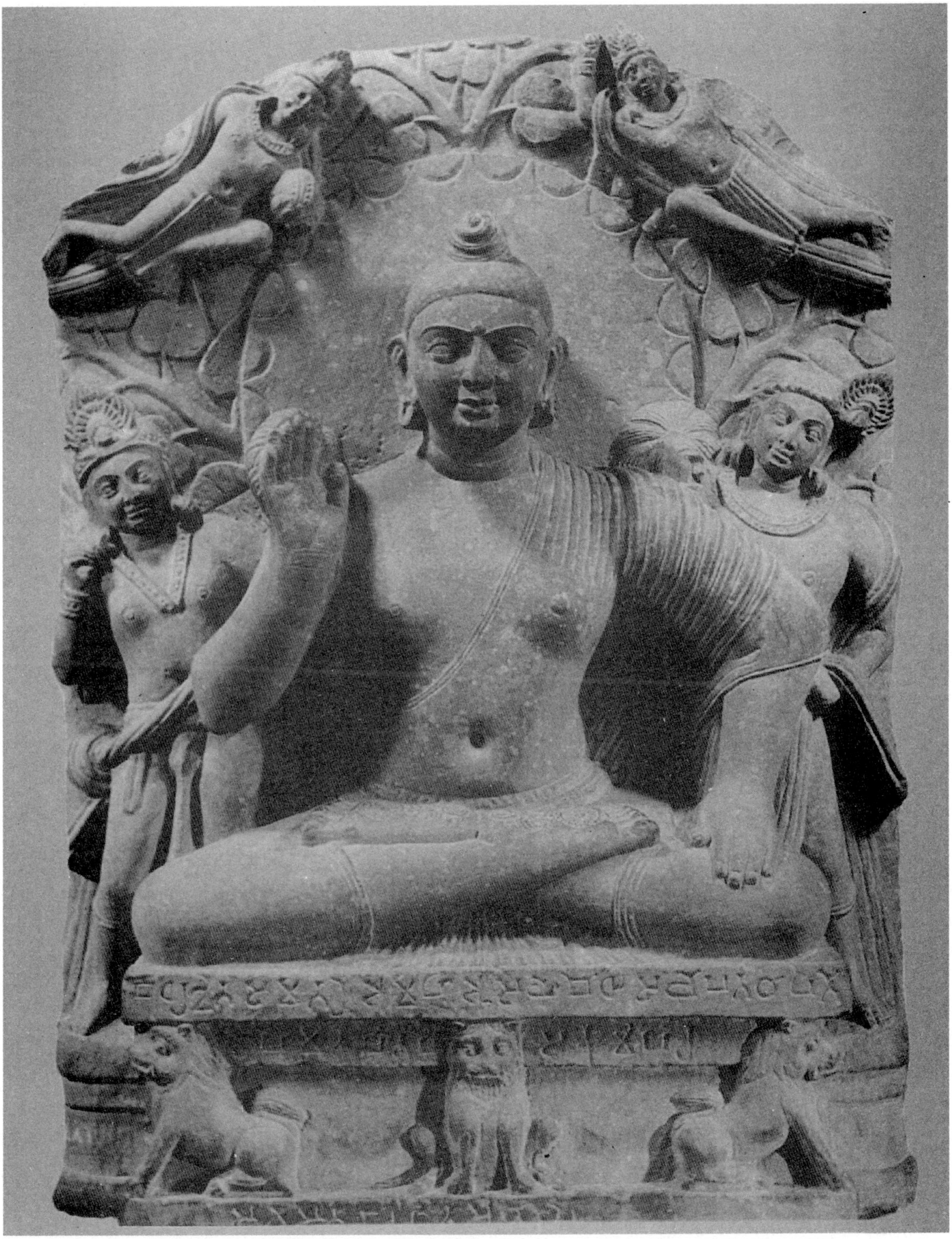

Pl. LIII : Inscribed image of Buddhisattva installed by Buddharakhita.

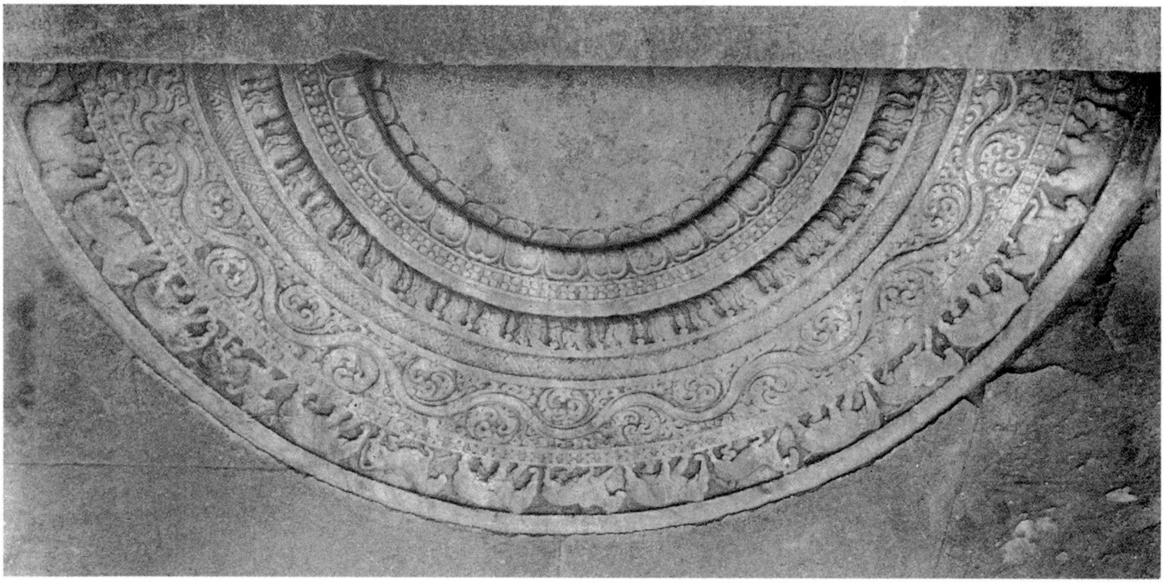

Pl. LIV : Moon stone, Sri Lanka.

Pl. LV : Buddhist railing South of Jetavana Dagaba.

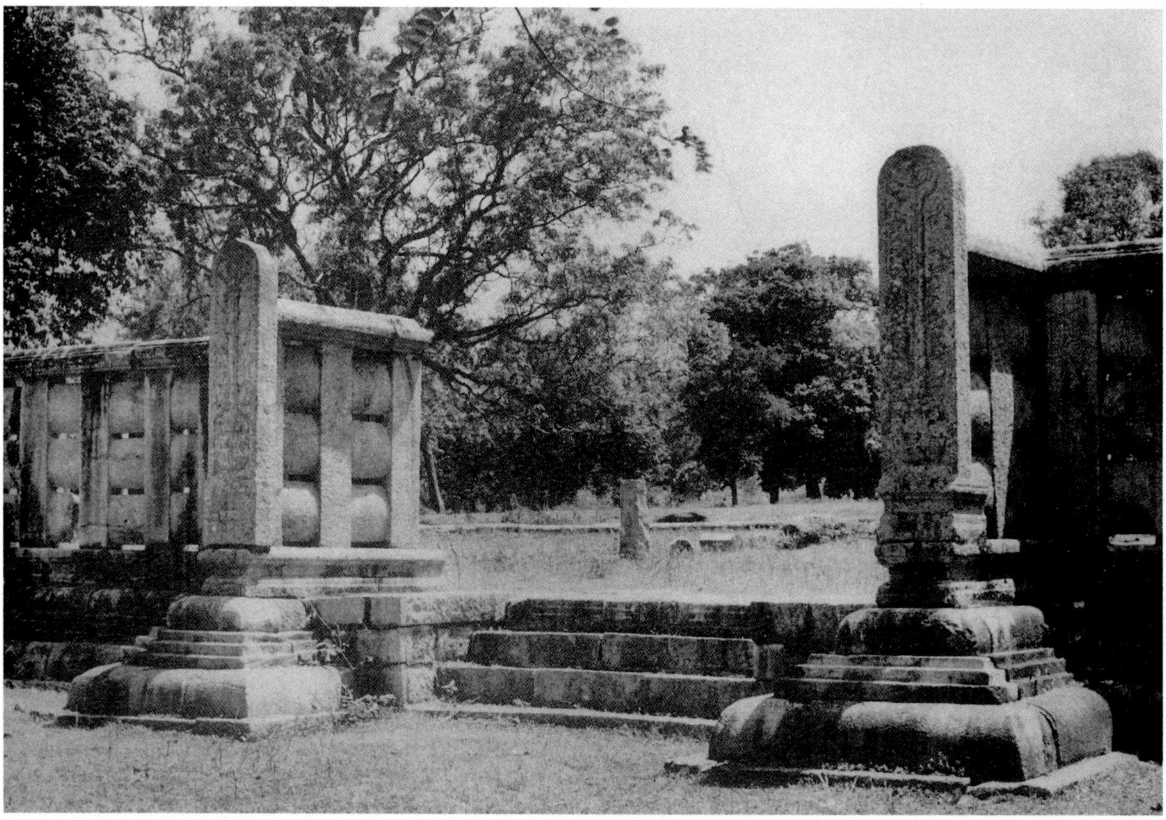

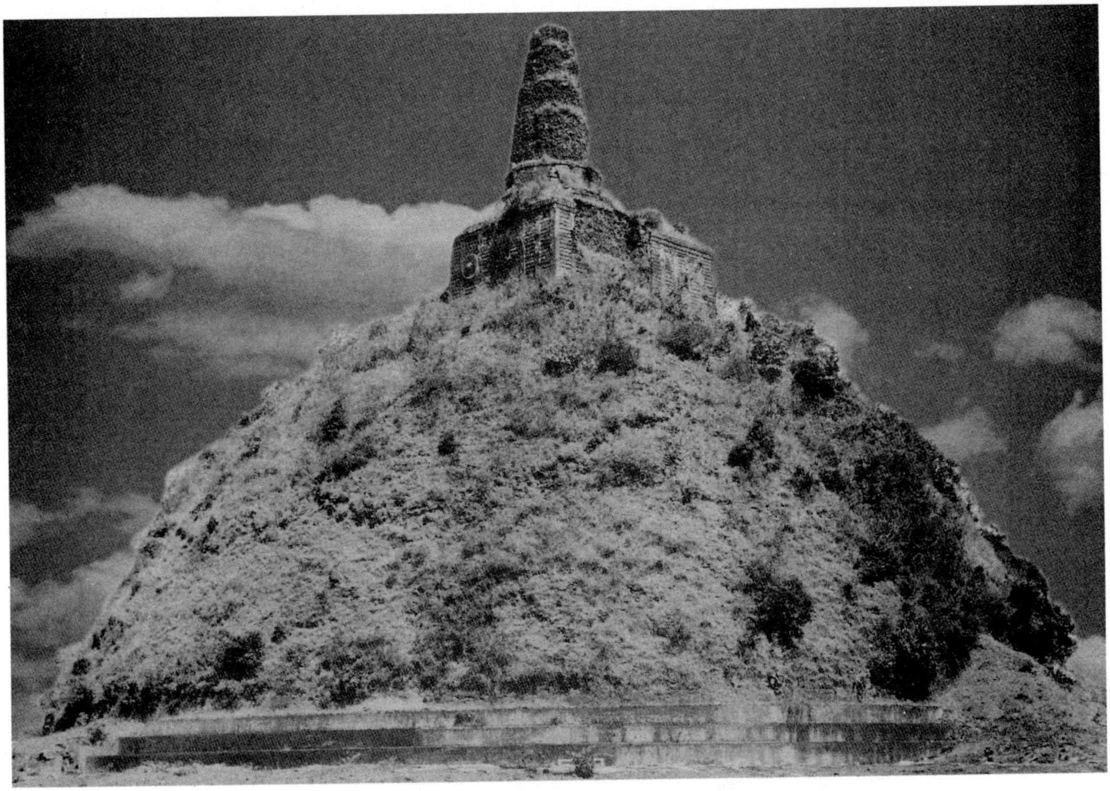

Pl. LVI : Abhayagiri Dagaba at Anurādhapura, Sri Lanka.

Pl. LVII : Jetavana Dagaba — General View, Sri Lanka.

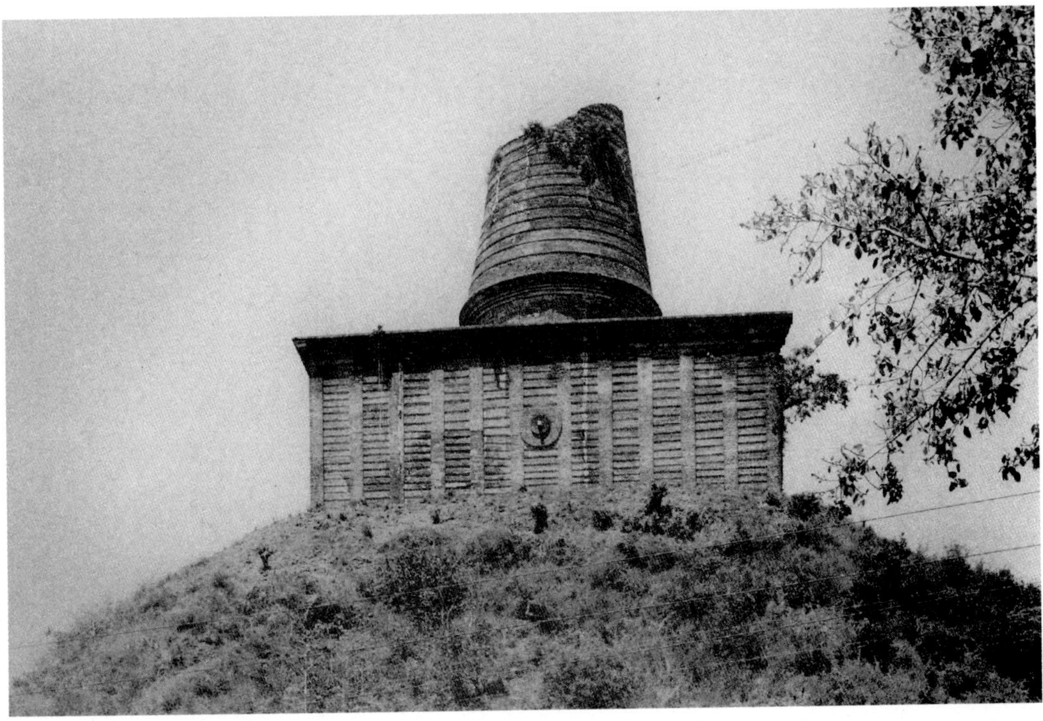

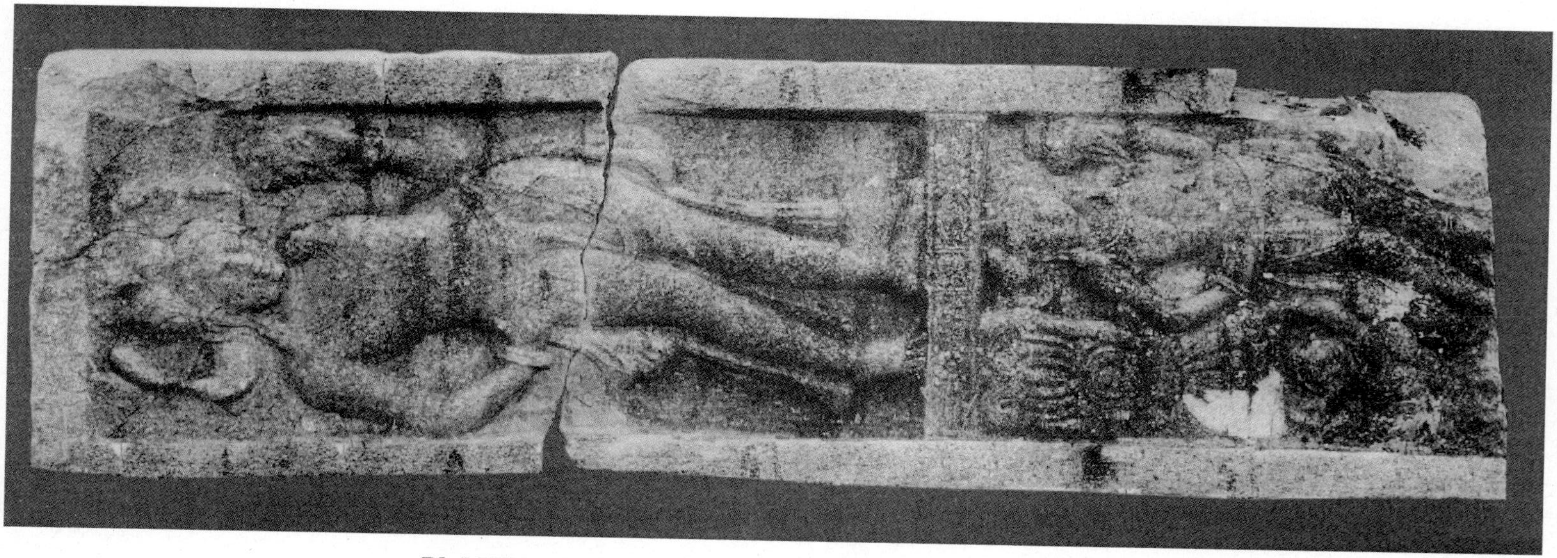

Pl. LVIII : Naga-dvārapāla, Jetavana Dagaba, Sri Lanka.

Glossary

Abacus : A square or rectangular table, An Abacus is a frame holding rods with sliding beads on them.

Abhisārikā : A damsel — a young unmarried woman. It is an old fashioned literary word.

Aisle : Lateral divisions; a narrow gap that separates rows.

Alignment : Correct position.

Ambulatory: Processional path.

Amorous couples : To express sexual love.

Amulet : An object that is worn to carry good luck and protection from evil.

Aṇḍa : The hemispherical dome of the *stūpa*.

Anklets : Foot joints.

Anthropomorphic : Resulting from a belief that a god resembles a human being in appearance, feeling; it is also a belief that an animal or object has feelings like those of a human being. Early Buddhist art of Bhārhut, Sāñcī, Bodh-Gayā and Amarāvatī and other places show no anthropomorphic representation of the Master. His presence is indicated by means of an empty throne, or a Bodhi tree or a pair of foot prints or a *dharma-cakra*, symbolising one or the other event of his life.

Apsaras : Celestial women dancers, usually dancing at the court of God Indra.

Arboreal : Arboreal which lives in the tops of trees; animal's life style.

Arcade : Range of arches supported on piers or columns.

Architecture : A particular style in which buildings were designed and constructed especially at a particular time.

Architrave : toraṇa.

Asura : demon.

Atibhaṅga : Woman's pose with one hip vaulted outward.

Avadāna : Life of Buddha in previous years.

Avantgarde : Style of art, fashion or writing whose methods and ideas are experimental or more modern than those generally accepted. The *avant-garde* are the artists, writers, musicians, etc., who introduce new and very modern ideas.

Balustrade: A small pillar or column.

Bangles: Band of glass that is worm round a wrist, generally Indian ladies are decorated with the bangles.

Baroque : Grotesque, fantastic.

Bas-relief : Bas-relief is a sculpture carved on a surface so that it stands out from the background.

Beaded : Cushion dress, decorated with beads.

Bodice : Above the waist; the bodice of a dress is the upper part of it.

Bodhi tree : (*Ficus religiosa*), *pīpal* tree, beneath this tree Buddha got enlightenment. The *bodhi* tree is not only sacred Buddhist symbol but Hindu also. In the *Bhagavad Gītā* Lord Kṛṣṇa proclaims 'of trees I am *aśvattha* (*bodhi* or tree of wisdom)'. The worship of the Bodhi tree have been prevalent and in the *Divyāvadāna*, it is mentioned that Bodhi tree was Aśoka's favourite object of worship.

Border lines : something that is border line is very nearly unacceptable.

Bust: It is a statue of the head, it is also used for women's breasts.

*Bodhisattva*s: One of the main interest of Bhārhut sculpture consists in the representation of the birth-stories of Gautama Buddha. These stories (or the *Jātaka*s) are of two main classes, those relating to the previous births of Buddha as a *bodhisattva* and his last appearance as Gautama when he attained Enlightenment of Buddhahood.

Cakravarti: In ancient times, a King got name and fame because of his charming manners and prosperity. He used to take care of the public.

Canopy : It is a cover in order to provide shelter or as a decoration.

Capital : Upper portion of a column.

Cakra : Sacred wheel of law.

Caitya : Prayer hall. Originally it was called *cita* — a tumulus.

Cankrama : Place of the promenade of the Buddha at Gayā.

Carving: A decorative object that has been cut out of stone, a design; it is the art.

Chef-d'oeuvre : Masterpiece.

Coral : A hard substance used to make jewellery. Coral is a small sea animal and its skelton forms Coral.

Crescent : Moonlike.

Crest jewel : Decorated with jewels; this happens to be a sign of a noble family; who belongs to a high social class.

Dagaba : *Stūpa*. In Sinhalese language, *stūpa* is called *dagaba*.

Dazzling colours : When one is extremely impressed by the skill, qualities and beauty of the pictures.

Dharmacakra : Wheel of the Law.

Dome: Round roof.

Drapery : A piece of cloth when hanged looks attractive. These are also called thick curtains.

Eaves : Lower edges of its roof.

Enamel : A substance like glass which is decorative.

Emerald : A precious stone bright green in colour.

Extant: Something that still exists in spite of being old.

Finial : Fishing portion of pinnacle.

Foliage : The green leaves of a plant are referred to as its foliage.

Gandharvas : Celestial musicians of Indra (Divine instrumental musician).

Garuḍa : *Vāhana* or vehicle of Viṣṇu.

Grotesque : Very exaggerated in an unpleasant way so that it looks as ridiculous.

Haṁsa: Human type based on features.

Harmika : The shaft the honorific umbrella on the *harmika* in a *stūpa*, a diminutive of *harmya* 'a small pavilion', in technical sense the pedestial on the top of a *stūpa* in which shaft of the umbrella was set.

Hellenic : Ancient Greek.

Hīnayāna : Earlier Buddhism was named as Hīnayāna.

Honey suckle : Border in Grecian art, decorative elements.

Icon : Image.

Iconography : Symbols of a subject shown through figures/drawings.

Jātaka : Stories of Buddha's past lives.

Kalaśa : Vase, pot.

Khīr: Ingredients of rice, milk, sugar or honey. Generally Indians relish this. In Sri Lanka it is prepared as salty.

Lalita : Delicate.

Mahābhārata: Famous epic by Vyāsa on the events of Kaurava and Pāṇḍava.

Mahāyāna : Later development of Buddhism, i.e., after Hīnayāna.

Mellowing of colour : Things objects princes appear golden, soft and rich in colour.

Mithuna : Loving couple.

Monastery : It is a building or collection of buildings in which monks live together and perform their religious activities.

Monolith : Single block of stone shaped into a pillar or a monument. Aśoka erected a large number of monolithic pillars.

Monument : A large structure made of stone which is build to remind people of an event in history.

Mudrā : Language of the hands and fingers.

Mural : Wall paintings, wall decorations. [The mural paintings in the Ajantā caves of the Vākāṭaka period have scenes from Buddha's life from the conception to enlightenment.] Mahāyānists defied Buddha and introduced *bodhisattvas*. Avalokiteśvara became most popular because of his great compassion for the living creatures.

Nāga : Semi divine snake.

Niche : A hollow area in a wall which can be used to hold a statue.

Nubile : Young physically mature and sexually attractive woman.

Palmette : Honeysuckle look like the snake hood. It is also called *nāgapuṣpa*.

Panel : Recessed compartment in a wall.

Pendant : Piece of jewellery which is attached to a chain or thong and is worn in a neck.

Pinnacle : *Guldastā*.

Pokuna : Bathing tank.

Portico : Space enclosed within columns.

Promenade : A place for a slow walk or pleasure.

Railing : A kind of fence made from metal bars.

raison d'etre: purpose that accounts for,

Rāmāyaṇa: The famous Indian epic, author — Goswami Tulsidas. Story of king Rāma and king Rāvaṇa (of Sri Lanka) make the epic more interesting.

Rampart : Broad mound or structure.

Rasa : Moods and emotions.

Refectory : Dining hall in a monastery.

Relic Chamber : A place where an object which has survived from the past into the present and is still used. Relic is a body or something closely associated with a saint, which is treated as holy.

Relief : It is a sculpture that is carved out of a flat vertical surface.

Roselte: Fixed to a doorleaf.

Śāla : Hall.

Scroll : A long roll of paper or other material with writing on.

Shaft : A portion of a column between base and capital.

Toraṇa : Architectural feature in Buddhist art, gateway.

Śālabhañjika : Damsels, *apsaras* or beautiful ladies, damsel under a *śāl* tree.

Vahalkades : Decorative projecting shrine in Sinhalese *stūpa*s or *dagaba*s.

Varnikabaṅga: Making of colours to produce effect of modelling.

Vihāra : Monastery.

Webbed fingers : Feet, toes or fingers having a piece of skin between them.

Yaksha : Semi-divine being.

Yogi: A person who has spent several years, practising meditation and he acquired of the Supreme Being.

Bibliography

Original sources

Culvaṁsa, 2 vols. (ed.), W. Geiger, London, 1925.

Mahāvaṁsa (tr.), W. Geiger, Colombo, 1950.

The Chronicles of the Island or *Dīpavaṁsa* (ed.), B.C. Law, Ceylon, 1959.

Dīpavaṁsa (tr.), Herman Oldenberg, New Delhi, rept. 1982.

Dhammapada, S. Radhakrishnan, Madras, 1977.

Works in Sinhalese language

Guruge, W.P. Ananda, *Buddhist Art of India*, Saman Publishers Ltd., Mahargama, Sri Lanka, 1962.

Nandadeva, Wijesekera, *Perini Singala Bitu Situbeen*, Govt. Department, Colombo, 1964.

Paranavitana, S., *Sinhalavo*, Colombo, 1967.

Suravir, A.V., *Anuradhpur Sanskriti*, Saman Mudralaya, Mahargama, 1961.

Wijayaratne, B.S., *History of Sri Lanka Art and Painting*, Lake House, Colombo, 1982.

Wickramasinghe, Martin, *Sinhala Lakuna*, Saman Publishers Ltd., Mahargama, Sri Lanka, 1947.

———, *Sinhala Sakaskada A Collection of Essays on Culture and Anthropology*, Saman Publishers Ltd., Mahargama, Ceylon, 1962.

———, *Ape Vitti*, compiled by ERS Sarachchandra, Saman Publishers Ltd., Mahargama, Sri Lanka, 1959.

———, *Atta-Yuta*, M.D. Gunasena and Co. Ltd., Colombo, 1957.

———, *Vichar Lipi*, Mount Yatralalaya, Galtissa, 1953.

Modern works in English language

Adikaram, E.W., *The Early History of Buddhism in Ceylon*, Colombo, 1953.

Agrawala, Prithvi K., *Early Indian Bronzes*, Prithvi Prakashan, Varanasi, 1977.

Agrawala, Vasudeva S., *The Heritage of Indian Art*, Publication Division, Ministry of Information and Broadcasting, 1964.

———, *Studies in Indian Art*, Vishwavidyalaya Prakashan, Varanasi, 1965.

———, *Masterpieces of Mathurā Sculpture*, Prithivi Prakashan, Varanasi, 1985.

———, *Sarnath*, Archaeological Survey of India, fifth edn., New Delhi, 1992.

Ahir, D.C., *Buddhist Shrines in India*, B.R. Publishing Corporation, New Delhi, 1986.

———, *Heritage of Buddhism*, B.R. Publishing Corporation, New Delhi, 1989.

Asher, Frederick, M., *The Art of Eastern India 300-800*, The University of Minnesota Press, Minneapolis, 1980.

Bajpai, K.D., *Five Phases of Indian Art*, Rajasthani Vidya Prakashan, Jodhpur, 1991.

Bandaranayake, Senake, Jaya Singhe, *Gamini, The Rock and Wall Paintings of Sri Lanka*, Lake House Bookshop, Colombo, 1986.

Bandaranaike, S., *Sinhalese Monastic Architecture: Vihāras of Anurādhapura*, Leiden, 1974.

Bapat, P.V. (ed.), *2500 Years of Buddhism*, Ministry of Information and Broadcasting, New Delhi, 1956.

Barua, B.M., *Bharhut Part I, II and III*, Indological Book Corporation, Patna, 1979.

Barua, Dipak Kumar, *Vihāras in Ancient India: A Survey of Buddhist Monasteries*, Indian Publication, Calcutta, 1969.

Benjamin, Rowland Jr., *The Wall Paintings of India, Central Asia and Ceylon*, Boston, 1938.

Basnayake, H.T., *Sri Lanka Monastic Architecture*, Sri Satguru Publication, Delhi, 1986.

Bhattacharya, Benoytosh, *The Indian Buddhist Iconography*, Cosmo Publication, New Delhi, 1985.

Biswas, T.K., Jha, Bhogendra, *Gupta Sculptures*, Bharat Kala Bhawan, 1985.

Brown, Percy, *Indian Architecture Buddhist and Hindu Periods*, D.B. Taraporevala Sons and Co. Pvt. Ltd., "Treasure House of Books", Bombay, 1965.

Burgess, James, *The Rock Temples of Ajantā*, Susil Gupta, Publishers, New Delhi, 1970.

Cave, H.W., *The Ruined Cities of Ceylon*, Asian Educational Services, New Delhi, reprint, 1984.

Chandra, Pramod, *The Sculpture of India 3000 BC-AD1300*, National Gallery of Arts (4B), 1985.

Codrington, H.W., *A Short History of Ceylon*, Macmillian and Co. Ltd., London, 1947.

Copleston, Reginald Stephen, *Buddhism Primitive and Present in Magadha and in Ceylon*, Asian Educational Services, New Delhi, reprint, 1984.

Coomaraswamy, Ananda K., *Yakṣas*, Munshiram Manoharlal Publishers Pvt. Ltd., New Delhi, 1980.

———, *Early Indian Architecture*, Munshiram Manoharlal Publishers Pvt. Ltd., New Delhi, 1991.

———, *Buddha and the Gospel of Buddhism*, Munshiram Manoharlal Publishers Pvt. Ltd., Delhi, 1985.

———, *History of Indian and Indonesian Art*, Dover Publications Inc., New York.

———, *Elements of Buddhist Iconography*, Munshiram Manoharlal Publishers Pvt. Ltd., New Delhi, 1972.

———, *Medieval Sinhalese Art*, New York, 1956.

Coomaraswamy, Ananda K. and Horner, I.B., *The Living Thoughts Gotama the Buddha*, Munshiram Manoharlal Publishers Pvt. Ltd., New Delhi, 1982.

Davids Rhys T.W., *Buddhist India*, Indological Book House, Delhi, 1970.

Dehejia, Vidya, *Early Buddhist Rock Temples — A Chronological Study*, Thames and Hudson, London, 1972.

Devendra, D.T., *Classical Sinhalese Culture*, London, 1958.

Dey, Sri Mukul Chandra, *My Pilgrimages to Ajantā and Bāgh*, Gian Publishing House, Delhi, 1986.

Ghosh, A., *Nalanda*, Director General Archaeological Survey of India, New Delhi, 1986.

Gokhale, B.G., *New Light on Early Buddhism*, Popular Prakashan, Bombay, 1994.

Grunwedel, Albert, *Buddhist Art in India*, Cosmo Publications, New Delhi, 1985.

Gunasinghe, Siri, *An Album of Buddhist Paintings from Sri Lanka*, National Museum, Colombo, 1978.

Gupta, S.P., *The Roots of Indian Art*, B.R. Publishing Corporation, New Delhi, 1980.

Gupta, S.P. (ed.), *Kuṣāṇa Sculptures from Sanghol* (first-second century AD), Vol. I, National Museum, New Delhi, 1987.

Harish Chandra, Brahmachari Walishinha, *The Sacred City of Anurādhapura*, Asian Educational Service, New Delhi, reprint, 1985.

Harle, J.C., *Gupta Sculpture*, Clarendon Press, Oxford, 1974.

Hart, R., Raven, *Ceylon — History in Stone*, n.p.

Havell, E.B., *The Ideals of Indian Art*, Indological Book House, Varanasi, 1992.

———, *A Handbook of Indian Art*, Reprint and Transpublications, Delhi, 1974.

Holden Lord, *Ceylon*, n.p.

Hulugalle, H.A.J., *Ceylon Yesterday — Sri Lanka Today*, Stureforlaget AB, 1976.

Humphreys, Christmas, *The Buddhist Way of Life*, George Allen and Unwin Ltd., London, 1969.

Huntington, Susan L., *The Art of Ancient India*, Weather Hill, New York, 1985.

Iyer, K. Bharatha, *Indian Art — A Short Introduction*, Taraporevala, Bombay, 1982.

Jayasekera, P.V.J. (ed.), *Security Dilemma of Small State*, South Asian Publishers Pvt. Ltd., New Delhi, 1992.

Jayatilleke, K.N., *The Message of the Buddha*, George Allen and Unwin Ltd., London, 1975.

Kail, Owen C., *Buddhist Cave Temples of India*, Taraporevala, Bombay, 1975.

Kausalyayan, Anand, *Desh Ki Mitti Bulati Hai*, Bhanta Anand Kausalyayan, Sanskar Sahitya Mala, Bombay.

Khosla, Sarla, *Gupta Civilisation*, Intellectual Publishing House, New Delhi, 1982.

Knox, Robert, *Amarāvatī, Buddhist Sculpture from the Great Stūpa*, The Trustees of the British Museum, London, 1992.

Kramrisch, Stella, *The Art of India*, The Phaiden Press, London, 1954.

Kurashi, Mohammad Hamid, *Rajgir*, Director General, Archaeological Survey of India, New Delhi, 1975.

Kuppuram, G. and Kumudamani, K. (ed.), *Buddhist Heritage in India and Abroad*, Sundeep Prakashan, Delhi, 1992.

Lewis, Frederick, *Sixty Four Years in Ceylon*, n.p.

Longhurst, A.H., *The Story of Stūpa*, Asian Educational Services, Delhi, 1979.

Ludowyk, E.F.C., *The Story of Ceylon*, Faber and Faber, London, 1962.

Maisey, F.C., *Sāñcī and Its Remains*, Indological Book House, Delhi, 1972.

Marshall, Sir John, *A Guide to Sāñcī*, Manager of Publications, Delhi, 1936.

———, *The Bāgh Caves*, Swati Publications, Delhi, 1982.

Masson, J.L. and Patwardhan, M.V., *Aesthetic Rapture*, Vol. I, Deccan College, Postgraduate and Research Institute, Poona, 1970.

Mendis, G.C., *The Early History of Ceylon*, Asian Educational Services, New Delhi, Reprint, 1985.

Mitra, Debala, *Ajantā*, Director General, Arachaeological Survey of India, New Delhi, 1992.

———, *Buddhist Monuments*, Sahitya Samsad, Calcutta, 1971.

———, *Sāñcī*, Archaeological Survey of India, New Delhi, 1978.

Mitra Rajendralala, *Buddha Gaya*, Indological House, Delhi, 1972.

Mitton, G.E., *The Lost Cities of Ceylon*, n.p.

Mookerjee, Ajit, *Art of India*, Oxford Book and Stationary Co., Calcutta, 1952.

Mookerjee, Radhakumud, *Ancient Indian Education (Brahmanical and Buddhist)*, Motilal Banarsidass, Delhi, 1951.

———, *Aśoka*, Motilal Banarsidass, Delhi, 1989.

Morley, Grace, *Indian Sculpture*, Lustree Press Pvt. Ltd, Varanasi, 1985.

Muller, Edward, *Ancient Inscriptions in Ceylon*, Asian Educational Services, New Delhi, Reprint, 1984.

Murthy, K. Krishna, *Glimpses of Art, Architecture and Buddhist Literature in Ancient India*, Abhinav Publications, New Delhi, 1987.

Murty, K. Satya, *Handbook of Indian Architecture*, Abhish Publishing House, New Delhi, 1991.

Nagpal, J.C., *Mural Paintings in India*, Gian Publishing House, Delhi 1988.

Nandadeva, Wijesekera, "Buddhist Art Painting and Sculpture", pp. 14-17, *All Ceylon Buddhist Congress Diamond Jubilee*, 2462-2522.

———, *Early Sinhalese Painting*, Saman Press, Mahugama, 1959.

Narain, A.K., (ed.) *Studies in History of Buddhism*, B.R. Publishing Corporation, Delhi, 1980.

Nath, Birendra, *Nalanda Murals*, Cosmo Publications, New Delhi, 1983.

Nell, Andreas, *The Influence of Indian Art*, Delhi Printers Prakashan, Delhi, rept. 1978.

Obeyesekere, Ranjini, *Sinhala Writing and the New Critics*, M.D. Gunasena & Co. Ltd., Colombo, 1974.

Pal, Pratapaditya, *Indian Sculpture*, Vol. I, University of California Press, 1976.

Pandya, Ravindra, *Cave Paintings of Sri Lanka*, Art Centre, Ahmedabad, 1981.

Pandey, G.C., *Studies in the Origins of Buddhism*, Motilal Banarsidas, Delhi, 3rd edn., 1974.

Pant, Sushila, *The Origin and Development of Stupa Architecture in India*, Bharata Mannisha, Varanasi, 1976.

Paranavitana, S., *Stupa in Ceylon*, n.p.

———, *Sigiri Graffiti I and II*, Oxford, 1956.

Parker, H., *Ancient Ceylon*, Asian Educational Services, New Delhi, reprint, 1984.

Raghavan, M.D., *India in Ceylonese History, Society and Culture*, Asia Publishing House, New Delhi, 1969.

Rahula, W., *The History of Buddhism in Ceylon*, Colombo, 1956.

Randhawa, Mohinder Singh & Randhawan Doris Schreier, *Indian Sculpture the Scene, Themes and Legends*, Vakils, Feffer and Simons Ltd., Bombay, 1985.

Ratan Parimoo, *Life of Buddha in Indian Sculpture*, Ashta-Maha-Prathiarya, Kanak Publications, New Delhi, 1982.

Ratan Parimoo and others (ed.), *The Art of Ajanta New Perspectives*, Vol. I and II, Books and Books, Delhi, 1991.

Ray, Niharranjan, *Idea and Image in Indian Art*, Munshiram Manoharlal Publishers Pvt Ltd., 1973.

———, *An Approach to Indian Art*, Publication Bureau, Punjab University, Chandigarh, 1973.

———, *Maurya and Post Maurya Art*, Indian Council of Historical Research, New Delhi, 1976.

Read, Herbert, *Education Through Art*, Faber and Faber, London, 1958.

Roy, C. Craven, *A Concise History of Indian Art*, Thames and Hudson, London, 1976.

Sahni, Daya Ram, *Catalogue of the Museum of Archaeology at Sarnath*, Superintendent Government Printing, India, 1914.

Sarkar, H. and Nainar, S.P., *Amaravati*, Archaeological Survey of India, New Delhi, 1992.

Sarkar, H. and Mishra, B.N. *Nagarjunakonda*, Director General, Archaeological Survey of India, New Delhi, 1987.

Schlingloff Dieter, *Studies in Ajanta Paintings Identifications and Interpretation*, Ajanta Books International, Delhi, 1987.

Senadeera, Karunaratne Gunapala, *Buddhist Symbolism of Wish-Fulfilment*, Sri Satguru Publications, Delhi, 1992.

Sharma, R.C., *Buddhist Art of Mathurā*, Agam Kala Prakashan, Delhi, 1984.

Silva, Chandra Richard De, *Sri Lanka A History*, Vikas Publishing House Pvt. Ltd., New Delhi, Reprint, 1994.

Silva, K.M. De, *A History of Sri Lanka*, Oxford University Press, Delhi, 1981.

———, "*Sri Lanka A Survey*" (A Publication of the Institute of Asian Affairs Hamburg), Hurst and Co., London, 1972.

Silva, R.H. De, *The Technique of Ancient Sinhalese Wall Painting Sigiri*, Parnavitana Felicitation Volume, Colombo, 1965.

Simon, Richard, *Sri Lanka the Resplendent Isle*, Times Edition.

Singh, Arun Kumar, *Archaeology of Magadh Region*, Ramanand Vidya Bhavan, Delhi, 1991.

Singh, G.P., *Early Indian Historical Tradition and Archaeology*, D.K. Printworld (P) Ltd., New Delhi, 1994.

Singh, Madanjeet, *The Cave Paintings of Ajanta*, Thames and Hudson, London, 1965.

Sirisena, W.M., *Sri Lanka and South-East Asia*, Leiden E.J., Brill, The Netherlands, 1978.

Sivaramamurti, C., *Birds and Animals in Indian Sculpture*, National Museum, New Delhi, 1974.

———, *The Art of India*, Harry, N. Abhrams Inc. Publishers, New York, 1977.

———, *Indian Painting*, National Book Trust, India, New Delhi, 1970.

———, *Sources of History Illumined by Literature*, Kanak Publications, New Delhi, 1979.

Smith, Vincent A., *A History of Fine Art in India and Ceylon*, Oxford at the Clarendon Press, 1930.

———, *The Oxford History of India* (ed. Percival Speer), Delhi Oxford University Press, 1982.

Sutherland, Gail Hinich, *Yaksa In Hinduism and Buddhism*, Manohar, 1992.

Thapar, Romila, *Aśoka and the Decline of the Mauryas*, Oxford University Press, Delhi, 1985.

Tucci, Giuseppe, *Stupa, Art, Architecture and Symbolism*, Aditya Prakashan, New Delhi, Translated into English, 1988.

Vatsyayan, Kapila, *The Square and the Circle of the Indian Arts*, Roli Books International, Delhi, 1983.

———, *Classical Indian Dance in Literature and the Arts*, Sangeet Natak Akademi, New Delhi, 1986.

Verma, T.P., *A Catalogue of the Seals and Sealings in Govt. Museum, Mathura*, The Government Museum, Mathura, 1983.

Warder, A.K., *Indian Buddhism*, Motilal Banarsidass, Delhi, 1970.

Wickramasinghe, Martin, *Buddhism and Art*, M.D. Gunasena & Co. Ltd., Colombo.

———, *Aspects of Sinhalese Culture*, Tisara Prakasakayo, Sri Lanka, 1973.

———, *The Buddhist Jataka Stories*, M.D. Gunasena & Co. Ltd., Colombo.

———, *Buddhism and Culture*, Tisare Poth Prakasakyo, Ceylon, 1964.

Williams Harry, *Ceylon Pearl of the East*, Robert Hale Ltd., London.

Zuber, Christian, *Sri Lanka Island Civilisation*, n.p.

Journals

The Ceylon Historical Journal, Ceylon, 1959.

India Perspectives, June, 1995.

Bulletin of Museums and Archaelogy in UP, June-December, 1985.

Bulletin of Museums and Archaeology in UP, June-December, 1970.

A Catalogue of the Seals and Sealings in Govt. Museum, Mathura, 1983.

Bulletin of Museums and Archaeology in UP, June-December, 1990.

Bulletin of Museums and Archaeology in UP, June-December, 1973.

Bhasha Manjusha SFL Journal, Ministry of Defence, 1990.

Marg, Vol. XV, No. 2

Dictionary/Encyclopaedia

New Gem Dictionary

Oxford

An English-Hindi Dictionary, Bulcke

Collins COBuild, *English Language Dictionary*

Encyclopaedia of Buddhism, G.P. Malalesekera

Robinson, F. (ed.), *The Cambridge Encyclopaedia of India, Pakistan, Bangladesh, Sri Lanka, Nepal, Bhutan and the Maldives*, Cambridge University Press, Cambridge, 1989.

Index